BALCHEN'S VICTORY

'A ship in distress, designed to represent the loss of HMS *Victory*
(1737) by a violent storm near Alderney.' Etching, 1745–6, by Peter
Monamy (artist) and Pierre Charles Canot (engraver). (PAH0712, ©
National Maritime Museum, Greenwich, London)

BALCHEN'S VICTORY

THE LOSS AND REDISCOVERY OF AN ADMIRAL AND HIS SHIP

ALAN M SMITH

Seaforth
PUBLISHING

Dedicated to Judith, my wife, for her patience and support,
and to Barbara, my late mother, for her legacy of belief and inspiration

First published in Great Britain in 2022 by
Seaforth Publishing,
A division of Pen & Sword Books Ltd,
47 Church Street,
Barnsley S70 2AS

www.seaforthpublishing.com
British Library Cataloguing in Publication Data
A catalogue record for this book is available from the British Library

ISBN 978 1 3990 9412 2 (HARDBACK)
ISBN 978 1 3990 9413 9 (EPUB)
ISBN 978 1 3990 9414 6 (KINDLE)

Pen & Sword Books Limited incorporates the imprints of Atlas,
Archaeology, Aviation, Discovery, Family History, Fiction, History, Maritime, Military,
Military Classics, Politics, Select, Transport, True Crime, Air World, Frontline Publishing,
Leo Cooper, Remember When, Seaforth Publishing, The Praetorian Press, Wharncliffe
Local History, Wharncliffe Transport, Wharncliffe True Crime and White Owl

Typeset by Mac Style
Printed and bound in Great Britain by CPI Group (UK) Ltd, Croydon, CR0 4YY

Contents

'History is in part the record of men's opinions.'

Voltaire

'What you leave behind is not what is engraved in stone monuments, but what is woven into the lives of others.'

Pericles

List of Colour Plates

'The Famous Ship Victory'. Woodcut to print, 1744, artist unknown. (PPA89760, © The Trustees of the British Museum)

'Admiral Sir John Balchen (1670–1744)'. Portrait, oil on canvas, circa. 1705, by John Baptiste de Medina. (BHC2525, © National Maritime Museum, Greenwich, London)

Memorial to Sir John Balchen, Westminster Abbey, North Transept, marble statue, commissioned by his wife, designed by Scheemakers, completed in 1746. (© Dean and Chapter of Westminster)

'Admiral Lord George Anson (1697–1762)'. (BHC2517, © National Maritime Museum, Greenwich, London)

Sir Thomas Slade (1703–71). (BHC3030, © National Maritime Museum, Greenwich, London)

'Lord Anson's victory off Cape Finisterre, 3 May 1747'. (BHC0369, © National Maritime Museum, Greenwich, London)

HMS Victory (1759). (Photograph of HMS *Victory* at the National Museum of the Royal Navy, Portsmouth, courtesy of Alan M Smith)

Timeline for John Balchen's Career

Year	Career and Commands	Wars/Battles/Monarchs
1669/70	Born and baptised in Godalming, Surrey	Charles II 1660–85
1685	Joined the Royal Navy	Louis XIV of France 1643–1715
		Nine Years War 1688–97 vs France
		James II/VII 1685–88
		William and Mary 1688–94
1690	Stationed in the West Indies	William III 1694–1702
1692	Lieutenant on *Dragon* (38 guns) then *Cambridge* (70 guns)	
1697	Appointed captain of captured *Virgin* (32 guns) in West Indies	Treaty of Ryswijk 1697
1700	Command of *Firebrand* fireship	
1701	Command of *Vulcan* (28 guns) fireship	
1702	Takes part in Battle of Vigo	War of the Spanish Succession 1702–13 vs France, Spain and Bavaria
		Anne 1702–14
1703	Command of *Modere/Moderate* (56 guns)	
1704	Command of *Adventure* (42 guns) cruising North Sea and Channel	
1705	Command of *Chester* (50 guns) cruising coast of West Africa	
1707	Balchen and *Chester* captured by French	Battle of the Lizard 1707

Year	Career and Commands	Wars/Battles/Monarchs
1709	Command of *Gloucester* (60 guns)	
	Balchen and *Gloucester* captured by the French	
1710	Command of *Colchester* (54 guns) in English Channel, then the Mediterranean	
		Treaty of Utrecht 1713
		George I 1714–27
		Louis XV of France 1715–74
1715	Command of *Diamond* (42 guns) in West Indies	
1717	Command of *Orford* (70 guns) guardship duties on the Nore, Thames	
1718	Command of *Shrewsbury* (80 guns) in the Mediterranean	
	Takes part in the battle against Spanish	Battle of Cape Passaro, Sicily
1719	Command of *Monmouth* (70 guns) cruising in the Baltic	War of the Quadruple Alliance 1718–20
1721	Command of *Ipswich* (70 guns) guardship duties at Spithead	
1726	Command of *Monmouth* (70 guns) cruising in the Baltic	
		George II 1727–60
1729	Promoted to rear-admiral, cruising in the Mediterranean	
1734	Promoted to vice-admiral	
1735	Flagship *Princess Amelia* (80 guns)	
1739–40	Flagship *Russell* (80 guns)	War of Jenkins' Ear leading to War of the Austrian Succession 1739–48 against Spain, then France as well

Timeline for John Balchen's Career

Year	Career and Commands	Wars/Battles/Monarchs
1743	Promoted to Admiral of the White Squadron, Flagship *Princess Amelia* (80 guns)	
1744	Retired, knighted and appointed Governor of Greenwich Hospital	
1744	Recalled as Admiral on Flagship *Victory* (110 guns), lost and drowned in storm	

Timeline for HMS *Victory*'s Career

Year	Career	Wars/Battles/Monarchs
1673	100-gun First Rate warship ordered	Charles II 1660–85
1675	*Royal James* launched at Portsmouth	
	Dockyard	Louis XIV of France 1643–1715
		Nine Years War 1688–97 vs France
		James II/VII 1685–8
		William and Mary 1688–94
1690	Renamed *Victory* after old 1666-built Second Rate *Victory* condemned	
1692	Flagship of Admiral Sir John Ashby at	Battle of Barfleur 1692
1694/5	Rebuilt at Chatham Dockyard	William III 1694–1702
1697	Vice-Admiral Matthew Aylmer complains of *Victory*'s instability	Treaty of Ryswijk 1697
		War of the Spanish Succession 1702–13 vs France, Spain and Bavaria
		Anne 1702–14
1705	*Victory* briefly decommissioned, then recommissioned	
		Battle of Vigo 1702
		Battle of the Lizard 1709
		Treaty of Utrecht 1713

Year	Career	Wars/Battles/Monarchs
1714	Given a new commission and renamed *Royal George*	
		George I 1714–27
		Louis XV of France 1715–74
1715	Again renamed *Victory*	War of the Quadruple Alliance 1718–20
1721	Caught fire while breaming in Portsmouth Harbour	
1721	Taken to pieces and stored in Portsmouth Dockyard	
1726	*Victory* ordered to be rebuilt as a 100-gun First Rate	
		George II 1727–60
1727	*Victory*'s new keel laid in Portsmouth dry-dock	
1733	Finally officially ordered to be rebuilt	
1737	'New' *Victory* launched and commissioned.	
		War of Jenkins' Ear leading to War of the Austrian Succession 1739–48 against Spain, then France as well
1740	Flagship of Admiral Sir John Norris in Channel Fleet.	
1740	Major accident off Portland when *Lyon* collided with and damaged her ·	
1744	Flagship of Admiral Sir John Balchen commanding Anglo-Dutch fleet to Lisbon	
1744	On return was lost with all hands in a fierce storm in the English Channel	

Year	Career	Wars/Battles/Monarchs
2008	Wreck of *Victory* found around 80km south-east of Plymouth, 75m deep	
2019	*Victory*'s 42-pounder bronze gun displayed at National Museum of the Royal Navy	

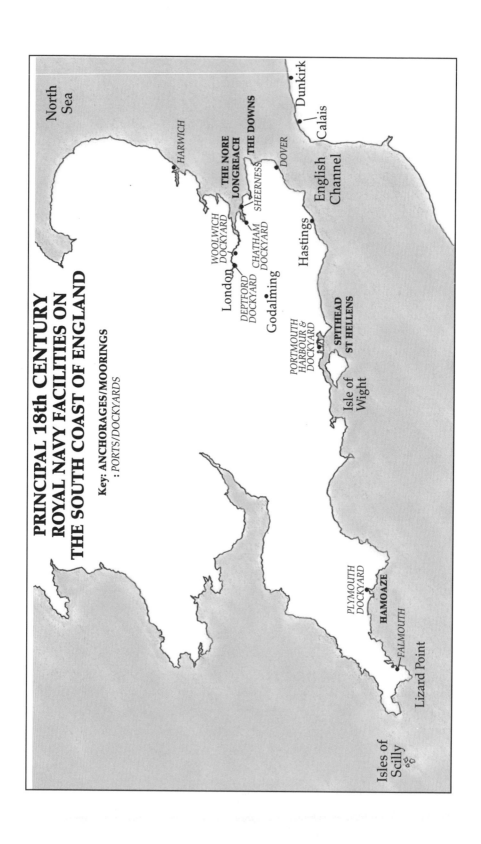

PRINCIPAL 18th CENTURY
ROYAL NAVY FACILITIES ON
THE SOUTH COAST OF ENGLAND

Key: ANCHORAGES/MOORINGS

: PORTS/DOCKYARDS

North
Sea

HARWICH

THE NORE
LONGREACH

SHEERNESS

THE DOWNS

WOOLWICH
DOCKYARD

DEPTFORD
DOCKYARD

CHATHAM
DOCKYARD

London

Godalming

DOVER

Hastings

English
Channel

Dunkirk

Calais

PORTMOUTH
HARBOUR &
DOCKYARD

SPITHEAD
ST HELLENS

Isle of
Wight

PLYMOUTH
DOCKYARD

HAMOAZE

FALMOUTH

Lizard Point

Isles of
Scilly

PRINCIPAL EUROPEAN
LOCATIONS WHERE
JOHN BALCHEN OPERATED
1685-1744

Atlantic
Ocean

North
Sea

The
Baltic
Sea

STOCKHOLM

LEITH

COPENHAGEN

REVAL
(TALLINN)

SCILLY ISLES

CHATHAM

PLYMOUTH

PORTSMOUTH

CALAIS

USHANT

BREST

ST MALO

NANTES

LA ROCHELLE

Bay of Biscay

CAPE FINISTERRE
FERROL

LA CORUNA

VIGO

BORDEAUX

LIVORNO
(LEGHORN)

PORTO

MARSEILLES

TOULON

BARCELONA

HYERES

LISBON

MINORCA
(PORT MAHON)

CADIZ
GIBRALTAR

MALLORCA

TANGIER

SICILY

CAPE
PASSARO

Mediterranean Sea

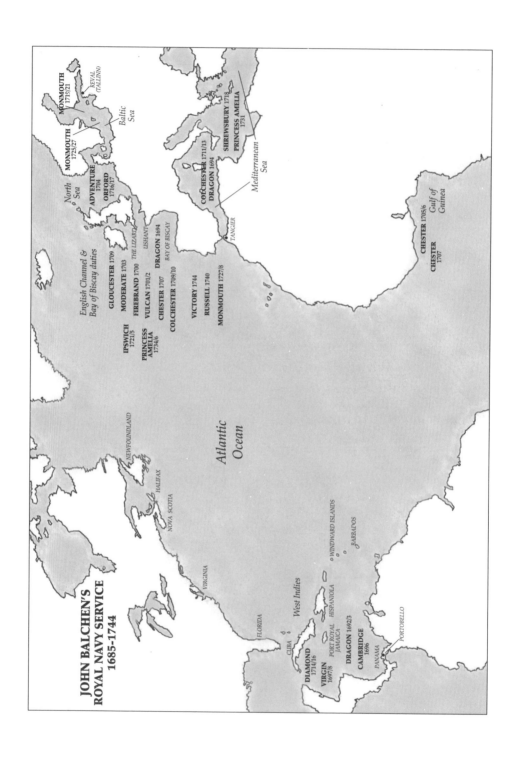

JOHN BALCHEN'S
ROYAL NAVY SERVICE
1685-1744

MONMOUTH
1719/21

REVAL
(TALLINN)

MONMOUTH
1725/27

Baltic
Sea

ADVENTURE
1704

ORFORD
1716/17

North
Sea

English Channel &
Bay of Biscay duties

GLOUCESTER 1709

MODERATE 1703

FIREBRAND 1700   THE LIZARD

VULCAN 1701/2   USHANT

CHESTER 1707   DRAGON 1694

COLCHESTER 1709/10   BAY OF BISCAY

IPSWICH
1721/5

PRINCESS
AMELIA
1734/6

VICTORY 1744

RUSSELL 1740

MONMOUTH 1722/8

COLCHESTER 1711/13

DRAGON 1694

SHREWSBURY 1718

PRINCESS AMELIA
1731

Mediterranean
Sea

TANGIER

CHESTER 1705/6   Gulf of
Guinea

CHESTER
1707

NEWFOUNDLAND

HALIFAX

NOVA SCOTIA

Atlantic
Ocean

VIRGINIA

WINDWARD ISLANDS

BARBADOS

FLORIDA

West Indies

CUBA

HISPANIOLA

PORT ROYAL
JAMAICA

DRAGON 1692/3

CAMBRIDGE
1696

PANAMA

PORTOBELLO

DIAMOND
1714/16

VIRGIN
1697/8

1

Introduction

'History abhors a vacuum, and as long as we don't know, there will always be those who want to know. A disaster of this scale looks for an explanation of equal magnitude. They must not have died in vain.'

Michael Palin, from his book *Erebus: The story of a ship*.

In 2018 two mighty eighteenth-century bronze naval guns lay on the concrete floor of Bay 3 in the Conservation Building at HM Naval Base, Portsmouth Harbour. Resting on simple wooden blocks and covered in plastic sheets, largely hidden by work benches and sheets of plywood and copper, these seemingly anonymous guns represented rare but tangible evidence of the lives of a gallant admiral and the finest First Rate warship of her time, both up until now lost in the mists of historical oblivion. This is the story of Admiral Sir John Balchen, his life and career, and of HMS *Victory*, the largest, finest ship of the line in the Royal Navy at the time, which he commanded when both were lost in a storm with all hands on the night of 3/4 October 1744. For more than 260 years the wreck of *Victory* and the remains of the entire crew of 1,100 sailors, including their captain, Samuel Faulknor, and their admiral, Sir John Balchen, have remained lost on the seabed of the English Channel. The wreck site was discovered in 2008 and formally identified in 2009 with the raising of these two guns. In 2019 the largest gun, a massive bronze three-tonne 42-pounder, was placed on public display in the National Museum of the Royal Navy in Portsmouth. That year also saw the conclusion of a 10-year legal and political battle that has eventually left the wreck and her remains to rest in peace where they lie, undisturbed, under the sea. So now is the time, at last, to swim back in time and to explore the significance of the admiral and the ship, what they achieved and why they should be better remembered by us all. It is now time that an observer of that great gun displayed in the museum can reach back and see, hear and understand the greater story of the long lives, adventures and tragic death of the man, his crew and his ship which are today represented in this seemingly anonymous slab of bronze. It must also resurrect interest in the glorious memorial to Balchen in Westminster Abbey and his portrait in the National Maritime Museum, Greenwich. It is time for him to re-emerge as a significant figure in the vast pantheon of British naval history of the eighteenth century.

This is in contrast to the much-recorded lives of Vice-Admiral Lord Horatio Nelson and his HMS *Victory*, where the glorious Battle of Trafalgar, Nelson's death and his relationship with Emma Hamilton combine to be completely incomparable to other maritime man-and-ship topics. With Nelson's great 104-gun warship *Victory* still visited by thousands of tourists in Portsmouth today, and Nelson's tomb in St Paul's Cathedral and his towering monument in Trafalgar Square in London, there can be little escape from their stories or their fame. But the stories of John Balchen and the other, previous HMS *Victory*, which concluded in their final, fateful voyage together, need to be told. They must not be lost, submerged in the clouds of time, only occasionally emerging simply as the story of a shipwreck. Their individual and remarkably parallel lives, including their tragic loss, can now be revealed as fundamental catalysts to the revolutionary reforms in naval shipbuilding, ship design and dockyard administration that transformed the Royal Navy after 1745. They were indeed major foundation stones for the glorious achievements of Nelson, Anson, Howe, Hood, Rodney, Boscawen and many more great admirals that followed.

Admiral Sir John Balchen, born in 1669, and his HMS *Victory*, the origins of which go back to 1673, had lived parallel, extraordinary and equally adventurous lives which, tragically, converged on that cataclysmic night in October 1744. This book challenges the absence of any meaningful references to the ship or admiral in recent naval history by unveiling a far greater depth of detail to the admiral's achievements which deserve more recognition than they have previously received. It also finds evidence of how his and *Victory*'s loss impacted Admiralty administration and later shipbuilding and design. They deserve their stories and legacy to be reconsidered as a great man-and-ship odyssey. They were both, in their own right, important pieces in the scattered jigsaw of British political and naval history in the late seventeenth and early eighteenth centuries. The circumstances and nature of their tragic loss, so widely reported and lamented across the nation, have resulted in their individual histories being largely overwhelmed by the shipwreck itself, thus submerging their own stories.

As recently as 30 April 2018, Dr Sean Kingsley, project lead archaeologist for the wreck, stated in *The Sunday Times* that *Victory* is 'arguably the most important shipwreck since the *Mary Rose*, Henry VIII's warship, lost in 1545 and raised in 1982'.[1] This in itself gives a reason to challenge why most of today's leading naval historians have chosen to ignore both Balchen and *Victory*. Evidence for this vacuum of knowledge is that most recent books on naval history, including twelve published on famous naval officers and admirals[2] and four published on famous naval shipwrecks,[3] make no reference to either Balchen or the tragic loss of *Victory*. This stark contrast between intrinsic importance and historical neglect makes it imperative to examine memorability and the use of history more broadly by seeking how the memory of the person, ship and event have been kept alive.

In January 2018 a survey[4] was undertaken amongst seven leading naval historians,[5] asking why the man and the ship no longer seem of any importance or relevance to naval history today. Among these historians, Sam Willis referred to both Balchen's memorial in Westminster Abbey and his portrait in the National Maritime Museum, concluding: 'I would argue that that means that they are fundamentally not forgotten. They are cared for and curated and on public display.'[6] However, although Balchen's memorial today stands proudly in the North Transept public entrance to the abbey, it is largely hidden behind security scanners and doors. This glorious memorial, erected in 1746, remains almost as obscure as his undisplayed portrait currently in storage. Nicholas Rodger responded that 'I don't at all agree that Balchen and the *Victory* are no longer of any importance to history', adding that 'even if ship and admiral had been quite forgotten, it would tell us nothing of their intrinsic importance'.[7] This book aims to ensure that they are not forgotten and that their 'intrinsic importance' is qualified. Observers may agree with Andrew Lambert's response that 'history remembers heroes and villains, not the solid sort who do most of the work, and carry the heavy loads', but may now disagree with his comment that Balchen 'teaches us no obvious lessons, and his career lacks both glory and humour'.[8] On the contrary, this book will demonstrate that both man and ship clearly taught us lessons. Given the recovery of these two guns and their public unveiling, it is timely to deliver what Lambert concludes: Balchen and *Victory* are 'long overdue for a serious reconsideration'.[9]

The most productive starting point in this task is to examine the actual event of their loss and, as important, the immediate reaction to that tragic event. The circumstances of the ill-fated voyage itself, the reasons why both ship and admiral were at sea on this commission and why this ship was the only one to be lost, all contribute to understanding their respective and collective legacy. At the time, the assumption and generally accepted cause of *Victory*'s loss was attributed to her being driven by the storm onto the infamous rocks of Les Casquets in the Channel Islands. All the immediate evidence, ranging from the reports by the inhabitants of Alderney hearing the constant firing of guns signifying distress throughout the night of 3/4 October, to the substantial amount of wreckage found upon the shores of Alderney, Guernsey and nearby French coastal beaches over the following days, all pointed towards her destruction on the reef. However, since the recent discovery of the wreck some 100km west of the Channel Islands and 80km south-east of Plymouth, and with hindsight, there are now many questions regarding her loss. Sean Kingsley, in his 2015 paper on finding the wreck, concludes that this 'unequivocally confirmed that the battleship never got within sight of Alderney, but was overcome in the midst of the sea, deep within the English Channel'.[10] Andrew Lambert echoed this view, claiming that 'Balchen did not do anything so un-seamanlike as to run into the well-known and widely avoided Casquets'.[11] However, it would be very convenient for the Admiralty, particularly the Surveyor of the Navy and Master Shipwright (already at loggerheads, as will be discussed in Chapter 4), for the ship to have foundered on the rocks rather than sinking mid-Channel as it would help deflect already the mounting public and Parliamentary criticism over current warship design and construction. So these evolving theories are further examined and analysed to establish how the ship may have been lost. Although since overshadowed by Nelson and his *Victory*, Balchen and his ship are beginning to emerge (with the guns) through those shadows as of greater significance than hitherto understood.

The British press, especially the London newspapers and journals, were keen followers of all things naval at that time. So when the battered ships of Balchen's squadron began to arrive in Plymouth, Portsmouth and Spithead in the days following the storm, the press expressed growing anguish and anxiety about the absence of *Victory*. When the wreckage was found and confirmed to be that of *Victory*, the consternation turned to outpourings of grief and lamentation, including songs, poetry and plays. That was followed by paintings, etchings and other manifestations of the widespread shock over the loss amongst the populace of the nation at large. Examining this material clearly demonstrates why the tragedy of the event itself came to dominate and even overshadow the histories of Balchen and *Victory*, even to the extent that they have become known only for a shipwreck.

By identifying the recorded achievements and individual legacies of the admiral and his ship, we can bring them out of the shadows of the shipwreck that took them away. Firstly, an examination of the chequered life of the ship itself, from her origins, through rebuildings, service activities and incidents from her 'birth' in 1673 through to her sinking in 1744, reveals a fresh view of contemporary ship design, shipbuilding and dockyard administration. This in turn helps link the loss of *Victory* to subsequent widespread reforms in dockyard practices and ship design, giving us a much better understanding of the significance of *Victory*'s newly restored guns and what they represent.

The same approach is taken to establish the importance or significance of Balchen himself and to identify his achievements that should have made him more recognisable, if not 'heroic'. A detailed examination of Balchen's life, firstly in the context of his birthplace, Godalming in Surrey, his family life and early records of his career,[12] leads us to analyse those aspects of his life that can now be 'reconsidered' in order to demonstrate the importance of his achievements and legacy. If Balchen was, in the opinion of Daniel Baugh in his latest biographical essay on the admiral, only 'best known to history by a shipwreck',[13] then the discovery and display of the guns call for a greater understanding of the wider significance of his life and legacy beyond his shipwreck. Balchen's part in questioning ship design and maintenance, his relationships with crew and officers and his undoubted courage revealed through the minutes of his two courts martial, as well as his actions in battle, all combine to confirm that he was much more than a run-of-the-mill naval officer whose place in naval history should rise above the ordinary and emerge above the story of a shipwreck.

By bringing together these threads leading up to the catastrophic event that claimed both their lives and how that was seen at the time as a national tragedy inevitably leads to the question of why the event itself, and its component parts, have since disappeared from historical significance. Indeed, we can now see how their story became a catalyst for naval and dockyard administration reform, shipbuilding practices and warship design following their loss. The sinking of *Victory* was almost predicted as inevitable by Admiral Vernon who had campaigned to reform warship design right up until the month Balchen's ill-fated fleet set sail in July 1744. He was backed by Commodore Charles Knowles and other serving officers at the time who severely criticised dockyard practices. Balchen himself actively criticised Sir Jacob Acworth, Surveyor of the Navy, over ship design. As we shall see, all this led directly to the monumental reforms that began only two months after the tragedy when a new Admiralty Board was created, which included Anson, who became the greatest reformer in Royal Navy history. It was Anson who captured the revolutionary French 74-gun two-deck ship *Invincible* in 1747 upon which the Royal Navy modelled its future fleet of warships and it was under Anson that Nelson's famous HMS *Victory* was ordered in 1759 and launched in 1765.

So we should begin to recognise that the story of Balchen and *Victory* does have significant and wider relevance. His loyal service, achievements and war record and their combined contribution to improved shipbuilding and design for the next era of British naval glory are highly significant. Since one of *Victory*'s great guns has recently emerged on public display, it can now be seen, at last, as a tangible representation of a truly significant and adventurous story about the admiral and his ship's new journey together, this time from obscurity to deserved recognition and, indeed, admiration.

In many respects this story echoes the recently published stories on the lives and wrecks of two other ships, their leaders and their crews: HMS *Erebus* and Sir John Franklin written by Michael Palin in 2018, and HMS *Royal George* and Rear-Admiral Richard Kempenfelt written by Hilary Rubinstein in 2020. Palin sums up his story, which ended with the wreck and loss of both *Erebus* and Franklin in 1848 in the North West Passage, with the words 'History abhors a vacuum, and as long as we don't know, there will always be those who want to know. A disaster of this scale looks for an explanation of equal magnitude. They must not have died in vain.'[14] Rubinstein's summary of her story, which describes the catastrophic capsizing, sinking and loss of both *Royal George* and Admiral Kempenfelt at Spithead in 1782, includes two quotes 'lamenting that Kempenfelt's name was known to the general public only because of his ship's sad fate' and 'we should still know from that acute intelligent face [in his portrait] that he had other claims to remembrance than the mere fact that he went down at Spithead'.[15] While those two books and this one are essentially about a ship and a great naval leader, the contrast between the events that led to their respective loss is stark, as are the lives of the three commanders in question. However, these books share the same objective in trying to build up an understanding of the achievements of each man and raise him up, as an individual, above his association with a fatal sinking, while revealing a greater knowledge of the ships themselves. Unravelling their stories and the legacy of their lives and loss must ensure that their names will resonate more proudly in future naval or maritime histories when they are written in years to come.

Note on Dates

In various parts of the text, as well as in many endnotes, readers will notice examples of 'Dual Dating' where either a document or an event is given a date such as 24 January 1725/6. Like many academically-inclined historians, this writer has adopted, where appropriate or when directly quoted, this dual dating. The rationale behind this rather confusing approach is due to the changes in the universal calendars across Europe over an extended period of time when the world gradually switched from the Julian Calendar to the Gregorian Calendar. In the case of Great Britain, this change followed the Calendar (New Style) Act of 1750, changing the start of the year from 25 March to 1 January, beginning from 1 January 1752. Scotland had already changed to 1 January in 1600. As a result, much of the late seventeenth century and early/mid-eighteenth century saw documents that were written, or events that had happened, between January and March being dual dated to cater for both the previous year ending on 25 March and the next year beginning on the earlier 1 January. Hence, for example, we have endnotes in this book relating to a log book entry on 23 February 1725/6. Where the dual dating has not been used in archive documents, the researcher has a challenge to decide which year to allocate the source!

2

The Shipwreck of 1744

'As with all shipwrecks, therefore, it is possible and rewarding to appreciate them on many different levels. Most obviously, tales of shipwrecks are attractive as straightforward descriptions of human tragedy, in which heroism, sacrifice and villainy all bubble to the surface in conditions of extreme physical and emotional suffering ... Shipwrecks can also be read as sophisticated allegories of contemporary issues in which the sinking itself and the death of those aboard are laden with symbolism and significance beyond the basic facts.'

Extract from Sam Willis, *Shipwreck: a History of Disasters at Sea.*

The circumstances leading up to the final voyage of Balchen and *Victory* can be seen in many respects as a reflection of the somewhat underfunded and disorganised state of Admiralty administration at that time. Their loss was a catalyst for the Government and Admiralty to begin major reforms which became a significant part of their legacy, which transformed the navy of 1713 to 1739 into the force that became commander of the oceans during the second half of the eighteenth century and the nineteenth century. Between the end of the War of the Spanish Succession with the Peace of Utrecht in 1713–14, through intermittent hostilities and the resumption of war in 1739, Britain was governed largely by the pacifist Whigs under Sir Robert Walpole, resulting in widespread cuts in military and naval spending. Although Britain was by now the greatest of the European naval powers, with the largest fleet in the world, the state of that fleet has often been questioned. In 1721, according to M S Anderson, Britain had 124 ships of the line and these figures were virtually unchanged when war broke out with Spain in 1739, 'but lack of maintenance under the Walpole regime meant that she had only 35 [ships] of the line fit for immediate use'.[1] Brian Lavery admits that the administrators of the navy in the long peace from 1714 to 1739 have attracted much criticism, and 'it has often been suggested that this period was the nadir of naval administration',[2] although he then adds that more recently, historians have placed greater emphasis on the positive side of the administration. Daniel Baugh's earlier interpretation weaved a more conciliatory path between the positives and the frankly shambolic administration based upon contemporary navy records. While discussing the Admiralty Board under First Lord Sir Charles Wager between 1733 and 1742, Baugh argues that Wager's reputation suffered from events such as the futile and costly naval mobilisation in 1734, the ensuing Opposition cries for war with Spain and the 'mistaken notion that the navy was materially unprepared for war in 1739', concluding that 'in some degree all these criticisms arise from Wager's association with, and loyalty to, Sir Robert Walpole'[3] and his pacifist foreign policy.

Unprepared as the country clearly was, the long drift to war had begun in 1738, driven by the pro-war press and many Tory MPs, and spurred on by the story of Robert Jenkins. Back in 1731, as captain of the *Rebecca*, Jenkins had been arrested by a Spanish officer and his ear slashed by a cutlass, then torn off by another Spaniard, allegedly bidding Jenkins to take the ear back to King George. It took until March 1738 before Jenkins was summoned to give evidence and 'the atrocity went gaily around, and to the war party was added the familiar, toxic thing, a war press'.[4] Meeting in June 1738, the British Cabinet, though not declaring war, agreed to send Admiral Nicholas Haddock down to Cadiz to support commercial interests and to intimidate the Spanish. The War of Jenkins' Ear, later merging with the War of the Austrian Succession (1739–48), was declared on 19 October 1739.

Walpole eventually resigned in February 1742, and with that First Lord of the Admiralty Sir Charles Wager stepped down. However, despite the earlier criticisms against Wager, when it comes to his successor as First Lord in 1742, the Earl of Winchilsea, Baugh pulls no punches, pointing out that he had no sea experience and 'was associated with a weak and fumbling ministry'. In summary, the 'indecisiveness

of Winchilsea's administration'⁵ reached its lowest point in 1744 –
coinciding with the widely criticised and mourned loss of *Victory* and
Balchen. Significantly, Winchilsea's Board collapsed and was replaced
on 28 December 1744, only two months after the tragedy. Of equal
significance, as we shall see, amongst this new Board of Admiralty
members appointed was Admiral George Anson.

Symptomatic of this administrative incompetence and indecision
was the objective behind Balchen's commission in June 1744 and his
fateful voyage that ended so tragically that October. Put simply, the
main objective for the mission was to relieve a large convoy of victualling
ships led by Admiral Sir Charles Hardy that was critically long overdue
to resupply the Royal Navy's Mediterranean Fleet, commanded then by
Admiral Thomas Mathews. Up until this point, the Victualling Board
had been providing regular convoys of provisions to the Mediterranean
Fleet and its bases in Gibraltar and Port Mahon in Minorca every
six months. However, it is clear that these deliveries were at least
unreliable and haphazard in the early years of the war, threatening
the very viability of the British naval squadrons in the Mediterranean.
Two years earlier, in September 1742, Admiral Mathews wrote to the
Admiralty Secretaries from his ship, *Namur*, anchored in Hyères Road
near Ile d'Hyères to the east of Toulon, expressing his despair over the
lack of cordage (i.e. rope) and sails to sustain his fleet at sea:

> I have given orders for the cordage being made with the utmost
> expedition, and to be sent to me in small quantities as it is made:
> for the squadron is in so miserable a condition for want of sizeable
> cordage and sails that if it blows a capful of wind, they are obliged to
> bear up and come in to me [from blockading the Port of Toulon],
> or go to leeward of the islands. Captain Cornwall on the 6th instant
> was obliged to quit his station with his whole squadron, which is
> off Toulon, and to send the *Nassau* into me, she having split her
> mainsail, and has never another on board; all her rigging is bad. I
> designed sending her to Minorca, but it is to no purpose, there being
> no rigging or sails to fit her or any other seventy-gun ship, nor is
> there one coil of rope or one sail for a seventy-gun ship coming out in
> the two storeships; that I dread the consequence, should I be obliged

to put to sea…. I must therefore desire their Lordships will hasten out two or three men of war with those absolutely necessary stores and sails for seventy and sixty-gun ships, in particular a mainsail for *Somerset*, there being not one in store.[6]

Clearly this situation was untenable. Despite Admiral Mathews' pleas for more rigging and sails, it appears that shortages continued. So it was hardly surprising that some seventeen months later a combined Franco-Spanish fleet successfully fought off the British fleet on 22 and 23 February 1744 at the Battle of Toulon, swinging the war in their favour. Unfortunately for Admiral Mathews, he was blamed for what was seen by the British press as cowardice in the face of the enemy, and he was court-martialled and dismissed from the service in 1746. Admiral Sir William Rowley, commanding the van squadron in that battle, was commended for his courage and succeeded Mathews as commander of the Mediterranean Fleet in August 1744. Thus depleted and faced with the threat of further challenges, the fleet was in even more desperate need of provisions. Significantly, in March 1744, while he was still in command of the Mediterranean Fleet, Admiral Mathews was fearful of losing Hardy's vital supplies, as recorded in a letter in the State Papers 'expressing Admiral Mathews' fears of the great danger of the interception of Sir Charles Hardy's victualling convoy'.[7]

By the time Hardy's convoy had at last set sail for the Mediterranean and become blockaded in the estuary of the River Tagus, Lisbon, by a large French squadron under Admiral M de Rochambault, in May 1744, Balchen's operation had become of vital consequence for the balance of forces between British and opposing Franco-Spanish fleets in the War of the Austrian Succession.

The letters addressed from the Victualling Board to the Admiralty Secretary and the minutes of the Admiralty Board itself tell a story of desperation which is then echoed in some of the earliest histories of the event. This was because the Mediterranean Fleet was close to annihilation for want of provisions for its 17,000 men as well as long overdue stores, sails and rigging for its ships; and the French were eager to capitalise on the situation.[8]

The latest six months' supply, ordered on 5 December 1743 and expected to sail on 20 January 1744,[9] did not sail until much later for fear of a large French squadron based at Brest. On 5 March, the Admiralty asked the Victualling Board what state Admiral Mathews' fleet would be in and the state of provisions in Port Mahon and Gibraltar if the victualling convoy was delayed longer 'and how the Admiral may get supplies otherwise'.[10] Their response was damning. They calculated that supplies then remaining at Port Mahon and aboard the ships would be 'insufficient' to serve 17,000 men until the middle of April while there were only sufficient provisions in Gibraltar to serve 18,000 men for between two and three weeks. They concluded:

> In case any accident should happen to delay the passage of the victuallers now at Portsmouth to the Mediterranean we are apprehensive it would throw the fleet there into the utmost distress, being humbly of the opinion that the admiral would not be able to get sufficient supplies of provisions anywhere in those parts to render the fleet capable of any kind of service but would be reduced to the necessity of sending the ships to different places for their present subsistence, where they would probably consume such supplies as they might be able to meet with as fast as they can collect them.[11]

Despite such a critical situation, the victualling convoy, escorted by Admiral Hardy, did not leave Portsmouth until 23 April. *The Biographical Magazine*, recalling these events in 1776, related the despatch of the convoy to Admiral Rowley (history had clearly disowned Admiral Mathews, for reasons described above, as Rowley did not take over command until August) 'who was in the utmost distress, his ships being almost destitute of provisions, and their rigging in a very wretched condition'. It also recorded that 'nor were the French either ignorant of this circumstance, or careless to profit by it', thus sending Admiral Rochambault with a fleet of fourteen ships of the line and six frigates to prevent Admiral Hardy from reaching Admiral Rowley.[12] Although the victuallers managed to arrive safely in Lisbon on 3 May, the French squadron had caught up with them and blockaded them and Hardy's escort ships in the River Tagus.

News travelled slowly at that time but even by 1 June, the Admiralty had resolved to call Admiral Balchen out of his recent retirement, aged 75, when Winchilsea's Admiralty Board 'signifyed his Majesty's pleasure that Sir John Balchen should be restored to his Rank of Admiral of the White Squadron of his Majesty's fleet and that a commission be made out accordingly'.[13] In the words of Baugh, 'it was unquestionably the greatest victualling failure of the war'[14] which led to Balchen's and *Victory*'s last voyage. In short, if these vital supplies failed to reach the Mediterranean, Britain was in danger of losing the War of the Austrian Succession. 'In this extremity', mentioned and then copied by three of the earliest publications on the lives of British admirals, 'the ministry cast their eyes on Admiral Balchen',[15] which clearly demonstrates the esteem in which he was held by the Admiralty who were not short of other senior officers.

Thereafter, conflicting instructions, ignorance of what was happening and increasing desperation unravelled. By 13 July, the Admiralty Board minutes noted that Admiral Balchen was 'on the point for setting out for Portsmouth and intending to hoist his flag on board the *Victory*'.[16] There followed a flurry of resolutions, all of which were translated into Admiralty instructions despatched almost daily to Balchen. Initially, Balchen's commission, issued on 14 July, directed him to 'repair down to Portsmouth and take command of his Majesty's ships there and at Spithead'.[17] He was provided with a list of ships at his disposal and his orders, which initially involved hastening the dispatch of several convoys for Newfoundland, New England and Virginia, added, 'afterwards cruising with a particular squadron in the Channel and Soundings in quest of the French Fleet'.[18]

On 18 July Balchen arrived in Portsmouth Harbour and reported back to the Secretary of the Lords of the Admiralty:

At half past 9 this morning I got to Portsmouth & have received their Lordships' orders of the 16th instant, accompanied with Twenty copies of his Majesty's Declaration of War against France & I have also your letter of the 17th with their Lordships' orders [for me] to Command in Chief & several other orders for my proceedings which came this morning by Express.

I herewith send the state of his Majesty's Ships at Spithead and in Portsmouth Harbour delivered to me by Vice-Admiral Steuart, who has acquainted their Lordships, with the arrival of six Dutch Men of War with two Vice and one Rear-Admiral.[19]

The records show that Balchen wrote letters of acknowledgement to the Admiralty in receipt of their Lordships' fresh orders every day from 19 July to 23 July, illustrating the constantly changing intelligence coming in about the whereabouts of the French squadron around the port of Brest. But on 23 July the Commissioners instructed Balchen to proceed to Lisbon and 'bring from thence a large convoy of Victuallers and storeships which lye there ... it being of the utmost importance to take all possible care of the security of the said convoy'.[20]

It was still not clear to the Admiralty exactly where the French squadron was since the Board minutes resolved on the same day that Balchen should be left to act 'according to the intelligence he receives of the Brest Squadron ... and to follow the enemy if they are at sea in such a manner as he thinks proper', adding the proviso that he 'be at liberty to call off the Rock of Lisbon, and if the Victuallers, etc are there, to take them out with their convoy and see them safe' to Gibraltar.[21] On receiving these instructions the next day, Balchen replied that he 'shall not loose a moment's time in putting these into execution so soon as Wind & Weather will permit me to put to sea, being now in readiness'. However, he cautiously added the proviso that 'as here are a great number of ships it will not be prudent to put to sea without a leading gale of wind down the Channel'.[22]

The Board then received an account from Captain Osborne of his situation in Lisbon, confirming that the convoy of victuallers destined for the Mediterranean was 'being kept in by the French and Spanish squadrons which are cruising to intercept him'.[23] On 24 August, when the Board received further confirmation of a 'considerable squadron of French ships' preventing the convoy's escape, they ordered Balchen to 'proceed immediately with his whole squadron off the Rock of Lisbon, and to take from thence Captain Osborne & the ships with him and the said convoy of victuallers & storeships and see them in safety to Gibraltar'.[24]

Balchen departed from the St Hellens (*sic*) anchorage off the Isle of Wight aboard his 110-gun flagship, *Victory*, with a fleet of seventeen British and six Dutch warships, on 28 July. Early records show that there were upwards of 200 merchant ships under the protection of this fleet heading for Portugal and the Mediterranean.[25] Documents record the official line of battle, where the Dutch were 'to lead with the Starboard and the *Princess Mary* with the Larboard Tacks on Board'.[26] This listed the formidable fleet and its commanders as follows:

Dutch ships under Vice-Admiral Hooft:

Damiate	64 [Guns]
Edam	54
Dordreght	54
Delft	54
Assendelft	54
Leeuwenhorst	54

Under Sir John Balchen, Admiral of the White:

Dreadnought	60
Hampton Court	70
Jersey	60
Augusta	60
Captain	70
Victory	100
Princess Amelia	80

Under William Martin, Vice-Admiral of the Blue:

Falkland	50
Suffolk	70
St George	90
Strafford	60
Exeter	60

Under Samuel Steuart, Vice-Admiral of the Red:

Sunderland	60
Monmouth	70
Duke	90
Prince Frederick	70
Princess Mary	60

On his way south, Balchen reported that on 2 August, 'not having gained any intelligence of the French Squadron, I sent the *Falkland* and the *Fly* Sloop off of Brest' in order to gain any further intelligence by intercepting and questioning merchant ships plying around the French ports. Subsequently, on 12 August his combined fleet captured six French merchant ships, two by the Dutch and four by the British[27] (more details of this engagement are in Chapter 6). Apart from this small fracas en route, Balchen and his vast fleet eventually arrived in Lisbon on 9 September and immediately met up with Admiral Hardy's squadron to break the French blockade. The only references to this engagement were in the early biographies on Balchen, which reported that Admiral Rochambault, on the first information of the approach of this formidable force, prudently decided to retire and secure his fleet in Cadiz, 'leaving the sea open to the British flag'.[28] In early September Balchen successfully escorted the vital replenishment ships to Gibraltar for their onward conveyance to Admiral Rowley's fleet in the Mediterranean. Having completed his primary mission, Balchen was then ordered by the Lords of the Admiralty on 13 September 'to rendezvous with Vice-Admiral Davers and Rear-Admiral Medley at Gibraltar'.[29] Further instructions came from the Admiralty the next day, ordering Balchen's fleet to sail with Vice-Admiral Davers from Gibraltar to the West Indies, 'being a consequence of the junction of the Combined Brest and Toulon Squadrons, and the Spanish out of Cartagena'.[30] He then left Gibraltar to comply with these orders and in the hope of drawing out and engaging the French fleet from Cadiz as well as intercepting any inbound treasure ships from Havana. By 25 September, the Admiralty issued further orders for 'Sir John Balchen to await the arrival of Vice-Admiral Rowley's squadron in the Straights of Gibraltar before attacking, taking in or otherwise destroying the combined Franco-Spanish fleet'.[31]

It should not be underestimated how important Balchen's successful mission was to the outcome of this war. Swamped by the ineptitude of constantly conflicting instructions amidst the dire state of the vital convoys, he had done his duty. Had he failed to relieve the convoy, the French and Spanish could have destroyed the Mediterranean Fleet and captured Port Mahon and possibly Gibraltar as well.

However, having vainly tried to entice the French fleet out of Cadiz, Balchen was forced to make an early journey home as the Dutch ships in his fleet were destitute of provisions.[32] The fleet left the coast of Galicia on 28 September and the next day entered the Bay of Biscay.[33]

On 3 October the fleet was caught in a ferocious storm as it entered the Channel, dispersing the ships. Badly damaged and dismasted in the gales, they all eventually returned to Plymouth or Spithead, with only *Victory*, last seen on 4 October, missing. The enormity of the storm can be felt in a letter written by Vice-Admiral Steuart of *Duke* on 8 October:

> On the 3rd instant we met with a hard gale of wind which tore our sails and rigging, so that we were obliged to submit to the mercy of the waves; on the 4th we had ten feet of water in our hold, which made our condition very bad, and the dread of death appeared in every face, for we momentarily expected to be swallowed up; the *Exeter*, Captain Broderick, was in more danger than we, she having lost her main and mizzen masts, and her upper guns were some minutes underwater, insomuch as they were obliged to throw 12 of them overboard to save her from sinking. Admiral Balchen was separated from us in the storm, and is not yet arrived.[34]

HMS *Victory*, the 'largest and finest ship in the navy', was lost. Balchen, described as 'so worthy and able a commander', together with 'a chosen crew of 1,100 men; and had, besides, upwards of fifty young gentlemen on board, some of them belonging to families of the first distinction, who entered as volunteers, anxious to serve, and learn the first rudiments of naval tactics under so worthy and able a commander',[35] had perished, with not a single body recovered. Despite the wreck recently being found far away in mid-Channel, it was reported that the inhabitants of Alderney 'heard the guns which the admiral fired as signals of distress; but the tempest raged with such uncommon violence, that no assistance could be given. The signal guns were continued during the whole night, but early in the morning the ship sunk, and every person on board perished.'[36]

Searches were undertaken by inhabitants of the Channel Islands. One of the reports came from Nicholas Dobree from Guernsey who was commissioned by the Admiralty to report on any findings from the wreck on the Channel Islands. In a letter to the Admiralty, he reported that on the morning after the storm, an oar was found in Alderney 'upon which the *Victory's* name is marked' and the next day a great quantity of broken wood, pieces of sash windows, a gun-carriage marked GR and also Captain Cotterel's (of Wolfe's Regiment of Marines) portmanteau were found on shore in Alderney.[37] Dobree also referred to the finding of a main topmast, a fore top mast and a yard in Guernsey and the top of the stern on the coast of France.[38]

Such was the interest in finding the wreck of *Victory* that the then famous veteran diver, John Lethbridge, approached the Admiralty in January 1745, seeking permission to find the wreck and recover her guns. Having invented his underwater diving machine (essentially a wooden barrel with a window and two arm holes that was plugged with the diver inside and lowered up to 60ft in the water) back in 1715, Lethbridge had made his fortune diving on sunken vessels around the world and recovering silver, lead, coins, guns, anchors and other valuables. In the 1720s and 1730s he was successfully diving on shipwrecks off the Cape Verde Islands, the Bahamas, Madeira, Outer Hebrides, Table Bay off Cape Town and the West Indies. His inventory of wrecks included British men-of-war and Dutch and British East Indiamen, as well as Spanish galleons.[39] He wrote to the Commissioners that he 'was desirous of searching for his Majesty's Ship the *Victory* lately lost in order to recover her guns'. He claimed he had been informed by a gentleman from Plymouth that a master of a ship reported that:

In the beginning of October in the nighttime being stormy near the Gaskets [Casquets reef off Alderney] he saw the lights of a stout ship go out who believes were the *Victory's* lights ... and he believes that the *Victory* was broke to pieces on them rocks (and not foundered) there being a great amount of wreck seen on the coast of Normandy about the time the *Victory* was supposed to be lost.

In the light of this information, Lethbridge believed he could 'find the place where the *Victory* was and also recover her guns, money and other valuable things that are sank in the sea'.[40] Although there is no record of whether Lethbridge did indeed begin a search as he had proposed, the navy clearly thought that efforts to find the wreck would be worth investing in. In response to a letter from the Board of Admiralty in February 1745 asking them for an 'account of the wreck of the *Victory*', the Navy Office responded that the only account they had of the wreck was the letter sent by Mr Dobree of Guernsey, a copy of which they enclosed, adding the question 'whether it may not be advisable to offer a Reward of One Hundred Pounds to any person that shall discover the said wreck'.[41]

Over 20 years later wreckage from *Victory* was still being found, with *The Leeds Intelligencer* newspaper reporting in September 1766 that 'a few days since the rudder of the *Victory*, a first-rate man of war, who was lost 20 years ago, and under command of the late Admiral Balchen, was towed on shore near Brighthelmstone [Brighton]'.[42] However, since the wreck of *Victory* was found in 2008, it appears that her rudder actually still remains with the ship at the bottom of the English Channel.

As was customary, the Admiralty Board was clinical in its reaction to the loss of *Victory*. The first mention in the Board minutes following the reported non-arrival of the ship was on 10 October when it is recorded that the Board 'resolved that Vice-Admiral Steuart be directed to send out the *Falkland* and *Fly* in quest of Sir John Balchen'.[43] It appears by the next day that news may have been filtering back to the Board as to the fate of the ship as it then ordered Steuart to take over 'all the matters lately ordered to be enquired into, by Sir John Balchen, he being not yet arrived'. A later resolution recorded at the same meeting was that Steuart also 'be directed to open the pacquets directed for Sir John Balchen, that lye at Portsmouth and if there is anything in them for His Majesty's Service, to put it in execution'.[44] There was no further reference to either Balchen or *Victory* in the next 20 days and, amazingly, there was never any acknowledgement of the tragedy recorded in the Board's minutes. The tone of the next two references was equally unemotional and clinical. The first was a resolution on

31 October that the wages of Lieutenant Hill, 'late Lieutenant of the *Victory*, be paid to him, if the Navy Board have no other objections thereto than the want of a Certificate from Captain Faulknor, who commanded her'.[45] Sadly, the final reference came on 17 December, only four days before the collapse of Earl Winchilsea's Admiralty Board and his dismissal as First Lord. Although these minutes reveal a system with scant regard to humanity with processes clearly undertaken 'by the book', the resolution was more sensitive. It was reported to the Board that the pension due to the late Sir John Balchen between 27 March and 31 May that year 'cannot be paid, by reason he had not qualified himself before he was cast away'. Unsurprisingly, the Navy Board was directed to 'dispense with the want of the usual Certificate' and to authorise payment.[46]

It is difficult to conclude how much influence the loss of *Victory* and her admiral had on the fall of Earl Winchilsea and his Board on 21 December, only two months after the tragedy, and how much could be attributed to Admiral Vernon's outright public hostility towards the Board. As detailed in Chapter 4, Vernon, sitting in Parliament, had voiced his opinions in the weeks leading up to the tragedy on the state of naval ships, their design and shipbuilding in general. His views were then widely publicised in Parliament, letters, newspaper articles and news-sheets immediately following the loss of *Victory*, pointing fingers at the Surveyor of the Navy as well as the administration of the dockyards. Clearly there were other factors in Winchilsea's dismissal, but this incident will be seen as the final straw that led to his fall and the subsequent rise of Admiral George Anson (as described in Chapter 8).

But the tragedy should not just be seen as the loss of the ship, her admiral, Sir John Balchen, and her captain, Samuel Faulknor. Even in the context of the huge loss of life at sea at that time, due consideration needs to be given to that catastrophic figure so often used in this context: the 1,100-plus crew that perished with them. Like the admiral and the captain, every one of these men had families, relatives and friends to grieve over their loss. Looking beyond the stark numbers, the grim reality of the enormity and scale of the disaster can be seen in the Muster Book[47] for *Victory* in the months leading up to her final voyage. The list of their names goes on, page after page, even indicating those who had been pressed into service and where from. It can then become even more poignant to see some of those names then appearing some time later in the growing list of their wills going through the Probate Courts, such as Thomas Crow on 26 November 1744 and William Newton on 1 February 1745. These are real people whose relatives sometimes had to wait months and years for Probate to approve their wills. For example, William Goddard on 3 November 1744, William Lockey on 16 March 1745, and William Pell, ship's carpenter, on 18 February 1746.[48] Between 23 October and 29 December 1744 alone, no less than twenty-seven names from the lost *Victory's* Muster Books appeared in the Probate Courts, including John Port, Robert Pain, William Garland, Daniel Langridge, William Tharpe, Stephen Mollandine, Thomas Adwinkle, Simon Fitzpatrick, Charles Carrow, William Potter, John Reid, Robert Strong, Nicholas Aspinall, John Quick, Edward Sparks, Jacob Jump, Francis Lakeman, Thomas Masters, Moses Wright, John Stonehouse, William Pearce, Isaac Robins, William Corp, John Crofts and John Burgess. Other lost crew members from the *Victory* are recorded by Probate as late as November 1748 and March 1752.

This had a profound effect on communities, towns and villages across a significant part of the country. At this point, it is appropriate to reflect on the lasting effects of the tragedy in one such town, Portsmouth. An article published in the *Hampshire Telegraph and Naval Chronicle*, so much later, in 1900, surmised that 'the grief and consternation of Portsmouth people can only be faintly imagined by those who have experienced the shock of other great naval calamities in which their relatives or friends were involved'. It continues by commenting that 'of the seamen, hundreds must have belonged to the town and of the officers there were probably not one who had not some connection with it'.[49]

One particularly moving piece of material in the Probate Court's documents was a letter written by Captain Samuel Faulknor, dated 12 September 1744 from the *Victory* in Gibraltar Bay, to his wife Fanny just before they sailed for home. In what can be interpreted as a premonition of his imminent death, Faulknor wrote:

Dear Fanny,

I am sorry I could not see you before we sailed and I am sorry that poor Dicky is not well God's will be done with him and me and in case I never see you more I leave you one half of the money I die worth and my part of the Falconthorp with all my plate household goods of every kind for your life and as to the rest of my efforts I leave as followeth that is to say To my son Sam: fifty pounds To my son Robt the same and to my son John the same and as they are all lieutenants they can't expect more To my son Jonathan I leave three hundred pounds and to my son Richard five hundred pounds and as I have not time to say more I must leave you to do them justice. God bless you, your aff't husband,

    S Faulknor

    My blessings to the dear boys.[50]

Since the great bronze gun recovered from *Victory* went on public display in Portsmouth Harbour in 2019, it is important that the human tragedy associated with it is fully understood; and the stories of Balchen and *Victory* should not detract from the terrible loss of those other sailors' lives. Furthermore, what has been learnt from the event is the importance of their last voyage in saving the Mediterranean Fleet from collapse and thereby changing the course of the war in Britain's favour. At such an advanced age of 75, Balchen and the fleet he commanded had captured several French merchantmen, relieved the victualling convoy and seen the French fleet flee into Cadiz, once again demonstrating his unwavering loyalty and bravery.

It is also important to put the scale of this disaster into the context of other major maritime disasters, both before and since, in order to understand the significance of the event. A simple, tragic selection is all that is required to give such perspective:

22 October 1707: Sir Cloudesley Shovell's fleet of *Association,*
    St George, Eagle, Romney, Phoenix and
    Firebrand destroyed on the rocks of
    Scilly Isles   Circa 2,000 souls lost
3/4 October 1744: HMS *Victory* (1737)
    lost in storm   Circa 1,100 souls lost

29 August 1782: HMS *Royal George* sank
  off Spithead   Circa 1,000 souls lost
14 April 1912: RMS *Titanic* struck an
  iceberg, Atlantic Ocean   1,500 souls lost
7 May 1915: Cunard liner *Lusitania*
  torpedoed by *U-20*   1,198 souls lost
9 July 1917: HMS *Vanguard* exploded in
  Scapa Flow, Orkney Isles   843 souls lost

3

The Lamentations, the Literature and the Artistic Legacy

'We are an island people. None of us is ever very far from the sea, whether geographically or inside our heads ... our literature is soaked in brine, the North Sea wind blows through its topsails.'

I Curteis, 'Introduction' in *A Prayer for all Seasons. The Collects of the Book of Common Prayer*

If the magnitude of an event can be measured by the scale of the consequent and related lamentations, national and local newspaper coverage and artistic manifestations, then the loss of Balchen and his ship was an immense one. Moreover, it is through the emotional nature and specific detail of those outpourings that we gain a much greater understanding of their significance at that moment in time as well as a much wider picture of their subsequent legacy. In virtually every piece of literature arising from the catastrophe we see not only references to the gallantry and the bravery of the admiral, but also the national esteem in which Balchen was held. Similarly, most mentions of *Victory* in this literature demonstrate the feeling of awe amongst observers that such a mighty, well-known and powerful vessel could possibly have been sunk in a storm. Shock and horror permeate every piece, balanced by admiration and respect for man and ship. So, as we undertake a survey of contemporary literature relating to Balchen and *Victory*, particularly following their loss, we can examine more closely the importance of their story and the significance of both of their lives and their loss. It is not just the sheer volume of such outpourings of sorrow but the very specific emphasis on the person himself, the tragic loss of the ship and the consequent impact on society at large in Britain. The British press in general gave great and consistent coverage at this time to naval activities, usually escalating at times of war or the threat of invasion. The navy, since the defeat of the Spanish Armada, was constantly seen by the populace as the bastion of an independent nation, keeping Continental rivals away from our shores, making the Channel a liquid wall and keeping the wider oceans protected for British trade and colonial expansion. In the event of their loss, the scale of the disaster and the shock of losing such a prominent admiral as well as the largest and greatest warship in the navy were met with escalating newspaper coverage. In the immediate aftermath of the storm, newspapers across the country were reporting on the reappearance of the bedraggled squadron in Plymouth and Portsmouth, with increasing anxiety over *Victory's* non-appearance. Once the fact of their loss became clear, coverage turned to lamentations as well as accusations. This in turn evolved into poetry, a play and even a sea-song ballad about the catastrophic event, accompanied by commemorative paintings and etchings. Significantly, in terms of legacy and historiography, such was the catastrophic importance of the event that newspaper references to Balchen's shipwreck continued well into the second half of the eighteenth century and sporadically through the nineteenth century, finally trailing off after 1900. Similarly, literature in the form of three short naval biographical essays,[1] based upon (and largely copied from) the earliest 1776 publication, were produced up to the end of the eighteenth century, with an 1808 publication[2] representing the last biographical mention given to Balchen until the 2004 *Oxford Dictionary of National Biography's* article on the admiral by Baugh.[3] References to *Victory*, however, have continued right up to the present in naval history publications. Unfortunately, in every case the emphasis of these histories has been focussed on the event of the shipwreck itself, not on the achievements or lives of either admiral or ship. This seems somewhat inevitable given the vast coverage in newspapers and magazines of their loss and the consequent plethora of emotive literature that somehow smothered the individual life

26

stories of those involved and brought to the fore the tragedy as a focal point. It is inevitable that, until now, Balchen has been 'best known to history by a shipwreck'.[4]

The navy in the mid-eighteenth century was viewed as a symbol of national culture in England and, as political history evolved over the second half of the century, in wider British society. During a period of almost constant war with France and/or Spain and with the constant threat of invasion, one of the greatest industries right across the country was that providing for and sustaining the Royal Navy's voracious needs: timber for shipbuilding, iron ore and foundries for the production of guns and shot, ports and harbours sustaining the Royal Dockyards, sailmakers, rope makers, agriculture providing livestock and grain for ships' victuals, and the list goes on. Few hamlets, villages or towns, no matter how far inland, were unaffected or unconnected with these endeavours as the navy went from strength to strength. To an island nation, the navy was also seen as a symbol of defence for the realm, whereas the army, as a standing army, seemed more of a threat at home, given its role in maintaining public order and suppressing recent Scottish and Irish uprisings, or Continental in terms of its militaristic objectives. A recent study into naval patriotism at the time concluded that a major factor that 'privileged the navy in patriotic culture concerned the fact that in wartime naval symbolism dovetailed with the interest in national defence, while in peacetime it could be attached to the concerns of commerce'. This same study argued that the growing historical success of the navy 'allowed the navy to occupy a singular place in late-eighteenth-century imaginings of national identity ... primarily because it functioned as an effective social analogue, as a metaphor for British society. The notion of the ship as a microcosm of society – a "wooden world" – was long held. So, too, were its constitutional associations as the "Ship of State".[5] Also of significance, a church is seen as a sanctuary, where the central aisle is called a nave after the Latin word 'navis', a ship. In this context, the populace had a deep interest in the navy, in its actions, in its victories and conquests, but equally in its failures, its tragedies or its losses. This was both an emotive and physical attachment as both success and failure would impact people across the nation. Society demanded constant news of happenings at sea, from the defence of the Channel and mainland Britain to the increasing spread of colonies and trade globally. It is therefore hardly surprising that the loss of a leading admiral and the navy's greatest ship at the time should spark a massive volume of press coverage, particularly as the public was already accustomed to, and interested in the exploits of Balchen and *Victory* leading up to the disaster.

The national newspapers and more niche magazines were aligned to the significance of the sea and the psyche of an island people, often using romantic prose in their coverage of naval activities, particularly where tragedies were concerned. *The Gentleman's Magazine* received regional

THE

BIOGRAPHICAL MAGAZINE;

O R,

COMPLETE HISTORICAL LIBRARY.

A WORK REPLETE WITH

INSTRUCTION AND ENTERTAINMENT,

AND ACCOMPANIED WITH SUCH EMBELLISHMENTS

As have not hitherto appeared in any PUBLICATION in EUROPE.

BY A SOCIETY OF GENTLEMEN.

VOLUME I.

L O N D O N:

Printed for F. NEWBERY, the Corner of St. Paul's Church-yard, Ludgate-street. 1776.

THE LIVES OF THE
BRITISH ADMIRALS.

DISPLAYING,

In the most STRIKING COLOURS,

THE

CONDUCT AND HEROISM

OF THE

NAVAL COMMANDERS OF GREAT BRITAIN AND IRELAND.

WHOSE INTREPIDITY

Has convinced the World, that BRITAN-NIA is the Sovereign of the OCEAN.

INTENDED

Not only to Instruct and Entertain, but also to animate the Youth of this Country with a becoming Ardour, to imitate the glorious Actions of these Heroes, if their Duty should hereafter call them forth in the Defence of their Country.

PART I.

L O N D O N:

Printed for E. NEWBERY, at the Corner of St. Paul's Church Yard.

M DCC LXXXVII.

Covers of the two earliest known biographies listing Admiral Sir John Balchen: The 1776 *Biographical Magazine* by a 'Society of Gentlemen' and the 1787 *The Lives of British Admirals*, both printed for Newberry, at the corner of St Paul's Churchyard, Ludgate Street, London.

and local newspaper articles which it reprinted and commented upon in the mid-eighteenth century and it was also deeply interested in naval activities, particularly given the continual threat of French invasion. Following the outbreak of war with Spain in 1739 and with France the following year, coverage of the escalating naval action increased. In August 1740, such were the months of comings and goings of Rear-Admiral Nicholas Haddock and Vice-Admiral Balchen chasing the Spanish warships in and out of their ports that it published a satirical poem, equating their voyages to a children's game and entitled 'On the Modern Method of Waging Naval Wars in Europe':

From Cadiz to Mahon see Haddock goes,
Balchen from Plymouth to Ferrol then hies,
Again from thence to Plymouth back flies,
Forth from Ferrol then straight the Spanish creep,
Say, children, is not this your play BO PEEP?[6]

Regional newspapers also kept the populace informed of naval activities and by then Admiral Balchen's name would have been very well known. This is exemplified by *The Birmingham Gazette*, which repeated reports coming from London in November 1741 that 'it is said Sir John Norris [on his flagship, *Victory*] is to sail with a New Reinforcement, and New Instructions, on another Secret and Important Expedition; and that Admiral Balchen is to command a strong Fleet in Observation'.[7] This reinforced and escalated the subsequent national coverage and grief that arose on Balchen's demise a few years later.

The first newspaper reports coming in of the unfolding disaster were both concerned and confused. As described earlier, the London *Daily Post* led the coverage on 10 October 1744, publishing a letter dated 8 October from Admiral Steuart aboard *Duke*, which described in detail the storm that the squadron had encountered on 3 October and how all the ships were severely damaged, ending 'Admiral Balchen was separated from us in the Storm, and is not yet arriv'd'.[8] The *Daily Advertiser* then reported on 12 October that following the storm, although most of Balchen's squadron had returned to port in a very bad state, 'there is no certain Account come to the Admiralty where Sir John Balchen is'.[9] Three days later the same paper reported optimistically that 'yesterday an Express arrived with Account that Sir John Balchen, in the *Victory*, was arrived at Plymouth, in a shattered condition'.[10] Another London paper, the *General Advertiser*, countered that same Monday that 'there is still no News relating to Sir John Balchen in the *Victory*, which greatly increases the Pain of the Publick for his Safety'.[11] As far afield as Edinburgh the story was unfolding with increasing apprehension, the *Caledonian Mercury* reporting on 16 October, that 'it was reported on Exchange, (which God forbid) that the *Victory*, Admiral Balchen, has been cast away on the Rocks of Scilly. As there is no Accounts arrived of him, People are under great Apprehensions.'[12] But that same day, back in London, the *London Evening Post* finally broke the news that, indeed, both ship and admiral were lost:

> The *John and Mary*, Miller [cargo vessel], is arriv'd there [Poole] from Guernsey, and has brought letters, dated the 14th instant, advising that a Fore-top mast, several oars, all mark'd *Victory*, have been drove on shore on the Isle of Alderney; and from many circumstances it appears, that his Majesty's ship the *Victory*, 110 guns, commanded by Sir John Balchen, and Captain Faulkner, was lost near the Island, in the night between the 4th and 5th instant; and as there was no Account of the crew when these letters were wrote, 'tis fear'd they all perished.[13]

The next wave of newspaper coverage focussed on the discovery of wreckage and a mournful acceptance of the loss. *The Gentleman's Magazine* reported on 19 October that two ships, the *Falkland* and the *Fly*, had been despatched to cruise around Alderney and Guernsey to 'get intelligence of the *Victory*', but only 'met with several pieces of a wreck and part of a carv'd work stern, which they judg'd to belong to the said ship'.[14] Finally, the *Westminster Journal* gave a conclusion to the event on 3 November, confirming at last that there was now 'no probability that a single soul has been saved'. It lamented that not only had the largest ship in the fleet and the finest set of guns, masts, rigging and yards gone to the bottom, 'but, sad disaster! With them are perish'd a considerable part of the flower of our mariners.'[15]

Such was the impact this tragedy had on the populace that poetic literature came to replace the reporting, reflecting the heartfelt angst felt in society over the losses. The very early release of the wood-cut print of *The Famous Ship Victory* capitalised on the outburst of mourning. This was followed by the more detailed and dramatic painting of the loss of *Victory* by Peter Monamy in 1745 and his collaborative etching the following year, both to immortalise the ship and the shipwreck. But parallel to this expression in art was the poetry and other popular literature produced immediately following the wreck. Even before the end of October, *The Gentleman's Magazine* seems to have produced the first poetry, entitled 'To Britain. On the loss of Adm. Balchen':

Portentous, Britain, were thy early fears
The sad, sad prologue of succeeding tears!
Thy after-hopes were as a chearing light'
To dying men's expiring sense and sight!,
The shatter'd planke confirm thy Balchen's fate,
A wreck like Shovell's, and a loss as Great.[16]

It must have been at this same time that what is called a 'broadside ballard' (not ballad), or popular song, was published about the catastrophic event, again giving popular access to lamentations of the occasion. Unlike sea shanties which were songs to accompany and coordinate heavy work such as hauling on board a ship, a broadside ballard, according to Julia Bishop, an expert in folklore and folk life,[17] is a song which may well have been sung by others besides sailors. They were, explains Steve Roud, also an expert on folklore,[18] 'cheaply-printed song sheets which were sold in the streets for a penny or less', making the subject a clearly popular and well-known event. Both of these experts agree that it is often difficult to discover the exact origins of a song such as this, categorised as 'street literature'. However, the broadside ballard entitled 'The Loss of the *Victory* Man of War' (see Appendix 2 for full text), though found most recently in John Aston's edited and collected *Real Sailor-Songs* of 1891, appears, in the nature of the genre with its obviously emotive and despairing tone, to have been written immediately after the event. The ten verses clearly attempt to relieve the distress of families hit by the disaster, displaying concern for 'their Widows left alone' and 'the fatherless have cause to rue' as well as referring to the 'grief of tender parents'. Although all reflect the enormity and tragedy of the loss, verse 6 sums up the event:

> The brave gallant Admiral Balchen,
>   With fourteen hundred Men beside,
> If she's lost, went to the Bottom,
>   And all at once together died:
> Oh! The dismal grief and Horror,
>   If one had been there to see,
> How they all were struck with Horror,
>   When sunk down the *Victory*.[19]

Verse 10 then turns specifically to the huge loss of life and, more specifically, what that loss meant to those left behind. The anguish and call to God drips with tragedy and pain felt far and wide across the country:

> Children crying for their Fathers,
>   Widows weeping in their distress,
> God will surely be their Comfort,
>   And protect the Fatherless,
> He'll be husband to the Widow,
>   That loves honest industry,
> And does give them his protection.
>   Farewell, fatal *Victory*!

Of a more personal nature, and one seeming to represent one of those people left behind to grieve, is an anonymous, undated but clearly contemporary song which is entitled 'Disconsolate Judy's lamentation for the absence of her true love Johnny, on board the *Victory*, with Admiral Balchen, now missing'. It also strikes true of the time, increasing the sense of tragedy by stating that her Johnny was press-ganged into the navy, as were many on board *Victory* on that last fateful voyage. It asks for the song to be sung to the tune of *Down by a Crystal River Side*:

Come pity me, young maidens all,
Who am brought into wretched thrall,
My love was prest away to sea, And
is on board the *Victory*.

When of him I did take my leave,
He said, 'Dear Judy, do not grieve;
Altho' I absent from you be, Stout is
our ship, the *Victory*.

'Brave Balchen is a gallant man,
And will conduct us safe to
land; Then my dear Judy I shall
see, When safe returns
the *Victory*'.

Ah! John, indeed my heart did fail,
When you to Lisbon was to sail,
For dangers they are great at sea,
Oh! Now where is the *Victory*?[20]

Reflecting the rising religious fervour pervading British society at that time, many of the poems and songs also contain references to God's grace and ardent prayer for the souls of the departed and comfort to those relatives left to mourn. This was a time when Charles Wesley was leading the evangelical Methodist movement across Britain, a time of new church-building and church-going. Nor should it be forgotten that only a few years before Balchen was born the new *Book of Common Prayer* of 1662 came to provide a whole series of 'Forms of Prayers to be used at Sea' which begin with two prayers 'to be used in her Majesty's navy every day'. Michael Brydon, writing about this, reflects that 'a ship in the midst of a storm would certainly appreciate a quick end to the distress of "raging winds and the roaring sea" and in a world of pirates and hostile foreign navies a request to the Almighty to "be a defence unto us against the face of the enemy" would have been heartfelt'.[21] Undoubtedly the writers and poets of the time would reflect on the religious passions connected with the sea and its dangers to all seamen of the time. Although it was some time before William Whiting, inspired by Psalm 107 with its maritime references, wrote the now famous naval hymn 'Eternal father strong to save ... for those in peril on the Sea', the navy of the mid-eighteenth century was very closely aligned with the Christian fervour of the period. So other semi-religious poems appeared in memory of others lost with Balchen, mostly mentioning his name as well. Such an anonymous poem was to the memory of the Reverend Charles Prince, the late Chaplain on board *Victory* (see Appendix 3 for full text). This, published in the November immediately after the wreck, concluded:

> Heav'n saw thy anguish, heard thy ardent pray'r,
> And snatch'd thee hence, his more peculiar care,
> To realms above; so his best servants fare.
> Nor think that Balchen, or his heroes, die;
> Led by their heav'nly guide, they triumph in the sky.[22]

Some two years later, in 1746, the place of Balchen, *Victory* and the shipwreck were still clearly established in British culture, being featured strongly in a play produced by William Hyland entitled *The Ship-Wreck: A Dramatick Piece* (see Appendix 4 for the relevant verses). Although this production was largely focussed on the plunder of Dutch shipwrecks on the coast of England, a significant four stanzas graphically describe the tempest swallowing up *Victory* and her crew. This reflects the continuing power of the loss in the public imagination, giving Hyland's play a reference point amongst the audience of how tragic such an event was and a tangible feel to his story. By equating his theme with Balchen's shipwreck, Hyland rekindles the emotions played out two years previously to heighten the tension and significance of his play, with the third and fourth verses reading:

> Wind, Lightning, Thunder, Rain and Hail,
> With furious Rage assault the Ship
> Now splits the Mast, now rends the Sail,
> And all are Swallowed in the Deep.

Thus Balchen and his hapless Fate,
And suffer'd an untimely Death:
A thousand Souls, the unhappy Freight,
All perish'd in a single Breath.[23]

All such literature helped immortalise the shipwreck among the nation and in British culture. It became a prominent landmark in popular understanding of naval history as a stand-out event, as much so as a major battle might feature prominently in the annals of military history. Eking out and unravelling the stories and characters consumed and overwhelmed by the shipwreck itself is the challenge of a scholar today. The historiography of the individuals, the admiral and the ship, has therefore been submerged in their tragic ending which became the emphasis of subsequent newspaper or journal articles as well as books and biographies. George Landow, in an article written about shipwrecks and English literature during this period, rightly pointed out that 'romance, satire and the literature of adventure have always relied upon the device of the shipwreck to isolate a character and place him in a new setting ... a convenient means of manipulating narrative'.[24] This is true in the case of Balchen and *Victory* in so far as the shipwreck has become their setting and their narrative ever since. But by the same token, Bernard Richards, in a review article about Landow's book on images of crisis as literary iconology in the period, declares that 'the various images of calamity besetting the voyager on the journey of life provide an excellent focus for investigation of the cultural paradigms',[25] which also chimes with how the populace perceived their loss at the time.

Over subsequent years the gradually dwindling written references to Balchen, as shown below, tend to relate only to his shipwreck. Even towards the end of the nineteenth century, it was the tragedy of the shipwreck, not the man or ship themselves, which became the story. In 1852, in its 'Calendar of the Week' section, *The Hampshire Advertiser and Salisbury Guardian* listed: 'The *Victory*, 110, wrecked near Alderney, and Admiral Balchen, with 1,100 men, perished, 1744.'[26] In 1877 an article appeared in *The Dundee Courier & Argus* under a series entitled 'The Romance of the Sea' and headed 'Loss of the

Victory, with Admiral Balchen, and 1,000 men'. This gave a detailed account of how 'the British Navy sustained a terrible disaster, which vividly recalled the fate of Sir Cloudesley Shovell, and the *Association*, the *Eagle*, and the *Romney*, in 1707'. However, it did describe Balchen as the 'gallant Admiral' and that *Victory* was 'considered one of the finest specimens of naval architecture in the world'.[27] The next significant reference to them was occasioned by another memorable naval catastrophe when, in 1893, Admiral Tryon drowned when his battleship *Victoria* sank in the Mediterranean following a collision with another Royal Navy ship. This prompted an article in a London journal, *The Graphic*, entitled 'England's Drowned Admirals',[28] which described Balchen's disaster and, like the earlier article, was largely a synopsis taken from the 1776, 1787 and 1795 biographies described later. The one and only newspaper or journal reference found by this study over the next 104 years appeared in 1900 when the *Hampshire Telegraph and Naval Chronicle*, in a series of articles on the 'History of Portsmouth', published a short piece on the shipwreck, but, unlike the previous articles, referred to the event in terms of the human cost: 'It is computed that not less than 1,100 souls perished in this terrible catastrophe, a greater number than in any single ship disaster in the annals of the British Navy.'[29] Significantly, as discussed earlier, this article placed the disaster into the context not of an admiral or a ship, but in the impact it had on the inhabitants of Portsmouth, describing how many of the seamen and officers came from the town and how the grief and consternation of Portsmouth people 'can only faintly be imagined'.

Another interesting account of the lamentations that followed the loss of Balchen and his ship comes from the chronicles of Greenwich Naval Hospital, where Balchen had been appointed to the prestigious position of Governor when he retired in April 1744, just a few months before his recall to the navy. These chronicles, published in 1886 by the Reverend A G L'Estrange, refer to 'Sir John Balchen, who held office for a shorter period than any other, and whose sad fate seemed to throw a shadow over Greenwich, though he never actually resided there'.[30] After briefly describing some of Balchen's naval exploits, the chronicles then go on to recall the subsequent outpourings felt across the country:

> What became of this splendid ship, freighted with so many precious lives, was never clearly known; not one of the men survived to tell the tale. No message from the sea was ever found to give the sad information.
>
> The whole of England was filled with grief at this disaster. Many of the principal families had to mourn for the young and brave, and the nation generally felt the loss of the grand ship and fine crew which had been the pride of the country.[31]

Given the national newspaper coverage of the tragedy and the amount of art and literature reflecting the outpourings of grief during the subsequent years, it is of little surprise that both Balchen and *Victory* are largely known to history today in the context of the shipwreck rather than as individual subjects. Although very few, if any, references to Balchen can be found between the 1900 article and Baugh's 2004 biography on the admiral, *Victory* has had a more continuous stream of references, though mostly confined to more specialist publications on naval ships, shipbuilding and design. Here again, as discussed later, these references tend to place the ship into the context of her flaws that led to her loss, thereby perpetuating the association with a shipwreck. The authors of most recent books in this category, published in 1979, 1983 and 1994,[32] have examined *Victory* in the well-recorded assumption that she perished on the rocks of the Casquets reef off Alderney. Since the finding of the wreck in 2008, only Rif Winfield's 2010 book[33] sees the ship foundering at sea rather than being wrecked. The discovery of the wreck and the finding and displaying of the two guns at the National Museum of the Royal Navy now gives historians a great opportunity to rectify their history by widening their knowledge about both the ship and the man so entwined with the guns. This survey of contemporary literature and art clearly demonstrates how important they were at the time by the impact their loss had upon the nation. It shows that this was no ordinary shipwreck nor was it just another loss of a naval crew at a time of war. The sheer volume, scale and reach of the reporting, prose and art that exploded across the country, with powerful local as well as national reach, echoes the enormity of losing the nation's greatest warship; their loss was undoubtedly represented a national disaster of immense scale and impact on the nation's psyche.

4

HMS *Victory*'s Story

Too proud, too proud, what a press she bore!
Royal, and all her royals wore.
Sharp with her, shorten sail!
Too late; lost; gone with the gale.

This was that fell capsize.
As half she had righted and hoped to rise
Death teeming in by her portholes
Raced down decks, round messes of mortals.

Then a lurch forward, frigate and men;
'All hands for themselves' the cry ran then;
But she who had housed them thither
Was around them, bound them or wound them with her.

Gerard Manley Hopkins (1844–89). Extract from his poem
'The loss of the Eurydice', *Foundered 24 March 1878.*

HMS *Victory*'s life began only a few years after Balchen's, on 1 April 1673, when the Admiralty ordered a 100-gun First Rate ship of the line to be built at Portsmouth Dockyard. She entered service at a volatile time in English history when the struggle between Catholicism and Protestantism tore the country apart and engulfed both Scotland and Ireland, as well as France and the Dutch Republic. The coming and going of monarchs over her following years of service was reflected in the changing names of the ship. She was launched in the reign of Charles II, on 27 June 1675, and named after his brother, later James

II, as *Royal James*. The 'Glorious Revolution' of 1688 saw William of Orange and Mary become joint monarchs (until 1694 when Mary's death left William III as king). Also, in September of that year the Nine Years War (otherwise called the War of the Grand Alliance, ending with the Treaty of Ryswijk in 1697) began, triggered by France's invasion of Cologne and the Palatinate which threatened the balance of power in Europe. The Anglo-Dutch William of Orange allied England and the Dutch Republic with Spain, Portugal, Savoy and the Habsburg Empire against Louis XIV's expansionist France. Coinciding with the outbreak of Continental war, as well as the Anglo-French colonial war in North America, were the Jacobite risings in Scotland and Ireland in 1689. It was following the Battle of the Boyne in 1690, when the invading James Stuart was defeated and returned to exile in France under the protection of Louis XIV, that the ship was renamed. A letter from the Admiralty to Chatham Royal Dockyard on 3 March 1690 confirmed that 'we thinke fitting that their Majesty's Ship now named the *Royal James* shall be named the *Victory*'.[1]

She took this name because the old Second Rate *Victory* of 1666, which was earmarked to be rebuilt upon her lower hull, was condemned. As the story of *Victory* unfolds here, the rebuilding of British warships will be seen as common practice during this time, as she herself underwent several such conversions. This practice, as well as the frequent re-use of timbers from condemned ships for new-build ships, is described in some detail by the letter from the Admiralty Office condemning the old *Victory* on 5 March 1690, only two days after ordering the renaming of *Royal James* to the new *Victory*:

> You have represented that their Majesty's Ship *Victory*, now in Woolwich Dock is upon a survey taken of her by their Majesty's Shipwrights of their Majesty's Yards at Deptford & Woolwich ... that her bottom is not fitting to be built upon, but that some of her Timber and Planck, may be useful in the building of another ship whereupon you propose the taking of her bottom in pieces for clearing the Dock of her.
>
> We do hereby advise and direct you to cause the said ship *Victory* to be cast and her bottom taken in pieces and that in this doing

thereof all possible care be taken for preserving such of her timber and planck as may be useful in other works, on one of an Third Rate Ship designed to be built this year.[2]

So the now newly-renamed *Victory* entered another of many phases of her life. She was placed under the command of Admiral Sir John Ashby, and participated in the huge Battle of Barfleur in mid-May 1692.[3] Under the threat of a French invasion being planned by Louis XIV, William III began to assemble a combined fleet of Dutch and British warships large enough to undertake a counter-invasion of France. This was a time when the British Government was weak and divided and there were still questions of naval loyalty to William amidst the continued struggle between Catholic and Protestant factions. When French Admiral Tourville entered the Channel off Plymouth he commanded a fleet of up to forty-four ships of the line which confronted an Anglo-Dutch force of some eighty-two ships. On 19 May 1692, off Cape Barfleur, the engagement took place. Despite early successes by Tourville's fleet, by evening he was being surrounded

'The Battle of Barfleur, 19 May 1692'. Seventeenth-century grisaille on panel, by Adriaen van Salm. HMS *Victory* was the flagship of Admiral Sir John Ashby at the epic Battle of Barfleur in 1692. She was part of a combined Anglo-Dutch fleet which heavily defeated a French fleet under Admiral Tourville, first at Cape Barfleur and later at La Hogue. (BHC0333, © National Maritime Museum, Greenwich, London)

and was forced to retreat under cover of darkness. While twenty-two French ships escaped into St Malo, over the next few days Tourville's damaged flagship and two others went aground and were burned by British fireships near Cherbourg and another twelve other ships of the line were burned at La Hogue, giving the Allies a notable victory.[4]

Nothing seems to have been recorded about *Victory*'s specific role in this battle, but her commander, Sir John Ashby, and Philip van Almonde, who commanded the Dutch fleet, were later criticised by Admiral Russell for not pursuing the rest of the French fleet before it escaped into St Malo.[5] But *Victory* had engaged in her first major battle and may even have been badly damaged, given the next stage of her life.

By May 1693, it had become apparent that *Victory* was having severe structural problems. Anthony Carey reported to the Navy Board that 'Admirals of the Fleet have found the *Victory* to be so unseaworthy that they have ordered her into Portsmouth Harbour. The Admiralty order that she be immediately careened and refitted.'[6] This seemed to have made matters worse because, only 20 days later, *Victory* was returned to port with more repairs required. Carey again reported to the Navy Board that 'Admirals are reporting that the Carpenter of the *Victory* has informed them that at her last refit at Chatham he notified the Master Shipwright of her defects and that significant repairs have not been carried out including to her Beach Plank and her Ironwork'. He continued that 'an instruction is given for an enquiry to be made, particularly as the ship has had to enter port again for further repairs'.[7] Things were clearly not going well for the ship and her very existence in her current form was being questioned.

From 1696 to 1745 Parliament did not vote for any investment in shipbuilding and, as mentioned earlier, the navy's needs were 'increasing met by "great rebuilds" of existing ships, which were largely or entirely broken up and reconstructed, sometimes on the old bottom, sometimes merely incorporating some of the old timbers.'[8] Thus it became the practice for the Royal Navy to take ships to pieces and either store the timbers for future need or rebuild them with fresh timbers or specifications.

So *Victory* ended up being rebuilt at Chatham Dockyard between 1694 and 1695. By August 1695 she was ready for relaunching but not before her hull had been sheathed. This was probably milled lead sheathing, which was often being used after around 1670 for Royal Navy ships or could have been the alternative solution, using sacrificial planking laid on a layer of tar, pitch and hair. The sheathing was to repel the blight of the Teredo worm boring through a ship's timbers below the waterline, particularly in warmer waters. Copper sheathing only became standard for Royal Navy ships much later, in the second half of the eighteenth century. Writing to the Navy Board on behalf of the Admiralty, John Lowther noted 'your letter to our Secretary informed us that the *Victory* will be in a condition to be put in the water and we wish to know whether she will be sheathed before she comes out of the dock. You are directed to have her sheathed before she is launched.'[9] So shortly afterwards, in October 1695, *Victory* did indeed enter the warmer waters as she had been ordered by the Admiralty to be fitted out 'forthwith' in Chatham for services in the Mediterranean; 'manned with her highest complement of men and furnished with six months dry and two months of wet Provisions, and that all possible dispatch be made therein'.[10]

By then *Victory* was the flagship of Vice-Admiral Matthew Aylmer. As such, the ship was frequently used as the 'court' for court martials, presided over by him. These were exemplified by two such trials undertaken on the ship in September 1696. A certain Thomas Freman, Pilot of the *Lynn*, was accused of running his ship ashore off Shoreham Harbour, but was acquitted on 2 September.[11] On the next day, however, the defendant was not so lucky. Thomas Sherman, Carpenter, was accused of misbehaviour and stirring up mutiny and was found guilty and sentenced to be hanged on board *Rose*, guardship, in Portsmouth Harbour on 17 September 1696.[12]

But it was only a year later that it became apparent that *Victory*, although newly rebuilt and therefore 'modernised', had some serious stability problems. These were the first claims that the ship was 'crank', or seemingly top-heavy and liable to roll in anything but calm seas, with great quantities of ballast required to keep her upright. Should the roll be worsened in rough weather, there was the danger of water entering her lower gun ports. The traditional way to rectify such 'crankness' at the time was to apply additional 'girdling' or extra strakes of timber along her waterline, in order to widen her base, providing greater girth and therefore stability. 'Obviously', states Baugh, 'ballasting may bring the lower tier of guns too close to the water. Increasing the beam prevented this, but ships that were too broad abeam often experienced a violent rolling action in heavy seas that loosened shrouds and stays, pried open hull joints (mainly by the working of the masts), and frequently led to the loss or damage of masts and spars.'[13] This was clearly the case with *Victory* when she was under the command of Vice-Admiral Aylmer in 1697. He wrote to the Lords of the Admiralty on 12 January 1697: 'My ship is so very cranke, that I think it absolutely necessary, she should have a good girdling, for in an indifferent Gale of Wind with my Topsails low sett, she conveyed her entering ports in the water & yet she cannot stow above forty tuns [of ballast] than she had in her.'[14]

The Admiralty Office responded to this request immediately, asking the dockyard shipwrights to respond to Aylmer's concerns: 'My Lords of the Admiralty, having read a letter from Vice-Admiral Aylmer touching the Crankness of the *Victory*, their Lordships command me to send you an extract of the letter, that you may consider thereof, and Report to them your opinion touching the girdling her, as the Vice-Admiral proposes.'[15] There is little doubt that this proposed action was taken on the ship since Josiah Burchett, who had been appointed Secretary to the Admiralty in 1694 (and was to hold the post until 1742), wrote in his covering note for Aylmer's letter of complaint about *Victory*'s crankness, that the Admiralty 'opines that she should be girdled'.[16] However, this issue clearly came back to haunt *Victory* again and it certainly appears almost as a premonition of later troubles arising from the ship's design. In the meantime other major works continued on *Victory* requiring her to be repaired in dry dock. On 11 June 1704 the Commissioner Captain Sir William Gifford of Portsmouth Dockyard reported that 'the *Victory* was launched on Monday' after one such refit.[17]

Although *Victory* was briefly decommissioned in February 1705 during the reign of Queen Anne (1702 to 1714), she was commissioned again and, in 1714, she was renamed *Royal George* when the Hanoverians came to the throne (George I reigned from 1714 to 1727). But within a year, she was again renamed *Victory*.[18]

'First Rate HMS *Victory* (1695), 104 guns'. Etching by Jan Kip after Isaac Sailmaker. (Image 70763, Object PAI6675, © National Maritime Museum, Greenwich, London)

Rather like Admiral Balchen's life of catastrophic events, as we shall see in later chapters, *Victory* clearly had her own. Already blamed for being crank, further problems were to beset the ship. In February 1721, she caught fire in Portsmouth while having weed burnt from her bottom (a procedure known as breaming) and burnt almost to the waterline.[19] In April that year she was taken to pieces and stored in the dockyard. In line with the Admiralty's peacetime practice between 1713 and 1739, she remained as the *Victory* on the navy list as a Royal Navy warship while in fact, comments naval historian Rif Winfield, 'she was simply a pile of re-usable timbers in a corner of the Dockyard'.[20] As recorded above, at the time warships above Third Rate were generally rebuilt and although more expensive and difficult to undertake compared to a new build, it was compensated for by the re-use of the salvaged timber. As described by Baugh, 'the largest pieces of a great ship – her keel members, stern post, stem pieces, knees and frame timbers – were exorbitantly expensive because of their unusual size or peculiar shape'.[21]

It wasn't until 1726 that the decision was made to rebuild *Victory* on the frame of the old ship[22] to the specifications for a First Rate 100-gun warship, and her keel was laid the next year in a Portsmouth dry-dock.[23] However, the official warrant 'directing his Majesty's Ship the *Victory* to be rebuilt of the Dimensions therein mentioned, or as near as agreeable thereto'[24] was not issued until September 1733 and she was not re-launched until 1737. Interestingly, before she was re-launched it was decided to alter an important aspect of the ship while she was still being built. The Commissioner of Portsmouth Dockyard, Richard Hughes, reported that 'the Master Shipwright has been preparing materials for a Lyon [Lion] for the *Victory* instead of a figurehead in accordance with the warrant and sketch previously sent'.[25] By 4 July 1737 the Navy Board was informed that 'the *Victory* is to be launched shortly but it will be difficult'.[26] Even from the day of her launch it seemed there would be difficulties with the rebuilt ship.

She was the last Royal Navy First Rate to boast a full, bespoke set of bronze guns, and one of the last to have a full deck of the massive 42-pounders. From this period onward, the cheaper iron guns were preferred to bronze for naval armament and the 32-pounder was preferred to the very heavy and difficult to handle 42-pounder. It was the 12-pounder and the 42-pounder guns that were brought up from the wreck site in 2009 that enabled the positive identification of *Victory* by the UK Receiver of Wrecks. Weighing over 3 tonnes, with a length of 3.4m (11.5ft) and a muzzle diameter of 17.8cm (7.0in), the 42-pounder is a wonderful display of craftsmanship, including elegantly ornate dolphin handles and an intricate Royal Crest of King George I (1714–27). The 12-pounder gun from the ship has the Royal Arms of King George II (1727–60). So the manufacture of the guns preceded the ship's construction by a number of years.

The base ring of the 42-pounder displays the name of the maker, 'SCHALCH'. Andrew Schalch was born in Schaffhausen, Switzerland in 1692 and was employed in the Douai cannon factory before coming to England. In 1716 he was engaged to build furnaces and other material for the new brass works being built at Woolwich. In May 1718 he was appointed as the first master founder to the Royal Brass Foundry in Woolwich (later Woolwich Arsenal). The name SCHALCH, together with the year 1723, also appears on a bronze 24-pounder currently in a museum storage facility in the Netherlands. This gun was allegedly illegally removed from the *Victory* wreck site by a Dutch salvage vessel in July 2011 using a hydraulic grab and taken back to Holland. Coincidentally, there is another bronze 24-pounder with the same name SCHALCH together with the year 1743 engraved on the base ring and sitting on its gun trolley in the grand cobbled courtyard of Henry VIII's Southsea Castle, close to the entrance to Portsmouth Harbour. Like the *Victory*'s great bronze guns, this one had also witnessed a similarly catastrophic event, having been on the mighty *Royal George* when she capsized at the Spithead anchorage in the Solent on 29 August 1782, with the loss of Rear-Admiral Richard Kempenfelt and some 900 crew. Ironically, perhaps, this gun was cast just the year before *Victory* and her guns were lost. Lying unassumingly on public display today, the gun was salvaged from the wreck site in 1834 by Charles Anthony Deane.

Victory's guns have been described as extremely rare examples of hybrid guns designed by Colonel John Armstrong based on the former Borgard system and a master template obtained from the French. Albert Borgard was a Danish mercenary soldier, joining the British Army in 1692, and in 1716 oversaw the standardisation of artillery. Under his method of reform, guns were thereafter known by the weight of the shot being fired (i.e. 12-pounder, 24-pounder, 32-pounder, etc). It was Armstrong, as the new Surveyor General of Ordnance in 1722, who then redesigned the Borgard system to incorporate further modifications.

After her recommissioning, *Victory* had an eventful though short life. In April 1740 Admiral Sir John Norris requested that *Victory* be fitted out in Portsmouth 'as a flagship for the Admiral of the Fleet'.[27] It was as flagship for the Channel Fleet under Admiral Sir John Norris that she had a major collision which brought her back to port for significant repairs. *The Gentleman's Magazine* reported the incident on 17 July 1740 thus:

The Fleet under Sir John Norris returned to St Hellens, having the night before met with a sad disaster off Portland, by the *Lyon* Man of War running foul of the *Victory*, and carrying away her Head, and doing her other damage; the *Lyon* lost her bowsprit, and 28 men who were thrown over by the shock, which was very alarming even to the oldest Mariner; the Sea poured into the *Victory* till by the immediate order of Sir John Norris it was stop'd.[28]

This incident, while *Victory* carried Vice-Admiral Norris and had Thomas Whitney as First Captain and the ill-fated Samuel Faulknor as Second Captain at the time, was captured in detail by *Victory*'s Lieutenant Sheldrake Laton's log book entry, which illustrates the seriousness of the occasion:

At 1AM a ship coming with her starboard tack on board run us on board; carried away our head & spreetsail yard: also her own Foremast and Bowspreet; altho we endeavour'd to make them see and hear us by shewing lights & hallowing as loud as the Watch was able and finding the most probable way to shun her was by putting our ship astays which we immediately did & had not our ship been very quick it might & would have been of worse consequence.[29]

A letter was addressed to the Commissioners of the Navy from Portsmouth Dock Commissioner Hughes, informing them about the inspected damage to *Victory*: 'I am now to inform you, the loss of her head, was occasioned from the *Lyon*'s running on board her; by which accident the latter's Foremast was carried away.'[30] This single event was so printed on the minds of observers that, after the loss of *Victory* in 1744, the author of a sea song lamenting her loss recalled the incident in one of 10 verses.

O *Victory*! Though wast unlucky,
But once before was out at Sea,
In the Night run foul of the *Lion*,
And her Carved-work took away:
Now thou art gone to the Bottom,
With a jovial Company,
An Admiral, Marines and Sailors,
Most Unhappy *Victory*![31]

Further problems then arose with *Victory*'s stability and sailing qualities. In February 1742, her now First Captain, Samuel Faulknor, reported that 'the tons of iron ballast assisted the ship during the last cruise, a view supported by John Norris' and he asked 'for an order for additional ballast',[32] implying that she required even more ballast to keep her stiff and upright rather than crank and wallowing.

There was an account of further damage done to the 'unhappy' *Victory* and several other ships in Admiral Sir John Norris's squadron in February 1744, due to a severe storm. A State Paper reported that 'the French Fleet has disappeared and the *Victory* and another ship have been damaged by the fierce storm ... the French ships in Dunkirk must have suffered'.[33] Reporting that the *Victory* had lost two anchors and three cables, William Moreland wrote that he had visited Sir John Norris on the *Victory* and was ordering ten anchors 'with hoops, Bolts & Treenails for the same'.[34]

Nevertheless, *Victory* was, according to Charnock's 1795 *Biographia Navalis*, 'the largest and finest ship in the navy'.[35] When Admiral Balchen was given his new commission and raised his flag on board *Victory* in the summer of 1744 in preparation for his final, fatal voyage to Lisbon, he and the Admiralty must have been confident that the fleet would carry out its mission successfully, led by the greatest warship in the navy and one of her most experienced and respected admirals as well as her highly regarded captain, Samuel Faulknor. The storm on the night of 3/4 October 1744, which severely damaged much of the fleet as it returned triumphant and so close to home, came to overwhelm *Victory* and engulf her and her entire crew; lost without a single survivor or body to tell the tale. Unfortunately, as will become clear, she had some serious flaws in her design and construction which certainly contributed to her tragic loss.

The wreck of *Victory* was discovered in 2008. She was found by Odyssey Marine Exploration around 100km west of the Channel Islands and 80km south-east of Plymouth. This, according to recent claims and despite contemporary reports, 'unequivocally confirmed that the battleship never got within sight of Alderney, but was overcome in the midst of the sea, deep within the English Channel'.[36] Naval historian Andrew Lambert echoed this view, claiming that 'Balchen did not do

The Logbook of Lieutenant Sheldrake Laton, 17 July 1740, describing the collision between HMS *Victory* and HMS *Lyon*. (ADM/L/V/60 Lieutenant's logs for HMS *Victory*, Caird Archives Library, National Maritime Museum)

anything so un-seamanlike as to run into the well-known and widely avoided Casquets'.[37] Frank Scott, nautical historian, is right to say that if a ship is 'lost with all hands', 'the circumstances of that loss can only be a matter of conjecture'.[38] But he also points out that, now we know she was not, as widely believed until the discovery of the wreck, driven onto the notorious Casquets reef, 'the assumption must be that she was overwhelmed in some way by the storm. Exactly how that took place', he concludes, 'is anyone's guess.'[39]

But no-one likes to 'guess' about such catastrophic events. Here, therefore, is a challenge for both historians and scientists to determine. One such scientific approach has been undertaken by a multi-disciplinary project undertaken by a team including the University of Greenwich's Computational Mechanics and Reliability Group (CMRG) and Nick Ball of the National Maritime Museum, using 'mathematical modelling and computer simulation' based upon a Computer Aided

Design (CAD) Model of the ship. This project, summarised in a paper given to the Royal Institution of Naval Architects' Historic Ships Conference in London in December 2016, identified five possible causes for *Victory*'s sinking:

1. Structural failure due to inherent design fault.
2. Inundation through the lowest stern window.
3. Structural failure due to use of inferior materials.
4. An external freak wave.
5. Seamanship error.

Illustrating the limitations of such a scientific approach, however, the team admitted that only 'the first two can be modelled using conventional engineering techniques, which is the focus of this paper'. This means that there are the three remaining scenarios that must still be considered. But in the meantime, this project calculated that during the storm at this particular location in the English Channel, there could have been a fundamental wave length of about 136m with a maximum height of 9.52m. One of their conclusions was that since 'the last sighting of the ship is described as "wallowing" which implies sinking while upright, rather than something more dramatic like a broach or a capsize'. In this case, they argued, two scenarios seem to be possible, namely:

1. The ship suffered structural failure of the hull under bending and shear from the large waves, leading to a massive leakage; probably the worst load case for this is with the crest of a wave at midships which would add extra hogging to the hogging inherent in such a ship.
2. The ship was flooded by waves smashing the stern lowest gallery and pouring water into the unpartitioned interior.

'The onset of structural failure', they stated, 'probably defined as enough structural disruption to allow uncontrollable leakage, is when treenails reach a critical load which is close to the ultimate failure load.'[40] There may well be some scientific and/or engineering, computer-aided explanations possible for the sinking of *Victory*. However, a historian would still prefer to look into the facts as they appear in historical documentation in order to analyse such an event. This sort of approach can also look at the wider picture of the historical circumstances in the building, maintaining and operation of such ships at that time and the opinions of the people involved. This also extends into the three other aspects or possible factors that computer and mathematical modelling cannot study, especially potential structural failures due to inferior materials and seamanship error. This leaves the extreme freak wave scenario.

Possible answers can be surmised on the basis of what evidence is actually available: she was too high, possibly top-heavy as well; she had been rebuilt on the frames of previous ships with timbers which, as evidenced below, could have been either green or rotten; she was already known to be unsteady or 'crank' and allegedly 'leewardly'. As early as 1740, Sir Jacob Acworth, Surveyor of the Navy, wrote to Joseph Allin, Master Shipwright at Portsmouth, asking for *Victory* to be fitted out for Admiral Sir John Norris, adding: 'He has promised to take the ship as she is, but complains much of her height abaft, treble balconies etc. which I was much surprised to hear of.'[41] This appears to be the start of an argument between the two over *Victory*'s construction, with Acworth remonstrating that 'our ships were [already] too heavy, too loose and too high without these additional encumbrances, which I am sure cannot add beauty, but must be in every respect disagreeable'.[42] Balchen himself, as discussed later in Chapter 6, had already criticised the instability of his ship, the 80-gun *Princess Amelia*, in 1735, telling the Admiralty that she was so tender or crank that she 'could have tumbled right over' and at the same time criticising Acworth.[43]

Most modern warship historians agree that the *Victory* was exceptionally high-sided and that this certainly contributed to her loss. Most 100-gun First Rate warships had, in addition to three decks, a quarterdeck and poop, an additional 'Poop Royal' or topgallant roundhouse, but, explains Lavery, 'the *Victory* of 1737, even had galleries in the poop-royal, giving her four tiers of windows and three open galleries'.[44] Commenting that she was the only British three-decker to have four complete tiers of quarter galleries, Winfield states that 'sadly this very characteristic compromised both her sailing qualities and her stability, causing her to roll in stormy weather',[45] and he concludes that 'it is a reasonable speculation' that this poor handling in heavy winds 'would have contributed to her tragic loss'.[46] Howard also describes the *Victory* as a 'high-sided ship for her draught' and this was believed 'to have made her leewardly and to have led to her loss'.[47] Writing more recently, Lambert also concluded that 'the top-heavy *Victory* was overwhelmed by a storm', adding that in his opinion Balchen's death 'was caused by sending out the ship in winter, when she was only fit for summer service'.[48]

The model of *Victory* which is today in the National Maritime Museum in Greenwich is an extraordinarily large scale contemporary 'full hull model' and gives us the best possible examination of the ship's design from keel to topmast and bowsprit to stern lamps and beam to beam. The model measures 2,037mm x 2,380mm x 990mm and is housed in a Perspex display case in the museum. Described by the museum's curators as being built in 'bread and butter fashion' and finished in the Georgian style, the model is partially decked, fully equipped and rigged. They go on to state that the large scale of the model supports the theory that it was once used as part of the equipment of the Royal Naval Academy at Portsmouth Dockyard for educating young gentlemen to the sea service. Though some have claimed that the model was specifically built as part of the Admiralty's investigation into her loss after the 1744 disaster, the museum curators clearly believe the model was made well before that, citing a letter written by six of these young gentlemen to the Navy Board in 1742 complaining that 'the model of *Victory* is so small, her rigging so slight, that we cannot learn anything from it, neither do we know anything of rigging or the stowage of anchors or cables, we are quite ignorant of everything that belongeth to sails'.[49] Rif Winfield also agrees that it is unlikely that the model was built to aid the enquiry into her loss 'given the length of time it would probably have taken to make the model', adding: 'but it certainly represents the ship as actually built. The hull, masts and rigging is contemporary with the ship itself.'[50]

The most accurate pictures available of the ship were drawn between 1741 and 1744 by Frederik Henrik af Chapman, an Anglo-Swedish ship designer who is now claimed to be the first 'proper' naval architect. The son of Thomas Chapman, a British naval officer who had joined

A drawing of the stern of HMS *Victory* produced by Frederik Henrik af Chapman, the foremost ship designer of his time, when he was working as a ship's carpenter between 1741 and 1744. Reproduced from Daniel G Harris, *F H Chapman – The First Naval Architect and his Work* (London: Conway Maritime Press, 1989).

the Swedish navy, and Susanna Colson, the daughter of a Swedish shipwright, Frederik Chapman was born in Gothenburg, Sweden in 1721. Between 1741 and 1744 he worked as a ship's carpenter in London, during which time he drew several detailed pictures of HMS *Victory* (and he was arrested more than once on suspicion of being a Swedish spy). Described as 'the foremost ship designer of his time, he owed his dominance to his extensive scientific training'.[51] His drawing of her stern (see the illustration above), clearly illustrates the dramatic height and range of her deck windows and galleries. This drawing, among others, is in the Sjohistorika Museum in Stockholm, while more of his drawings showing the plan of the body of HMS *Victory* are in the

National Maritime Museum, though strangely dated circa 1754,[52] and also demonstrate the unusually high stern galleries.

Given her disproportionate height and the clear violence of the storm, a closer look at the technical problems of sailing-ship stability focusses on the effects of a 'squall'. Expert in the field of square rig operations and safety Frank Scott comments that while a sailing vessel may operate perfectly safely in 'normal' conditions, squalls have caused the knockdown and loss of a number of ships. 'The impact of a squall in any case causes a greater heeling moment than a steady wind of the same force', he advises, adding, 'certain combinations of circumstances will result in knockdown even for the best vessel, and the degree of resulting down flooding is critical to her ability to recover.'[53]

It appears that such a squall led to the *Victory*'s fate, illustrated perhaps by the painting of her loss by Peter Monamy. It may be no coincidence that this painting's scene is described by the National Maritime Museum as being 'in the van de Velde tradition'.[54] There is a Willem van de Velde painting, completed in 1680, currently in the Rijksmuseum in Amsterdam entitled 'A Ship on the High Seas Caught by a Squall, known as *The Gust*', and depicts a large 70-gun British warship clearly in distress. The two paintings, though one perspective is from the bow and the other from the stern, are remarkably similar in showing the power and impact of a storm and, in particular, a 'gust' on a large warship and it might be speculated that Monamy may, through his painting, have considered a squall as the possible cause of *Victory*'s loss.

There could well have been other contributory factors to her loss, especially concerning overloading ships with guns and the quality of timber used for their construction. Indeed, Lavery concludes that 'the shipbuilders and administrators of the long peace from 1714 to 1739 have attracted much criticism, and it has often been suggested that this period was the nadir of naval administration'.[55] This conclusion was clearly partly based upon Admiral Edward Vernon's bitter criticism of the Admiralty, naval adminstrators and ship design at the time. Ironically, even as Admiral Balchen's fleet was setting sail for Portugal, on 18 June 1744 Vernon was writing to the Lord Commisssioners of the Admiralty complaining about the strength and durability of warships:

'It is certain those complete ships [*Royal Sovereign* and *Royal Oak*] were of great strength and long duration: and that our modern ones are famous for neither: But to great cost of the Crown, have been found eminently defective in both', adding that the French 'don't generally crowd their ships with guns as we do, in which I think them much in the right, and that we cripple our ships by it.'[56] Going on to castigate the Surveyor of the Navy, Acworth, whom he said 'has halfe ruined the Navy', Vernon concluded prophetically that an enquiry should be made 'before it be too late; as I apprehend our Royal master's true interests are most likely to be the fatal sacrifice of not making some such timely inquiry'.[57]

The largest capital ships of the earlier eighteenth century were generally too small for their armament, particularly the 80-gun three-deckers, making their higher guns disproportionate to the ship's length and breadth and the lower guns too close to the water to be opened in anything but a flat calm sea. This need to carry the heavy guns as high out of the water as possible, explains Baugh, resulted in 'ships of the line were more likely to be "crank" or "tender", that is to roll or heel easily and excessively'. To remedy this, the options were either to add more ballast, which inevitably made the lower guns too close to the waterline, or to add exterior belts of timber, which gave a wider beam, but which could also lead to an even more violent rolling. Baugh states that this view was 'expressed by people who sought improvement in the 1740s', and he related this to the dispute between Admiral Balchen and Sir Jacob Acworth in 1735 over the defects in the 80-gun *Princess Amelia*.[58] The fundamental flaw in these large ships was that 'they carried too much armament for their capacity, and the answer was to increase their displacement and give them rather full bodies amidships'. This happened soon after the lessons learned by *Victory's* loss, and 'when this was done with the *Royal George* (100 guns), which was laid down in 1746 ... the result was a fine ship which acquitted herself admirably'.[59] This is a key legacy, as the new Establishment of 1745, in the wake of *Victory's* sinking, sparked a wave of reform and innovation in ship design, albeit delayed by the conservative-minded Acworth who held his office from 1715 to 1747.

The proximity between Vernon's vociferous criticisms of naval shipbuilding and the loss of *Victory*, only four months later, was instantly picked up by the media. In particular *The Gentleman's Magazine* for October and November 1744 led the charge to support Vernon's demands for reform. It cited the 19 October edition of *The London Evening Post*, reminding readers that as Admiral Vernon 'had represented some defect in the building and managing the royal ships ... it was hoped that the loss of this ship [the *Victory*] would cause an enquiry into this worst of grievances to a maritime power'.[60] In November, the magazine then cited the *Westminster Journal*, commenting on *Victory*'s 'misfortune' and with 'reflections occasion'd by the loss of his Majesty's ships of war, with Admiral Vernon's opinion on the late method of building them', adding that, as 'has been suggested, if our ship-building for the Royal Navy has been many years universally bad, ought we not to fear that the structure of this great vessel partook of the general mistake'. It therefore demanded 'the necessity of looking into causes, especially as they had been before more than hinted to those in authority, by a gentleman of unquestion'd judgement'.[61]

The wider community of seagoing naval officers also seized the opportunity provided by *Victory*'s loss and Vernon's accusations against the Admiralty to add their own views. In January 1745, Commodore Charles Knowles wrote to Lord Winchilsea, First Lord of the Admiralty (though Winchilsea had been replaced the previous December): 'The many great complaints that have been made of late years about the badness of our ships of war, both in regard to their figure as to sailing, and to their incapacity for lodging their men, as well as the badness of materials, and the manner in which they have been built, are not without just foundation.'[62] His lengthy letter covers a series of 'innumerable other faults' which he believed contributed to the 'badness' of naval ships, but he ends with this more serious accusation: 'The reason for our ships not being so durable as the enemy's, is that the timber as it is purchased and brought into the yards is laid in heaps, and not regularly expended according to its ages and the times of it being cut down.' He concludes: 'I have often seen green timber (which has lain uppermost) used soon after it has come into the yards, and the old timber which has lain undermost (and been seasoned fit to use) lay till it has rotted, or been so bad that it has decayed soon after it has been converted to use.'[63]

Charles Knowles, later Admiral Sir Charles Knowles, 1st Baronet, was certainly someone to be listened to and it was he who later added to the positive and constructive legacy of *Victory* and Balchen's loss as will be shown later. Indeed, Knowles was present with both Balchen and Anson at the Battle of Cape Passaro in 1718 where he was temporarily aboard Admiral Byng's flagship *Barfleur*. Significantly, he was also commander of the 60-gun *Weymouth* in 1740 as part of Sir Chaloner Ogle's fleet sent to reinforce Vernon in the West Indies during the War of the Austrian Succession. It was from the West Indies that he wrote his letter of complaint to the Admiralty, clearly already aware of Vernon's more vocal criticisms from his acquaintance with him on this commission, 'to give my opinion of the questions I see the late Admiralty asked of Mr Vernon'.[64] So his comments about the state of the yards and his criticism of the class of vessels would lend considerable weight to the evidence mounting up against the Admiralty at that time.

In this context, Winfield's comment can be recalled: that between 1721 and 1733, *Victory* 'was simply a pile of re-usable timbers in a corner of the Dockyard'.[65] It can legitimately be asked whether indeed *Victory's* timbers could have been of suspect quality when rebuilt from this 'pile' between 1733 and 1737, as alluded to by Commodore Knowles. This is a fascinating extra dimension to her loss. Indeed, a picture in the British Museum of *The Famous Ship Victory*, produced in 1744 by an unknown artist who, according to one description, 'rushed this woodcut to print, capitalizing on the mourning expressed throughout the nation',[66] gives further credence to this speculation. Looking more closely at the picture, there appear to be battle-scarred holes all over the ship. Interestingly, 'this woodcut', comments the British Museum, 'was made from an old worm-eaten block, pressed into service to illustrate a topical event'.[67] This may well be a satirical take on the state of *Victory's* timbers, with the unknown artist deliberately using worm-eaten wood to imply that the ship's loss could be attributed to rotten timbers.

Perhaps the worst aspect was that the authorities were well aware of such defects, even at the time *Victory* was built. Addressing the Master Shipwright, Storekeeper and Clerk of the Survey in Portsmouth on 17 March 1737, the Commissioners of the Navy directed them to undertake a 'strict and careful survey' of all the timber knees in the store and to send an account of their condition 'and particularly those complained to be daily Rotting and Perishing, and to consider and let you know in what manner they may be preserved and season'd for future service'.[68] Also in the year of *Victory*'s launch, there was further evidence that the Commissioners were aware that poor ventilation of naval ships was contributing to the causes of rotten timbers. Admiral Haddock wrote to the Navy Office that the Master Shipwrights and their Assistants were worried that since some forty-three ships listed at Portsmouth, Woolwich, Chatham and Plymouth, 'have not been open'd since they came into harbour', they 'may receive considerable damage' if they remained closed. An order was sought 'for the taking down of their bulkheads in holds, & opening the proper Strakes of plank on their gun decks ... that it is absolutely necessary for the Preservation of his Majesty's Ships, that they be open'd to give all air that is possible whilst they lye in harbour'.[69] A little later Admiral Haddock wrote to the Commissioners complaining that the defects discovered in the *Berwick*, 'occasioned by some rotten & worm-eaten planck, were also repaired; but she was obliged to take out everything and heave almost keel out'.[70]

The design and strength of the navy's ships were also the subject of some discussion in the years immediately leading up to the shipwreck, sparked by Admiral Balchen's bitter complaints about the *Princess Amelia* in 1735, even before Admiral Vernon began his attacks on the Admiralty. In 1740 the Admiralty Board wrote to Sir John Norris, Commander-in-Chief, asking him to examine and consider some plans drawn up by Sir Jacob Acworth, Surveyor of the Navy, and several Master Shipwrights for standard methods of building ships for the navy. Citing the many different dimensions of ships, the Board added their observation that 'the scantlings [structural timber beams] of his Majesty's ships, in general, are not so large and strong as they should be, and it is also a general complaint that the ships are crank, and heel so much in blowing weather, that they cannot open their lee-ports'.[71] Such a description of the general faults in their ships is, in effect, an indictment that the Board was almost anticipating a disaster to befall one or more naval vessels. But it was also a recognition that the design and methods of shipbuilding had to change. The event on the night of 3/4 October 1744 was the spark for that change which was quickly acted upon. Thirty years later this was admitted in a memorandum addressed to the King from the then Surveyor of the Navy, Sir John Williams: 'About the year 1745 a general complaint was made of the ships of the Royal Navy, that they did not carry their guns a proper height above the water, and that they were crank ... on which the Right Honourable the Lords Commissioners of the Admiralty gave directions to the Flag Officers, to the Surveyor of the Navy, and to the master shipwrights of the dockyards to prepare and lay before them a scheme'[72] to improve ship design and building.

Whether it was her faulty design, her rebuilding or her timbers that led to *Victory*'s loss can only be surmised. But it is clear that at the time of her building, her launch and then during her short active service, there were serious issues around the integrity of the ship that could have contributed to her sinking. The retrieved bronze guns in Portsmouth Historic Dockyard today, whilst being tangible props in rebuilding the history of the ship and Admiral Balchen, are also important in recollecting the state of shipbuilding and dockyard administration in the first half of the eighteenth century. It is also clear that so many complaints being levelled at the Admiralty Board about the state of ship design, shipbuilding and dockyard administration, heightened by the loss of *Victory*, certainly contributed to the fall of Winchilsea's Board in December of the same year. The new 1744 Board,[73] and particularly its new member and future First Lord, Admiral George Anson ('a decisive force behind the movement for naval reform, not only in shipbuilding but also in tactics and organisation',[74] and who, in 1759 commissioned the building of Nelson's *Victory*[75]), was to introduce many reforms that laid the foundations for the future Royal Navy ships that were to be so successful between 1759 and 1805 at the Battles of Quiberon Bay, The Saintes, The Glorious First of June, Cape St Vincent, The Nile and Trafalgar. The *Victory*'s guns, it is argued, represent an event that was a mighty catalyst for change and reform in the navy which ultimately led to those victories by Admirals Hawke, Rodney, Hood, Howe, Jervis and Nelson in the next phase of British naval history. Indeed, as described in Chapter 8, many aspects emanating from *Victory*'s flawed design, building history and eventual loss as well as Balchen's career, achievements and final fateful voyage contributed enormously to such reforms that produced the glorious future of the navy, thereby sealing, without doubt, the strength, depth and significance of their legacy.

5

Captain John Balchen's Adventures

'... fame is a strange thing. Some men gain glory after they die, while others fade. What is admired in one generation is abhorred in another. We cannot say who will survive the holocaust of memory. Who knows? ... We cannot say. We are men only, a brief flare of the torch. Those to come may raise or lower us as they please'.

Madeline Miller, in her book *The Song of Achilles*, 2011.

John Balchen is largely unknown. Put simply, his life and service to the crown, spanning the reigns of seven British monarchs from 1669 to 1744, have been swallowed up by the mists of time into virtual obscurity. And yet there is a glorious memorial to him in Westminster Abbey and a magnificent portrait of him in the National Maritime Museum in Greenwich. He also has the distinction of having a few pages to his name in the prestigious *Oxford Dictionary of National Biography*. So John Balchen must have been, in his time, more than just a 'somebody' and clearly more outstanding than just another Royal Navy admiral. Is it simply time which has eroded what was certainly a prominent figure's presence in history? Or has that presence been subsumed and gradually buried under the drifting sands of more prominent, more successful and more victorious figures that have emerged since his death? If others have survived time and built such a tremendous reputation that retains their importance alongside succeeding figures, then why not John Balchen? The underlying truth is that his life and achievements were not so remarkable as to shine through those of more famous seafarers. It is only when one pieces together the story of his life, inextricably linked with that of his ship, *Victory*, and their combined catastrophic loss on 3/4 October 1744, that the significance of his importance truly comes to light. It was John Balchen's death and the circumstances surrounding it that lit the volatile touchpaper on explosive repercussions throughout the Admiralty, and indeed the country, which, within weeks, began a decade and more of massive change and reform to the navy and its future. It is, therefore, the legacy of Balchen's life, achievements and death that should be seen through the hubbub of later rising stars of the Age of Sail. Only by fully understanding this can we reassess and perhaps reinstate him, even though his name has since been superseded and consequently submerged by greater naval men and their actions.

Indeed, observers of the Age of Sail may look to the names of Nelson, Hawke, Hood, Howe, Jervis and Boscawen amongst others as the pre-eminent naval heroes of the time. This is largely due to their tremendous victories at their battles of the Nile, Trafalgar, Quiberon Bay, The Saintes, The Glorious First of June, Cape St Vincent, Lagos and Louisbourg. Or they could name George Anson for his several naval victories and also his famous circumnavigation of the world and capture of a Spanish galleon. Edward Vernon's capture of Porto Bello and his prominent political as well as naval career is another admiral whose name still lives with us today. It could never be claimed that Balchen should ever be included in such a hall of fame simply because he did not achieve such definitive victories or other significant accomplishments, but, even without any hint of 'fame', he does need to be recognised for his service and especially for the legacy of his life on the future navy.

In truth, there are many other admirals who served during the lifetime of John Balchen, many of whom, at some stage in their careers, were involved in great naval battles, but, like Balchen, remain largely unknown. Sir Stafford Fairborne (1666–1742) fought at the Battle of Barfleur and, in the War of the Spanish Succession (1701–13), the Battles of Cadiz and Vigo Bay. Like Balchen, Fairborne has a memorial in Westminster Abbey. Sir John Norris (1670–1749) also fought in the Battle of Cadiz, was commander of the Channel Fleet at the outbreak of the War of Jenkins' Ear in 1739, and under whom Balchen served several times. Sir William Rowley (1690–1768) fought in the Battle of Toulon in 1744 and in the same year went on to be commander-in-chief of the Mediterranean Fleet for which Balchen's last, fateful, voyage was undertaken in order to release their supply convoy blockaded in Lisbon by the French. James Steuart (1678–1757) had accompanied Balchen on that same voyage as second-in-command and survived the terrible storm that overwhelmed Balchen and the *Victory*. George Byng, 1st Viscount Torrington (1663-1733), fought in the Battle of Vigo and was commander of the Mediterranean Fleet at the Battle of Cape Passaro in 1718 under whom Balchen served as Flag Captain to Vice-Admiral Sir Charles Cornwall on the *Shrewsbury* (it was Admiral John Byng, his son, who was shot for cowardice in 1757 at the outbreak of the Seven Years War). All of these undoubtedly successful and brave commanders have been left in the shadows of some of their immediate contemporaries such as Anson, Hawke, Howe, Vernon and Boscawen. Indeed, Admiral Edward Boscawen (1711–61) is not only known for his several victorious engagements including the successful capture of Louisbourg, Nova Scotia, in 1758 (which led to the capture of Quebec the next year, and ultimately Canada, from the French) and the Battle of Lagos in 1759, but also for being the officer who signed the death warrant for the execution of Byng for failing to engage the enemy. As will be shown later, Boscawen also crops up in some of the significant changes sparked by the death of Balchen in subsequent years.

Two other admirals amongst those whose careers overlapped with Balchen's have certainly retained more prominent recognition: Sir Cloudesley Shovell (1650–1707) and Rear-Admiral Richard Kempenfelt (1718–82), both of whose lives and deaths are more closely aligned with those of Balchen. Like Balchen, Shovell boasts a grand memorial in Westminster Abbey and, again like Balchen, died in a shipwreck of possibly equal prominence. In 1707, during the War of the Spanish Succession, he commanded an expeditionary fleet in an unsuccessful attempt to capture Toulon and on the way back to Plymouth encountered a storm in the Channel. This blew the fleet onto the reefs of the Scilly Isles during the night, when Shovell's flagship, *Association*, sank with all hands, followed by *Eagle* and *Romney*. Some 1,300 men perished and Shovell's body was washed ashore and is buried in Westminster Abbey. His loss amidst a series of catastrophic shipwrecks in many respects shares with Balchen a historical significance reflected mainly through the event itself rather than his individual achievements or his legacy. Again in common with Balchen and Shovell, Kempenfelt was drowned in the accidental sinking of his flagship *Royal George* off Portsmouth in 1782. Like both Balchen and Shovell, Kempenfelt also has a grand memorial in Westminster Abbey. However, unlike Balchen or Shovell to date, Kempenfelt's life and achievements have been rediscovered recently by Hilary L Rubenstein's book *Catastrophe at Spithead: The Sinking of the Royal George*, which includes much information about him not previously known or recorded.[1]

Unsurprisingly, recent surveys confirm that not only is Balchen unrecognised by the general public, but even by those visiting naval and maritime establishments, and also by the community of his birthplace, in Godalming.[2] However, State and Admiralty archives from the period, as well as contemporary newspapers and early biographies, reveal clearly the story of his life and his adventurous naval service. Until now, Baugh's short article on Balchen in the *Oxford Dictionary of National Biography* has been the most definitive summary of the admiral's life and loss. His sources include his own two publications on naval administration in the period,[3] Balchin's 1994 article in the *Mariner's Mirror*[4] and several older books on naval warfare.[5] He does not mention any of the three earlier biographies from the eighteenth century (mentioned in previous chapters) in his list of sources although much of the material in his narrative seems to reflect their observations, particularly about Balchen's early naval career. However, he brought much new evidence and anecdotes about Balchen's service and character from The National Archives' Admiralty documents.

It is not clear from a scholarly point of view how valid the sources are for the earlier biographies. The authors of the 1776 biography ('a Society of Gentlemen') give no source for their material on Balchen, though on its title page it claims much of the content has 'not hitherto appeared in any publication in Europe'.[6] The 1787 biography[7] lifts most of its narrative and all of the 'facts' and dates directly from the 1776 version, with some minor tweaks throughout ensuring it is not a verbatim copy. Charnock's 1795 *Biographia Navalis*[8] draws upon both earlier publications but clearly contains added research to give a more detailed view of the admiral's service. Much greater detail is now known of Balchen's family life and service following a more rigorous examination of primary sources at both The National Archives and the National Maritime Museum.[9] This chapter and the two that follow can therefore give a more rounded story of his life and character alongside the most pertinent aspects of his service life to assess his achievements.

So, John Balchen was born in Godalming, Surrey, in 1669, where today his portrait hangs prominently in the Borough Hall. The accompanying script for the portrait, which is in the Godalming Museum, states that: 'It is said that the portrait originally hung in the Godalming King's Arms Hotel where it was recorded that it was given to the father of the nineteenth-century landlord in respect of a debt by Mr Garthwaite of Hall Place, Shackleford. It is believed to be a copy in the style of Godfrey Kneller.'[10] But this script also refers to the 'original' portrait which now hangs in the National Maritime Museum, Greenwich.[11] This latter portrait, painted circa 1705, begins to throw more light on Balchen. According to the curatorial description of the painting, the identification of the subject is based on a lengthy inscription added to the portrait which reads: 'Vice-Admiral John Balchen, was born of very obscure Parentage February 4th 1669 at Godalming in Surrey, and rose to Eminence noticed above solely by his own Exertions and Services, for which he was rewarded by his Sovereign with the Governorship of Greenwich Hospital.'[12] The painting came to the museum as part of the Greenwich Hospital Collection and Sir Henry Austen gave it to the Naval Gallery there in 1852.

Though first attributed, as mentioned above, to the famous artist Sir Godfrey Kneller, the painting was later reattributed to Jonathan Richardson. However, the National Maritime Museum has more recently suggested that Sir John de Medina is the more likely artist. In

1703, the then Captain Balchen was appointed commander of HMS *Adventure* in which he served in the North Sea and English Channel until 1705. 'This would have provided the opportunity', states the museum, 'for the ship to have anchored in Edinburgh docks for an encounter between Medina and Balchen ... the ship in the background is perhaps meant to represent the *Adventure*'.[13]

To have his portrait painted and later to have it displayed in the great Naval Gallery at Greenwich Hospital, which opened in 1824, is a good indication of Balchen's importance to the navy. Describing the collection, Geoff Quilley claims that the portraits are of 'principal naval commanders together with "Representations of their Warlike Achievements"', as the title to the catalogue put it, and a major function of the gallery was, likewise, to ensure that 'the eminent services of the Royal Navy will never lose their interest in the view of those who visit Greenwich Hospital'.[14] The significance of Balchen's portrait being included here is emphasised by a further description in this catalogue, written in 1836, which demonstrates the larger, spiritual purpose, where the paintings:

> Serve to rekindle the gratitude of this highly-favoured nation, in whose cause our brave countrymen fought and bled, we may ever remember that far higher debt of gratitude which is due to God, who mercifully guided them through all the perils of the deep, and nerved the arm of every fearless seaman in the day of battle.[15]

Clearly then, Balchen's life and achievements were perceived to have been of sufficient substance for his portrait to be included in such a hall of fame as Greenwich Hospital's gallery. As we begin to unfold his life and his naval adventures, the latter being a mixture of both disastrous and yet bravely accomplished activities, it becomes clear why his portrait was elevated to such a place and also why it remains in the National Maritime Museum today, albeit in storage and not on public display.

To return to his early days, John Balchen is recorded in the parish registers as being baptised on 14 February 1669 (1670 in the present calendar), son of 'John Baltchin and Ann'.[16] His mother was Ann Edsur and his father was John Balchin (baptised in Godalming on

18 October 1640, the son of Lawrence Balchin and Abigail, both of Godalming[17]), who came from 'farming stock and was a member of the Balchin "dynasty" of yeoman farmers who held land in the Godalming-Bramley area of Surrey for several hundred years from 1530 onwards'.[18] Though the 2004 biography refers to the Admiral as their 'fourth and only surviving child',[19] the Parish Register records there were five children: John, baptised 9 June 1665 and his twin Ann (they were both buried on 12 June 1665), Ann, baptised on 24 February 1666, John (the Admiral), baptised 14 February 1669 and William, baptised on 22 January 1670.[20]

We will investigate more of Balchen's character and personality as well as revealing aspects of his home life and about his close and extended family later, but suffice it to say that in his youth, there were many factors which could have influenced his choice of a career in the navy, rather than for him to stay and be employed locally. Not least of these influences came from a close association that his home town had with surrounding industries and trades linked with maritime England at that time and with the naval dockyards at Portsmouth Harbour in particular. These came through its busy transport links between London and Portsmouth, providing trade with locally-grown grain and other victuals, powder from the nearby extensive gunpowder works and timber supplies as well as guns and shot from the local iron foundries; all providing for the growing demands of the navy (see Appendix 5 for more detail). So, the next phase of his story was about to begin – at sea.

Having joined the navy at the age of 15 in 1685, Balchen's subsequent 58 years of service were during some of the most volatile times in England's naval history, through the sometimes turbulent reigns of seven monarchs, and several periods of war with the Dutch, French and Spanish both in Europe and, increasingly, across the globe in the struggle for colonies and trade. These early years witnessed the on-going religious struggles in England, including, in 1688, the Glorious Revolution with James II being replaced by the Protestant William and Mary. Having fled to France, James II then landed in Ireland the next year, just as Jacobite risings broke out in Scotland as part of the struggle for control of England and Ireland. The defeat of

James and the Catholic army at the Battle of the Boyne entrenched William, but the subsequent Franco-Jacobite alliances continued the internal troubles even after William III's reign ended in 1702. Also beginning in 1688 was the Nine Years War, with the growing might of France being opposed by an alliance of Austria, the Dutch Republic, England, Spain, Portugal and Savoy. This was, in effect, the first war that could be described as truly global, being waged in Europe, North America, the Caribbean and India. The colonial and trading battles for control of the lucrative West Indies and the Anglo-French colonists' skirmishes for lands in North America were joined by many European nations trying to establish footholds across the coasts of the Indian sub-continent. It was a time when France, under the great 'Sun King' Louis XIV, was being transformed into a supremely powerful nation, with ambitions for European supremacy.

In the context of the challenges for the Royal Navy and the young Balchen in this period, France had taken advantage of the earlier Anglo-Dutch wars, in which the two most powerful maritime and trading nations tore each other's navies apart, to rebuild and expand her own navy. The contemporary French writer, Voltaire, described in detail the rise and fall of Louis XIV's navy and his battles with the English on land and sea in his book *The Age of Louis XIV*, published in 1751. He wrote that in 1664 and 1665, 'whilst the English and the Dutch were overrunning the seas with nearly three hundred large ships of war, he [Louis XIV] had as yet but fifteen or sixteen vessels of the poorest class' but then 'with incredible activity Louis set about re-establishing the navy and providing France with everything she lacked'.[21] The scale and rapidity of this naval building programme was such that by the time Balchen entered service in the Royal Navy, France had become a formidable naval power, as was described by Voltaire:

Building commissions were set up in the ports so that ships might be constructed on the best possible lines. Five naval arsenals were built at Brest, Rochefort, Toulon, Dunkirk and Havre-de-Grace. In 1672, there were about 60 ships of the line and 40 frigates. In 1681, there were 198 ships of war, counting the auxiliaries and 30 galleys in the port of Toulon, either armed or about to be so; 11,000 of regular troops served on the ships, and 3,000 on the galleys. 166,000 men of all classes were enrolled for the various services of the navy. During the succeeding years there were a thousand noblemen and young gentlemen in this service.[22]

During the Nine Years War (1688–97) this rejuvenated and still expanding French navy was unleashed upon her enemies across the oceans as Louis 'sought by every means to redress the folly and misfortunes which France had brought upon herself by ignoring the sea, while her neighbours were founding empires at the ends of the world'.[23] Balchen's naval career, starting in 1685, coincided with this escalating maritime endeavour. The earliest known biography of Balchen, dated 1776, described his early naval training and deployment in these words: 'During his youth ⌈he was⌉ properly instructed in the several arts necessary to form a complete seaman' and 'when he had attained the knowledge of the arts and sciences requisite in a seaman, he was placed on board the Royal Navy, where he served several years in inferior stations.'[24] Early records show that he served during much of the 1690s in the West Indies where, in 1692, he was made lieutenant, first on a 38-gun frigate, *Dragon*, originally launched in 1647 as a Fourth Rate ship then rebuilt in 1690.

The death rate of officers and men in the West Indies Squadron was horrific. We know that Horatio Nelson, stationed there between 1784 and 1787 as commander of the Leeward Islands Squadron, hated the place. Writing to his fiancée, Frances Nisbet, from his frigate HMS *Boreas* anchored in English Harbour, Antigua, Nelson complained of being 'woefully pinched by mosquitoes'[25] in this 'vile place'.[26] Being a lieutenant in the *Dragon* in the West Indies was clearly a posting with the danger of death by yellow fever, malaria and any number of other tropical ailments. Indeed, such was the fear of the place that many sailors would desert rather than sail there, as evidenced aboard *Dragon* at the time of her departure from Portsmouth to the West Indies in August 1692, when her captain, William Vickars, wrote to the Navy Board asking that 'his men are sent back from the ships they deserted to when they heard the ship was going to the West Indies'[27] and the next day reported that he 'is sending his Lieutenant to London to make an application to get the *Dragon's* crew back from the ships they have deserted to because the *Dragon* is going to the West Indies'.[28] Nevertheless, it was not long before she was deployed in the Leeward Islands, Martinique, St Christopher, St Kitts and other parts of the Caribbean as part of Rear-Admiral Sir Francis Wheeler's formidable West Indies Squadron, alongside the *Tiger, Chester, Ruby, Mold, Dromedary, Norwich, Advice, Experiment* and *Resolution*.[29]

Balchen and his fellow lieutenants' worst fears about their well-being in the Caribbean were clearly realised. The Probate Courts reveal the will of Chief Lieutenant of *Dragon*, Thomas Day, granted on 28 October 1693,[30] followed on 13 December 1693 by the will of Lieutenant Peter Devett of *Dragon* in Barbados.[31] Later, the will of a mariner 'bound for the West Indies' in *Dragon*, Charles Vickars, was also granted Probate[32] (and it could be speculated that this gentleman may have been related to the ship's captain, William Vickars, as some senior officers at the time were known to employ young relatives on their ships in support of their early careers). But Balchen survived and would certainly have benefitted from the passing-away of his more senior lieutenants, thereby giving him more opportunities for instant promotion as well as greater officer experience and learning. Indeed, the following year saw *Dragon* back from the West Indies and escorting a merchant convoy to the Mediterranean, first to Messina and then to Venice, Italy.[33] By 22 December 1694, *Dragon* could be found cruising off Cape Finisterre on the west coast of Galicia, Spain, to protect merchant shipping from French privateers.[34] Five days later it was reported that the French warship *Sphaere* had been captured by *Dragon*, giving Balchen his first taste of a prize.[35]

Although it is unclear exactly how long Balchen stayed on board *Dragon*, his next commission saw him transferred as lieutenant onto the new 70-gun Third Rate *Cambridge*, launched in 1695. This was to provide him with another opportunity to gain experience and demonstrate his potential for further promotion. The *Cambridge* was the flagship of Rear-Admiral Sir John Neville and initially formed part of a nine-ship 'Spanish Expedition' fleet under the command of Vice-Admiral Mitchell in 1696,[36] before she sailed to the West Indies. It was probably here that Balchen actually joined the ship's company.

In April the next year, the then Vice-Admiral Neville wrote from *Cambridge*, then anchored in Barbados, that he was preparing to sail and was trying to muster his men again, expressing his belief that many were determined to remain on the island in the hope of joining a trading ship 'because of the merchantmen's temptations'.[37] When, in December 1697, *Cambridge* arrived back in Portsmouth as part of a fourteen-ship squadron from the West Indies,[38] Balchen had remained in the Caribbean.

Amongst the decimation of fellow officers on the West Indies station, 'Balchen was a survivor', comments his latest biographer, 'and thus, though he lacked influential connections, made post [Captain] aged twenty-seven'.[39] His first command came there on 25 July 1697, when he was appointed by Admiral Sir John Neville as captain of a captured prize ship, the 32-gun *Virgin*. Clearly, Neville had seen enough of Lieutenant Balchen in action and in his performance as an officer to merit his promotion to command a ship of his own. It was reported that *Virgin Prize* was in Port Royal, Jamaica, in August 1697,[40] so Balchen continued operating with the West Indies Squadron. 'From that time', states the 1776 biography, 'he was always considered as one of the most active commanders in the British navy.'[41] In the same year as his appointment, however, the Peace of Ryswijk ended the Anglo-Dutch war with France and many ships were laid up and officers, including Balchen, relieved from duty. Frustrated at this and eager for another appointment, he wrote to the Admiralty on 12 June 1699 requesting employment and summarising his earlier career, concluding: 'I continued in command of the *Virgin* till September 1698, then being paid off, and never at any time have committed any misdemeanour which might occasion my being called to a court martial, to be turned out or suspended.'[42]

He was subsequently appointed commander of the fireship *Firebrand* in 1700 and the next year of the 28-gun fireship *Vulcan*. It was aboard this small ship that Captain Balchen began to make his mark more forcefully in the navy. On 20 December 1701 in Portsmouth Harbour, he proudly entered in the ship's logbook 'this day entered on board the *Vulcan*'.[43] In January he loaded eight months' provisions of beer, pork and beef, loaded on board his guns and then, on 23 January sailed out of the harbour heading for the west coast. The year 1702 was momentous for Britain as well as for Balchen. In his logbook he noted that on 11 March we 'struck our colours at half mast and fired 7 guns for the Proclamation of Queen Anne' and on 23 April 'fired 9 guns for the Queen's Coronation'.[44] William III's reign was over, Queen Anne ascended the throne and a new era began, along with a new war and new opportunities for Balchen to progress in his career.

The War of the Spanish Succession came about after King Charles II of Spain died childless in November 1700, resulting in both France and Austria hoping to inherit Spain through their royal relatives. Neither Britain nor the Dutch United Provinces wanted either of them to obtain the inheritance as it would lead to a virtual hegemony over Europe. One of the three candidates was Philip of Anjou, the French King Louis XIV's grandson. When he was proclaimed King Philip V of Spain in April 1701, Louis XIV determined to combine the powers of the two nations. So in May 1702 the two maritime powers, England and the United Provinces, together with the Austrian Emperor, simultaneously declared war on France and, by default, Spain. Eventually, the combined forces of France, Spain and Bavaria faced Britain, Austria, Prussia, Hanover and the Dutch Republic and the war was to last until 1713.

It was relating to this period of Balchen's career that the 1776 biography summed up how he was seen as a young officer and commander:

> At this early time of life he gave many indications of a tenacious memory, sound judgement, and the most intrepid courage. He was alarmed by no dangers, intimidated by no difficulties. He pursued his purposes with the greatest perseverance, steadiness, and resolution, and rarely failed of seeing them succeed according to his wishes. But though he was thus resolute and intrepid, he was far from being petulant, nor ever willingly affronted any.[45]

The *Vulcan's* logbook reveals that between May and October 1702 Balchen and his crew were cruising between the Lizard in Cornwall, the Isles of Scilly and Cape Finisterre on the west coast of Spain. Then, on 12 September, Lieutenant Robert Caslaign's log entry describes the capture of *Vulcan*'s first prize: 'At 3 yesterday in the afternoon we saw a sail bearing WSW bearing down to us, we gave chase to her, ye *Bonaventure* being to Leeward of us, att 5 we fired 3 guns att her, then she strook [struck her colours] to us. She proved to be a French barque laden with fish bound to France.' Balchen's own logbook entry was a little less dramatic: 'Att 3 saw a sail bearing WSW at 4 gave chase – at 5 she struck – at 7 saw two sail move to Windward.' Unfortunately, in the next day's log entry, Balchen reported that in very thick fog 'in the morning lost sight of my Prize, she having broke her towrope'.[46] However, it appears that they managed to find their prize again. In their 1702–03 records, the High Court of the Admiralty's Commission of Appeals for Prize Monies report that a French ship, the *Gabriel en Paix* (Master, Gabriel Ernand), which was a 60-ton vessel laden with 10,000 codfish from the Newfoundland fisheries and bound for Nantes, was 'taken by HMS *Vulcan* Fireship and brought into Portsmouth'.[47] So Balchen had his first capture of an enemy vessel as captain of his own ship and he gained his second award of prize money, a portion of which was shared amongst the rest of his crew.

Apart from such minor skirmishes at the start of the war, one of the earliest major naval engagements was the attack by Sir George Rooke's Anglo-Dutch fleet on French and Spanish ships at Vigo, on the northwest coast of Spain, on 23 October 1702. Attached to this fleet was Balchen's *Vulcan*. Following an unsuccessful attempt to capture Cadiz, Rooke's fleet spotted a convoy of Spanish transport ships escorted by French ships of the line as they entered Vigo Bay in Northern Spain. The resulting Battle of Vigo Bay saw the entire fleet of transports and the French escort ships either captured or destroyed in what was an overwhelming naval victory. Six French ships of the line were captured and six others burned or wrecked, while nineteen Spanish ships were taken or burned: 'the French navy suffered heavily, and the Spanish navy was virtually eliminated'.[48] Whether or not he was directly involved in this action is uncertain but it was during this battle that the Royal Navy captured the 56-gun French ship *Modere*. Baugh's biography states that Balchen captured the ship himself[49] though it seems amazing for an 28-gun fireship to take a 56-gun man-of-war. Unfortunately Balchen's logbook for his service in *Vulcan* was signed off seven days before the battle, on 16 October 1702, and there is no record of a follow-on logbook. What is known is that the prize *Modere* was renamed *Moderate* and taken into Portsmouth Dockyard. Here, in May 1703, directions were given for her and another ship, *Assurance*, also a prize, to be altered 'as proposed by the Master Builder ... as Sir George Rooke is pressing for the work to be done'[50] and she was launched on 20 June,[51] when Balchen was given command of her until 1704.

He was then transferred to cruising duties in the North Sea and Channel in command of the 42-gun *Adventure*[52] which had been rebuilt in 1691. The only substantive record of Balchen's command of this ship is a letter he wrote while anchored at the Nore anchorage on the Thames estuary, requesting 'an anchor having lost his at Scarborough while ordered to attend a Russian ship sailing for Portsmouth'.[53] And if the curators of the National Maritime Museum are correct, it was during this time that Balchen took the *Adventure* into Edinburgh's Leith Docks and where his portrait may have been painted by Sir John de Medina, with his ship in the background.[54]

The next stage of Balchen's career and war record came with mixed and contrasting experiences. He took command of the 50-gun *Chester* in 1705 in Portsmouth Harbour and his first commission was to sail to the coast of Guinea in West Africa. This immediately caused Balchen and his Master problems as neither had any experience of cruising along that coast, known to be a more dangerous and disease-ridden place than the West Indies station. They both wrote on the same day, 9 July 1705, to the Navy Board Commissioners, with Balchen's letter reading:

> I understand that the ship I command is ordered to fit for Guinea and Mr Hockaday who is now Master of her informs me that he is not in any ways acquainted with that coast and can't take charge there, therefore pray their Honours will be pleased to order me a Master that is acquainted – myself going wholly a stranger there.[55]

John Hockaday himself reinforced this plea in his own letter: 'Now I am informed by my Commander that this ship is bound upon the Coast of Guinea which is a place [I] never was att: I therefore as in duty

Bound ... please to fortrust me farther as Master to any place where I have already been.'[56] Clearly, West Africa was a destination, as was the West Indies earlier, which was not popular with either officers or crew. One such example was James Conch aboard Balchen's ship *Chester* who, knowing they were due to sail to Guinea, wanted to leave the ship and join a merchant ship, claiming that 'I am on board deprived of my liberty to follow my privet occasions for merchant [service]'.[57] While in the meantime, by 2 September, Balchen was again writing to remind the Board that he was still awaiting a replacement Master, adding also that his Surgeon was complaining that part of his medical equipment was 'worn to pieces; desire your honours will give your Directions that he may have a new one'.[58] Two weeks later, just as he was preparing to sail, Balchen was still without a new Master and pleaded with their honours that they should act before he sailed: 'Yesterday I received her Royal Highness's Instructions for my sailing to Guinea, I shall go out of this Harbour Monday next as soon as the *Poole* comes from the Downs and the Guinea [merchant] shipps joyne me, I shall sail on my Voyage, therefore I pray your honours will be pleased to order me a Master that's acquainted on the coast, for I have not anybody that has been there.'[59]

By 18 September Balchen had been informed that the Board could not find a Master familiar with navigating the Guinea coast and that he should go about looking for someone himself – even at this eleventh hour as he was about to sail! He made it his business to do so and had more luck doing so himself. He reported back that he had found a man, John Stanton, who was Master of the *Norris and George* and had been trading on that coast and that 'he is willing to serve and has a good character' and seeking the Board to send down a warrant for him to serve on *Chester*.[60] So off he eventually set to cruise the coast of West Africa.

Balchen returned from his first cruise on 19 July 1706, when it was reported that he and *Chester* had arrived back at Spithead from the coast of Guinea, but, unfortunately, 'has buried his Surgeon on the voyage and taken the Surgeon of the *Poole* in his place',[61] clearly demonstrating the dangers to be encountered in those waters and ports of call. However, he then spent the next year back cruising the coast of West Africa, where Britain's trading interests needed protection.[62]

Meanwhile the land war still raged on, with the Duke of Marlborough decisively defeating a French army at the Battle of Blenheim in 1704 followed shortly after by his victory at the Battle of Ramillies. Then the navy was to benefit from one of the greatest victories – the capture of Gibraltar on 4 August 1705. Immediately after this capture, wrote Voltaire, 'the English fleet, mistress of the seas, attacked the Count of Toulouse, Admiral of France, in sight of Malaga; the battle, it is true, was indecisive, but it marked the last phase of Louis XIV's power'.[63] From then on the overwhelming power of the Royal Navy meant France and Spain avoided full fleet battles, instead employing squadrons to disrupt enemy trade, largely through privateering activities.

Balchen was back in Portsmouth in April 1707[64] and spent the next few months refitting and readying for Channel service. If the vagaries of attaining fame between two people can be seen to swing on the outcome of a single incident or action, then Balchen's next two engagements represent just such events. They led his adversary on both occasions to achieve legendary status in France but for Balchen the ignominy of defeat, the loss of his ships, his capture and subsequent courts martial; not the best foundations for fame. Having returned to home waters, Balchen and his ship *Chester* were assigned to be part of a small squadron of five warships under Commodore Edwards which was sent to escort a large convoy of between 80 and 130 merchant ships carrying armaments and provisions to Lisbon, Portugal, to support the land war in the Peninsula. This convoy 'was not only of a very considerable intrinsic value, but of the highest consequence and importance, considered in a national light, for all the provisions, stores, and upwards of one thousand horses for the service of the ensuing campaign in Spain were embarked upon it'.[65] Alongside *Chester* was Edwards' flagship, the 80-gun *Cumberland*, the similarly armed *Devonshire*, the 76-gun *Royal Oak* and the 50-gun *Ruby*. On 10 October 1707, having proceeded only as far as the Lizard, along the Cornish coast, the convoy was intercepted by the combined French squadrons of Admirals de Forbin (Admiral Claude Count de Forbin-Gardanne) and Duguay-Trouin (Vice-Admiral René Duguay-Trouin),

The 12-pounder (left) and 42-pounder bronze guns, both retrieved from the wreck of HMS *Victory*, being restored at the National Museum of the Royal Navy, Portsmouth. (Photographs courtesy of Alan M Smith)

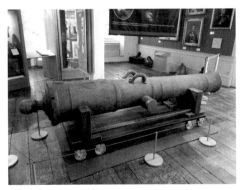

The 42-pounder bronze gun from *Victory* on display in the National Museum of the Royal Navy in Portsmouth. (Photograph courtesy of Alan M Smith)

The remains of HMS *Victory* on the seabed in the English Channel, photographed in the summer of 2020 during a dive by the Plymouth Sound Branch of the British Sub-Aqua Club. (Photographs courtesy of Dominic Robinson, Joint Service Sub Aqua Dive Centre, JSSADC Devonport)

Opposite page: 'Calm: HMS *Royal James* (1675)'. Detail of oil painting, 1678, by Willem van de Velde the Elder. (BHC3608, © National Maritime Museum, Greenwich, London)

Model of First Rate 110-gun warship *Victory* (1737), Scale 1:34.3. A contemporary full hull model. (SLR0449, images D3816-4 and L3241-004, © National Maritime Museum, Greenwich, London)

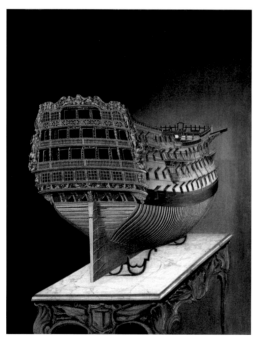

'Painting of the Model of *Victory* 1744'. Shows the splendour but also the height of the galleries on the stern of HMS *Victory*. The painting was in the collection of George III and was donated to the Science Museum by Queen Victoria. (Image 10325752, source 1864–0012, © Science Museum/Science & Society Picture Library – All rights reserved)

Opposite page: 'Loss of HMS "Victory", 4 October 1744'. Oil painting, by Peter Monamy. (BHC0361, © National Maritime Museum, Greenwich, London)

'Admiral Edward Vernon (1684–1757)'.
Oil painting circa. 1730s–1748,
by Charles Philips. (BHC3068,
© National Maritime Museum,
Greenwich, London)

'The Famous Ship Victory'. Woodcut to print, 1744, artist unknown. (PPA89760, © The
Trustees of the British Museum)

'Admiral Sir John Balchen (1670–1744)'. Portrait, oil on canvas, circa. 1705, by John Baptiste de Medina. (BHC2525, © National Maritime Museum, Greenwich, London)

Memorial to Sir John Balchen, Westminster Abbey, North Transept, marble statue, commissioned by his wife, designed by Scheemakers, completed in 1746. (© Dean and Chapter of Westminster)

'Admiral Lord George Anson (1697–1762)'. (BHC2517, © National Maritime Museum, Greenwich, London)

'Sir Thomas Slade (1703–71)', Britain's greatest naval architect of the eighteenth century. (BHC3030, © National Maritime Museum, Greenwich, London)

'Lord Anson's victory off Cape Finisterre, 3 May 1747'. In the War of the Austrian Succession, Cape Finisterre was the scene of a naval battle between a British fleet of fourteen ships of the line commanded by Sir George Anson, who had recently been promoted to Vice-Admiral of the Blue, and two French squadrons. The great victory for the Royal Navy included Anson's capture of the 74-gun *L'Invincible*, which was to become the model upon which Nelson's navy was largely built. (BHC0369, © National Maritime Museum, Greenwich, London)

Nelson's famous flagship at the Battle of Trafalgar in 1805 had no name when her keel was laid in Chatham Dockyard in November 1759. The Admiralty only named her HMS *Victory* in 1760 following a year of great victories over the French which removed some of the ill omen and stigma attached to the name that lingered after the tragic loss of the previous *Victory*, her admiral and 1,100 crew. Admiral Lord Anson was First Lord of the Admiralty when she was ordered and she was designed by Anson's Surveyor of the Navy, Sir Thomas Slade. (Photograph of HMS *Victory* at the National Museum of the Royal Navy, Portsmouth, courtesy of Alan M Smith)

with a total fleet of twelve large warships. While de Forbin's squadron of six vessels included his own 60-gun *Mars* and two recently captured 54-gun British ships, Duguay-Trouin's squadron led by his 74-gun *Lys* included the *Achille* (66), *Jason* (54), *Maure* (50), *Gloire* (40) and *Amazone* (36). Charnock's 1795 account records that the small British squadron 'was unable to contend against an enemy so wonderfully superior; the commodore's ship, the *Cumberland*, as well as the *Ruby* and *Chester*, after having separately made a most gallant, and, indeed, desperate defence, fell into the hands of the enemy. The *Chester* itself became the prize of the Count de Forbin himself.'[66] Only the *Royal Oak* escaped, while the *Devonshire* exploded and twenty-two of the merchantmen were captured. However, shielded by the gallant efforts of their warship escorts, nearly all of the other transport ships escaped.

Balchen's *Chester* was directly engaged by the *Jason* and the *Amazone*, and then a third ship before being boarded and captured.[67] Balchen was released on parole in September 1708 and formally exchanged in 1709. The court martial for the loss of his ship took place on 27 September 1708, on board the *Royal Anne*, chaired by Admiral George Byng. Balchen asked for ten of his ship's crew to be with him at the court proceeding and such was the widespread and often uncontrolled use of press gangs in London at the time that he 'had special protection for ten of his ship's company whom he desired to bring to London as witnesses in a suit then pending against him'.[68] The court confirmed that *Chester* and the other escort warships were attacked by twelve enemy warships but also recorded the brave conduct of Balchen and his crew against overwhelming odds:

> The *Chester* was in her proper station, & was engag'd till being boarded by three of ye enemies ships, & att last they having entered many men, and his own men driven off ye deck, and the ship much disabled, Captain Balchen was seized on ye quarterdeck and ye enemy then got possession of ye ship. And the Court being satisfied that Captain Balchen in all particulars discharged his duty on this occasion ... the Court did acquit Captain Balchen.[69]

In contrast to Balchen and Edwards, de Forbin and Duguay-Trouin were hailed as heroes back in France. During much of the War of the

Spanish Succession, the French and Spanish fleets could not face the English and Dutch fleets in open-sea fleet battles so they had resorted to privateering. De Forbin and Duguay-Trouin, both employed as privateers, or corsairs, and based in St Malo, became the most successful at this strategy. Indeed, these twelve ships which were engaged in what was to be called the Battle of the Lizard, were actually French naval vessels, but were employed on the account of private adventurers.[70] This privateering, particularly aimed at seizing British merchant ships and their precious cargoes rather than for military or naval purposes, clearly upset the traders of Britain who relied on naval protection. This perceived imbalance of strategy between near-sea trade protection and distant military adventure by the Royal Navy in 1708, was described by a writer in 1779, particularly referring to both Forbin and Duguay-Trouin:

> The manner in which the trading vessels of England were made prize of by the French cruisers, might well draw forth complaints from the merchants; and indeed, the interests of that useful and respectable body of men, were shamefully slighted by the council of Admiralty, who suffered the two French partisans, Forbin and Gue [*sic*] Trouin, to ride triumphant in the British seas, whilst our formidable naval force was making conquests in the Mediterranean.[71]

Nevertheless, after his release and being fully exonerated by his court martial, Balchen seemed desperate to secure another command, writing letter after letter to the Lord High Commissioners of the Admiralty. Clearly making enquiries at the various naval dockyards across the country about progress being made on new ships being built or ships under repair, he was eager to spot a likely warship which he could command and sought such an appointment as soon as possible. Writing on 4 February 1709, he beseeches the Admiralty: 'I have heard that the *Antelope* which is att Portsmouth will soon be repair'd. I prey your honour to move my Lords of the Admiralty that I may have Command of her when their Lordships shall think fit to commission her if not provided for otherwise.'[72] By 2 May his desperation for a ship was demonstrated in a somewhat garbled letter to them in which he intimated that other officers who had lost their ships in the recent engagement had gained new appointments while he was still waiting:

Your honour is no stranger to my misfortune and that I have been a great sufferer, I may say a great deal now than any that was taken at the time I was upon the act of that voyage ... therefore hope I shall not be forgot when any vacancy [for command of a ship arises]. I know not whether I am misinformed or not but am told there is a ship building in Mr Buschels yard at Deptford of the 4th rate which will be ready as soon as any that is now on the stocks or repairing if your honour shall feel fit. I prey I may be [considered] for her if nothing should happen in the meantime before she launches. I submit myself to your disposal.[73]

Scribbled in the margin of his letter was a note from their Lordships indicating that Balchen should be recommended 'for the ship he desires, if nothing happens beforehand'. However, it was not until August that he was finally given his ship, as indicated by several of his letters from Deptford dockyard between 11 and 15 August trying to get crew members from two other ships, including *Scarborough*, to man his next ship, *Gloucester*.

So we find Captain Balchen once again commanding a warship, being the brand-new 60-gun *Gloucester* lying at moorings in Deptford. However, even before he could leave Deptford his ship was damaged by a merchantman which had cast off and bearing away from the moorings when it 'fell foul of the starboard gallery [of *Gloucester*] and broke the lights and all toptiers. I ordered my carpenter ashore to get those repaired.'[74] Reporting the damage to the Navy Board on 24 August, Balchen was clearly trying to find and confront the Master of the merchantman that 'did damage to my gallery', concluding that 'I have made enquiry but can only find that the ship's name is the *Barbados*. She was off the moorings and be foul of the *Gloucester*.' He then asks the Navy Board to find out from the Master of Attendance, whose role it was to supervise ships using the moorings, to 'enquire the Owners of the ship are – for I was not on Board when it was done'.[75] He was clearly incensed by the damage to his new ship.

Things continued to bedevil Balchen in his new ship. Having eventually set out from Deptford, *Gloucester* arrived at the Longreach moorings on the Thames, where the busy task of loading provisions, guns and powder for the voyage began. It was here that he found he had lost his Surgeon's First Mate, John Herring, whom he had given permission to go to London 'as he said to pass his examinations for to be a surgeon of a ship, promising to return in a day or two'. Much to Balchen's displeasure, Herring had not returned as promised and clearly had no intention of doing so. There were several issues arising from this that were of concern to Balchen. Firstly, there was the issue of safety for his crew and those stevedores involved in loading the ship, a time of frenetic and dangerous activities: 'att this time there is as much occasion for Surgeon's Mates as at anytime', he wrote, 'for taking in the guns and provisions accidents happen daily'. So he needed a replacement from the Navy Board as soon as possible to cope with such accidents. Secondly, Balchen did not suffer fools gladly, as we shall see later in his career. He was always a stickler for duty and for loyalty, so Herring's non-appearance was unforgiveable. Rather than seek to have the surgeon's mate returned, he wanted him away, to be replaced and not to be employed by the navy again: 'Since he does not see fit to give his attendance to his Duty', Balchen told the Navy Board, 'I can't think him worthy of his employ.'[76]

By 13 September he was completing the final provisioning of the ship at the Longreach moorings. He reported that 'this morning came on board 22 Guns which is the last of what is designed for the ship. I have sent my gunner to the Ordnance Officer to hasten down the powder which as soon as I have it on board, I shall proceed to the Nore with the first opportunity if wind and weather [allow].'[77] But his first foray to sea, seemingly for what today would be known as 'sea trials', did not last long and he was back at the moorings in Longreach a week later. He reported to the Navy Board that with 'a fresh gale of wind the ship goes very well I think, but', he added, 'I think but only wants more canvas'. He then explained that the *Gloucester*'s topsails and topgallant yards were all too small and her sails not 'proportioned to the rest of her yards'. So, having just received orders from Sir William Jumper to proceed to the anchorage at Spithead, he asked the Navy Board 'to give directions to the proper officers of Her Majesty's Yard there that my yards and sails may be enlarged, if I stay there time enough to have it done'.[78] No documents appear to suggest whether the ship's sails and yards were replaced with larger versions or not, but the ill-fated *Gloucester* was about to lose some completely anyway.

Indeed, the equally ill-omened Balchen then almost lost his ship the following month in a storm in the English Channel, largely due, he claimed, to an inadequate crew. In a letter to the Admiralty describing how the wind 'blew hard and continued all day on Sunday blowing a very hard storm which made a very great sea', Balchen complained that 'with the very bad ship's company I have I should have lost all my masts. I have 450 odd people on board and I am sure 350 were sea sick and those I took for sailors prove bad fellows ... I have not above 50 able seamen. I have lost my long boat, spritsail yard and flying gib boom.'[79] In another letter written on the same day, this time to the Navy Board, his description of the storm was even more graphic and it had clearly horrified him. Not only did he describe how the 'wind came to the SW & SSW and blew hard which made a great sea', but also that the motion of the ship broke away the large sheet anchor 'caused a great deal of trouble with my bad ship's company' and 'I was fear full it might do the ship damage'. Demonstrating his own very real personal trauma, Balchen continued by relating that all day 'it blew very hard' and that as the ship rode the storm, it was 'the hardest rode that ever I was riding in my life'. He concluded: 'but thank God made the ship to get in here [the Downs] today'.[80] The Downs anchorage is a roadstead in the English Channel, off the Kent coast, north of Dover. So Balchen and his ship had survived, albeit with a crew that he was not happy with.

But only a couple of weeks later, on 10 October, he did lose his ship and was again captured when he ran into his old adversary Admiral Duguay-Trouin. His orders were to take *Falmouth* under his command as well as his *Gloucester* and proceed on the instructions of the East India Company to escort a convoy of merchantmen 20 leagues west of the Scilly Isles, where and when his instructions could be opened. What happened en route is best described through the records of the subsequent court martial which Balchen faced for losing his ship. This took place on 14 December 1709 on HM Yacht *Peregrine* on the River Thames, headed by Admiral Sir John Jennings. For his defence in the proceedings, he had asked the Lords of the Admiralty to have his Second Lieutenant, Master, a Midshipman and the Lieutenant of Marines to attend at the court martial if they 'shall think those people sufficient for my trial. I pray your honour to move their Lordships that I may be tried next week'.[81] The court documents revealed that Balchen's ship was engaged with Duguay-Trouin's own 74-gun ship *Lys* for over two hours with 'another French man of war firing at her at ye same time, and three other ships very neare & ready to board her'. Again, there is evidence of Balchen's courage and tenacity in this engagement, with the court reporting that *Gloucester* 'had her fore-yard shot in two so that her Head-Sailes were render'd unserviceable, & had also received much damage in her other yards, masts, Sailes & Rigging; and it is ye opinion of ye court that ye said Captain Balchen & ye other officers and men did discharge their Duties very well in this action', adding that there was no possibility of saving his ship from 'so unequall a Power of ye enemy'.[82]

While Balchen was fully exonerated and soon given his next command, Duguay-Trouin's fame and fortune grew. Even by 1694 Louis XIV had awarded him with the sword of honour and by 1709 made him a nobleman after he had captured 16 warships and over 300 merchant ships from the Dutch and the English.[83] It was, however, his victory at the Battle of the Lizard that was his greatest engagement, though quickly followed by his capture of Balchen's *Gloucester*. Over the subsequent years, no less than ten ships of the French Navy have been named after him, an accolade which clearly reflects his importance to the nation. Ironically, one of these ships, the 74-gun *Duguay-Trouin*, built in 1795, survived and escaped from Nelson's great Battle of Trafalgar on 21 October 1805 but soon afterwards, on 3 November, was captured along with the fellow surviving French ships of the line *Formidable*, *Mont Blanc* and *Scipion*. Renamed HMS *Implacable*, she remained in the Royal Navy's fighting line until 1855 when she became a training ship for boys at Devonport for another 50 years. Described by *The Times* in December 1919 as 'one of the great historical treasures of the nation – or of two nations, for the French have an almost equal interest in the last survivor of their Fleet at Trafalgar',[84] the old *Duguay-Trouin* was towed to Falmouth for restoration. She was the oldest ship of the line after Nelson's *Victory* when, in 1948, she was scuttled.

Meanwhile, back in 1709, Balchen was fully exonerated and appointed to the 54-gun frigate *Colchester*, which had been launched in 1707, and aboard which he would sail for the next five years. It was at this time, during the final three years of the War of the Spanish Succession, that Balchen truly made his mark as a successful commander, beginning with the capture of four enemy ships, including both merchantmen and privateers, in 1710 alone. In May that year, the High Court of Appeals for Prizes, a division of the High Court of the Admiralty which administered the handling and disposal of ships captured by the Royal Navy, adjudicated on the distribution of prize monies for the captured French merchant ship, *L'Aurore Josephus de Dieppe* (Master – Johannes Godebout). This 60-ton vessel, armed with six guns, had been loaded in Dieppe, France, with beer, cider, iron pots, bale goods and other merchandise, bound for Saint Domingue on the Island of Hispaniola in the West Indies. The court records show that the ship was 'taken by HMS *Colchester* (John Balchen commanding) and HMS *Litchfield* (Joseph Taylor commanding) and brought into Plymouth'.[85]

Also recorded in the High Court of Appeals in the same year was a larger captured merchant ship, the 70-ton *St Claude* (Master – John Mathe), which was laden with 40 tons of salt and bound for Newfoundland on a fishing voyage. It was noted that the ship was 'taken in a fight by HMS *Colchester* (John Balchen commanding) and HMS *Litchfield* (Joseph Taylor commanding) and brought into Plymouth'.[86] It seems Balchen and his counterpart on the *Litchfield*, Joseph Taylor, were on a mission to capture as many prizes as they could together, as a third ship then appears to have been captured by the pair, this time a more formidable French privateer of 70 tons and armed with 24 guns. This was *Count de Vassy* (Master – John de Marquerye) and again being recorded as 'taken in a fight by HMS *Litchfield* (Joseph Taylor commanding) and HMS *Colchester* (John Balchen commanding) and brought into Plymouth'.[87]

In November 1710 the prize court recorded the capture of another French privateer, this time taken by Balchen and his *Colchester* alone, when he 'chase'd him Large with a very strong gale of wind'.[88] This was the 100-ton, 18-gun *Chevalier de St George* (Master – Tobias Dossche), taken in a fight by HMS *Colchester* (John Balchen commanding) and brought into Spithead. The subsequent Letter of Attorney, which was to be executed 'when the Prize taken is a Man of War, a Privateer or a Merchant ship' noted in its legal-speak that 'the commander and officers, or the majority of them, and the Ship's Company, and other, or the major part of them, of or on board Her Majesties Ship the *Colchester* entitled to the Prize and Bounty hereafter mentioned ... dispose of the ship called *Chevalier de St George* of Dunkirk together with her stores, Tackle, Apparel, Guns & Furniture and the Goods, Wares and Merchandize on Board then taken as Prize'.[89] It then lists all the officers and crew entitled to prize money, starting with J Balchen, Captain, Jonathan Edwards, First Lieutenant, Samuel Tilley, Second Lieutenant, E Allen, Master and so on down the ranks to the ordinary seamen in the crew. At last, Balchen had not only enhanced his reputation in the navy, but he had also accrued significant prize money to improve his home and his family's fortunes beyond his salary alone.

It was around this time that Balchen seems to have acquired a reputation for his activities protecting English trade and merchantmen. The 1776 biography described his service in this way:

He never sacrificed the honour of his country to the designs of a party, or his own private interest, nor sought stations that might be attended with greater advantage than those where his superiors thought proper to place him. The true interest of his country, and the honour of the British flag, were the grand motives that influenced his conduct, and to promote these was the greatest pleasure of his life. The merchants were highly sensible of the advantages which the commerce of the nation derived from his care and vigilance; and the privateers of the enemy felt so often the effects of his courage and intrepidity, that they dreaded even the name of the ship which Balchen commanded.[90]

It was not long before Balchen and *Colchester* were switched from Channel duties to join the Mediterranean Fleet, where they served until the end of hostilities with the Treaty of Utrecht in 1713. Records show that they were in Lisbon, Portugal, in May 1711[91] and then in

Leghorn, Italy, in March 1712.[92] They were attached to Admiral Sir John Jennings' (the same man who had presided over Balchen's court martial in 1709) Mediterranean squadron for most of 1713 and Balchen's orders from the Admiral took him to Valdo Bay and to Barcelona,[93] Port Mahon in Minorca and cruising off Toulon[94] among other duties.

But peace also brought unemployment to many, both officers and seamen alike. Many officers went on half-pay and into 'reserve' while many of the older officers were dismissed and left unemployed at the end of the war. There seemed to be a detailed mathematical and financial formula to the decision-making on the number of ships to be employed and therefore how many men were needed to service those ships in peacetime. At a Council meeting at the Court of St James, attended by King George I, who ascended the throne in 1714 not long after the Treaty of Utrecht, a debate arose as to the distribution of monies that Parliament had agreed to give the Admiralty to cover the costs of half-pay to flag officers, captains, lieutenants and the eldest of the masters of the navy who shall be unemployed. The Order in Council

> considered that his Majesty's service may require during the time of peace the following ships and vessels to answer all occasions both at home and abroad, though possibly the same may vary according as unforeseen circumstances or accidents may happen, viz.

Ships and Vessels

Rate	No.
4th	10
5th	15
6th	24
Yachts	5
Sloops	6
Guardships	10
	—
	70 in all

On this basis, the Council concluded that these active ships 'will employ 70 captains and 98 lieutenants, so that of the whole number there will be unemployed of the former 188 and of the latter 261'.[95] Luckily for Captain Balchen, his experience and reputation garnered by the end of the war were such that he escaped the axe and remained in employment; a remarkable demonstration of how important he had become to the navy in wartime and then in peace.

A year after the Treaty of Utrecht Balchen was given a new commission as commanding officer of the 42-gun *Diamond* then fitting out in Woolwich Dockyard. His attention to detail in fitting out his ship for service and his meticulous reporting of the minutiae of these activities back to the Commissioners of the Navy Board is well illustrated at this time, when he wrote to acquaint them that 'His Majesty's Ship the *Diamond*, under my command, came out of the Dock at this place the 9th instant, since which I have enter'd my complement of men, but as yet have not a Master, Surgeon or Surgeon's Mate, Therefore pray you'l give directions that they may be order'd for the ship.'[96] He followed this with an update a few days later:

> This comes to acquaint you that since my last [letter] we have completed the rigging of His Majesty's Ship I command; our anchors, and all our cables (but 2) are on board, as they are not yet made. I have one whole suit of sails aboard fit for service, others that was not I acquainted Mr Ackworth [later, as we shall see, Sir Jacob Acworth, Surveyor of the Navy, and whom Balchen was to have a major falling-out with] with when here, who gave directions in that affair. Most of the Boatswain's Small Stores are aboard and Carpenter's, the Ship is ready for taking her beer and provisions, but that I have no directions for as yet. I should desire, if you think proper, to have another Spare Topmast, for now we have but one.
>
> The Surgeon appeared Saturday last, and is gone to London by my leave to prepare his things for the voyage, I desire your Board will be pleased when he applyes, to give directions that he may be supplyed with the Necessary for the intended voyage.[97]

It seems that this latter request was not met with the urgency required because a few weeks later Balchen wrote to the Commissioners again, this time while taking on final provisions for *Diamond*, now moved downriver to the Longreach moorings on the Thames. He complained that while he was under orders to sail 'at the first opportunity for Jamaica; my Surgeon acquaints me that the Necessaryes which were ordered some time since are not yet come aboard'. He asks with clear urgency that they give directions 'to hasten them down to me, or if I should saile without them that you'l order [that] I may be supplyed at Portsmouth, where my Lords of the Admiralty's Orders direct me to go', adding by way of warning: 'I design to saile tomorrow if the weather will permit.'⁹⁸

The next thing we hear from Balchen is that he has arrived in Port Royal, Jamaica, at his old stomping grounds in the West Indies. He reports to the Board that while he is sending back to them his ship's Monthly Books on *Biddeford*, 'My self, Officers and Ships Company continue in a good state of health'.⁹⁹ So it seems that the surgeon's 'Necessaries' must have reached the ship before she sailed from Portsmouth! Such good health never did last long in the West Indies, as noted previously, and not much later Balchen was reporting crew deaths on the station.

It was not only disease which threatened seamen's lives in the Caribbean, but, even in peacetime, many pirates roamed the seas trying to intercept trade between there, South America and Europe and North America. A letter from Samuel Page, the Deputy Commissioner of Jamaica, based in St Jago de la Vega (later renamed Spanish Town, then the colonial capital of Jamaica, just west of Kingston and Port Royal), to the Navy Board in August relates to 'three pirates having been met with by some of our Sloops near this island, Captain Balchen is now at sea convoying several merchant ships through the Windward [Islands] passage'.¹⁰⁰ So Balchen and his crew in *Diamond* were thus kept busy cruising to inhibit the pirates' activities and ensuring merchant convoys could sail safely amongst the widespread British colonial island ports in the West Indies, from Barbados in the south-east to Jamaica in the north-west, including several Leeward and Windward islands in between such as St Kitts, St Lucia and Antigua. The main naval bases from which they operated were English Harbour in Antigua and Port Royal in Jamaica.

Over the ensuing months it appears that Balchen was given greater responsibilities in his role in the West Indies, both in commanding more than just his own ship, but others in company, as well as being given more land-based jobs to do in Jamaica. Reporting to the Navy Board in November 1715 he related that Captain Knighton and his Majesty's Sloop, *Jamaica*, 'had the misfortune of being cast away on the Grand Camanos' (today's Grand Caymen Islands), but had managed to save much of the ship's stores which he had brought back to Port Royal, 'which I have disposed of'. Whilst Balchen was sending Knighton back to England, he explained that 'the greatest part of his men I have kept here to make good my complement and the Sloop *Tryall*'s [complement], which have been very much weakened by death', presumably by disease and accidents. Obviously still pestered by pirates in the region, he added that because of 'several complaints being made of Piratts molesting the trades of this Island', he had ordered the cleaning of the *Tryall* sloop to get her back into service.[101]

'View of Port Royal and Kingston Harbours', Jamaica. Eighteenth-century etching by engraver Peter Mazell. As a young officer, Balchen spent much of his early naval career in the West Indies, often based in Port Royal, Jamaica, or English Harbour, Antigua. (PU0930, © National Maritime Museum, Greenwich, London)

Foreign trade, whether during wartime or peace, was seen as being indispensable to Britain's ongoing power and wealth and this was enhanced by the self-interests of merchants and traders, both back in Britain and the colonists abroad. Thus naval protection was an economic as well as a political necessity. The wider Britain's colonial and trading activities became across the oceans in the peace after 1714, the greater the need to sustain a naval presence in those waters. 'Consequently', states Baugh, 'maritime outposts, always expensive to maintain and defend, came to be seen more as assets than liabilities.' Such assets included the major naval bases in Port Mahon, Minorca, and, more recently, Gibraltar. But having increased her possessions and consequently her trading interests in the West Indies and North America, Britain began consolidating and expanding her bases along the American Atlantic coast and in Jamaica and Antigua in the Caribbean. 'In each case', concludes Baugh, 'they were immediate strategic concerns in view, but the intention of permanence is unmistakable and could only have arisen from a sense of maritime destiny.'[102] The duties of naval officers therefore increasingly extended beyond simply cruising the trade routes in defence of merchantmen with duties involving the operations of the developing colonial naval bases and dockyards.

So it was unsurprising that towards the end of Balchen's time in the West Indies, in February 1716, he received detailed orders from the Admiralty 'to be in charge for the repair of His Majesty's Naval Storehouse at Kingston on the Island of Jamaica'.[103] However, he left Jamaica bound for home a couple of weeks later, not having completed his orders. As we have now become familiar with Balchen's obsession with doing his duty and his attention to detail, it comes as no surprise that he was determined to explain exactly why he had not completed his orders and why he thought that not doing so was not necessarily a bad thing for the interests of the Lords of the Admiralty. Arriving back in British waters, off the coast of Dover in May, he wrote to the Navy Board, as required of him by the Admiralty orders:

To acquaint you of my arrival here, with his Majesty's ship under my command and *Tryall* Sloope from Jamaica, which place I left on the 9th of March. Some time before I came away I received Orders from the Rt Hon'ble the Lords Commissioners of the Admiralty for repairing his Majesty's Naval Store House there and letting the same, if convenient, and to give your Board account of what I did in it, and the Charge; the workmen could not get lime to do it before I sail'd, so have left it to one Mr Coleman which I thought would be more to his Majesty's Advantage than repairing and letting it, for nobody would give so much for the King's Store House by the year, as his Majesty must do for a month, in case his ships should have occasion for the Storehouse room, as they will clean; as I presume they will do, for I had their Lordships' Order for cleaning his Majesty's ship under my command twice a year and Sloopes every four months, which order I suppose other ships will have to attend on that Island.[104]

In other words, he felt that rather than letting the store rooms to a third party, it would be better to keep it to serve the needs of Royal Navy vessels when they frequented the island for regular cleaning. There is no evidence of Balchen being in trouble for this so it seems his logic may have been accepted, though his next posting certainly lacked the intensity of either the West Indies or the Mediterranean squadrons.

However, before Balchen left *Diamond* in May, he was anchored off the Nore when he had an angry confrontation with a Customs Officer which earned a complaint against him to the Admiralty while also throwing some light on Balchen's own personality. Moored at The Nore fleet anchorage in the mouth of the River Thames, Balchen's ship was boarded and searched by a Customs Official, a Mr Bowen. As ordered by his captain, Balchen, the ship's 'Master stay'd with him [Bowen] sometime 'till Bowen was angry at his being with him' whereupon Balchen answered: 'you give me reason to suspect whether you are the officer you claim to be, or not'. Bowen's response was to point to his boat at the side of *Diamond*, to which Balchen responded 'I answer'd that anybody might get a Customs House Boat and [do] a mischief with her, that severall people had broke prison lately and as far as I knew he might be one of them, and I told him I must be further satisfied, or otherwise I would confine him'.[105] Having repeatedly asked Bowen in vain for his credentials and official documentation, Balchen ordered him to be put in irons in the bilges of his ship. Bowen subsequently accused Balchen of 'trying to evade excise duty, slandering Customs Commissioners, striking Bowen and drawing his sword'.[106] In the subsequent enquiry, where several of Balchen's officers and crew denied any drawing of swords, the Admiralty replied to the Commissioners of His Majesty's Customs, that Balchen was 'a sober man, of honest principles to the Government, and one who hath always behaved himself so as not to give any grounds for exceptions', effectively admonishing the Customs Officers for not behaving 'mannerly and civilly to the Commanders of His Majesty's ships'.[107] So the Admiralty were certainly fully supportive of Balchen, who then went on to his next commission.

Between September 1716 and November 1717 he was to remain in British waters commanding the 70-gun *Orford*, largely on guardship duties at The Nore. Amongst the logbooks of his officers, the Journal kept by his First Lieutenant, George Protheroe, reveals what a boring, uneventful service this was. From his first report on 17 September 1716 that 'This day Captain Balchen came aboard with commission to Command this ship' to his last entry in January the next year, he plots the *Orford*'s short voyages between the Nore anchorage, the Longreach moorings, Sheerness Harbour and various obscure anchorages and minor ports along the south-east coast.

Perhaps the boredom of this commission got to Balchen as he does seem to have run into some serious confrontations with one crew member who then lodged a formal complaint against him to the Lords of the Admiralty. In many ways these confrontations reveal something of his personality. The letters he wrote in his defence show an understanding of his duties and responsibilities but also a belligerent spirit, prepared to fight his corner and uphold his integrity. In a letter he wrote to the Lords of the Admiralty on 26 January 1717, he explained his side of a complaint made against him:

The Petition of Guyco Mahanto complaining of his hard usage received from me; I am sorry such a complaint should be made to the Rt Hon'ble the Lords of the Admiralty, but it is from an Insolent fellow that deserves a great deal, and had butt little ... going ashore again without asking my leave or any Officer on board ... this fellow took liberty of going ashore without leave, as appears by the Books he was ashore all Christmas ... this Machanto [*sic*] went in the boat to put me ashore, I ordered the boat to go aboard; notwithstanding as soon as my back was turn'd, he ran away from her, and stay'd all night; when he came on board the next day, my Lieutenant Protheroe ordered him to be whip't. I have observ'd, since I have had the ship, this fellow, to be a very Impudent Rascall.[108]

Balchen was soon rid of the 'Impudent Rascall' as he shortly afterwards left *Orford* to take up a new command, this time the 80-gun *Shrewsbury*. On 10 March 1718 he received orders for *Shrewsbury* to be fitted out for service in the Mediterranean.[109] As part of a large Mediterranean squadron under Admiral Sir George Byng, *Shrewsbury* became the flagship of Vice-Admiral Sir Charles Cornwall, with Balchen serving as his Flag Captain. Despite being officially 'at peace' with Spain at the time, Britain, now under King George I, was allied to Emperor Charles VI who controlled Southern Italy, when Spain occupied Sicily. In an attempt to recover territories lost under the agreement reached by the Peace of Utrecht in 1713, Spain had recaptured Sardinia in 1717 and then seized Sicily. What later became known as the War of the Quadruple Alliance (between 1718 and 1720) saw the Triple Alliance of Britain, France and the Dutch Republic joined by Austria against Spain. As tensions mounted, Charles Drummond, Third Lieutenant in *Shrewsbury*, recorded in his logs that the fleet left Malaga in July 1718 and soon arrived off Cape Passaro on the southern tip of Sicily.[110] Here, on 11 August, Byng's fleet of twenty-two ships of the line met up with a Spanish fleet of twenty-seven ships of the line and frigates commanded by Vice-Admiral Antonio de Gaztaneta and Rear-Admiral Fernando Chacon. Although there was no declaration of war, and Byng did not signal his fleet into battle, an exchange of gunfire was the excuse for him to fully engage the Spanish fleet, with Balchen and *Shrewsbury* in the heart of the battle. It was a decisive victory in which both Spanish admirals were captured and sixteen Spanish ships of the line and frigates and more smaller ships were either captured or burned. It is recorded that in this action, Captain Balchen again 'behaved with the greatest courage and intrepidity'.[111]

'The Battle of Cape Passaro, 11 August 1718'. Pen and ink drawing by Peter Monamy, circa. 1720. Captain John Balchen commanded HMS *Shrewsbury* as the flagship of Vice-Admiral Sir Charles Cornwall in this battle. The British Mediterranean Fleet under Admiral Sir George Byng destroyed a large Spanish squadron off Cape Passaro, Sicily. (PW5730, © National Maritime Museum, Greenwich, London)

A powerful insight into the intensity of action at this battle, as viewed from Balchen's and his Vice-Admiral's ship, is given by Third Lieutenant Drummond's log book (and echoed by Second Lieutenant Henry Power's log entry):

At 5AM we saw several men of war and the galleys of the Spanish stand in close to the shore, upon which our admirals made signal for the *Canterbury, Dunkirk, Rippon, Dreadnought, Argyle, Rochester* and *Looe* to stand in shore after them and att 7 we see they have engaged the Spaniards and that one of them had struck to the *Argyle*. The main body of the Spanish fleet which consisted of 11 sail from 80 to 44 Guns stand away to the southward and we are in chase of them with Admiral & Rear-Admiral and 11 men of war and 2 fireships, att 11 the *Orford*, *Kent*, *Grafton* and [another] at the headmost of our ships are engaged with the enemy, att noon the *Orford* and *Kent* has taken the Spanish man of war from 54 to 60 Guns, all this [time] we had no signal for a line nor any for Battle. Att 2PM a ship of 44 guns struck to the *Montague* and *Rupert* and att half past another of 44 guns struck to the *Essex*, at 3 the *Cumberland* and the *Grafton* fought [their] Rear-Admiral for one hour and is now in chase of another ship, att 4 two Spanish men of war came from the SW into the fleet and fired a broadside at which time ... the *Grand Phillippe* 74 guns struck to the *Superb* and *Kent*, at half past 4 the Rear-Admiral and *Royal Oak* are in chase of a ship to SE of us, and we and *Grafton* are in chase to the SSE and SE, att 8PM finding our chase gaind of us the *Grafton* and we left off the chase and att 12 we joined the fleet again ... we have six Spanish men of war as prizes.[112]

In March the following year Balchen was back home and fitting out *Shrewsbury* for Channel service when, just a few days later, he received 'Orders for removing myself and Company into His Majesty's ship *Monmouth*, and two press warrants for the manning of the said ship'. He immediately despatched his now Second Lieutenant, Mr Drummond, to London in order to 'hasten down what men he can find belonging to the *Shrewsbury* and to enter what he can more'.[113] The issue of finding sufficient crew members was a recurring theme during this period, with all commanding officers constantly under pressure to press men into service in order to reach their ship's full complement. Even when this was achieved, many such pressed men were either ill-equipped to be seamen or deserted at the first opportunity.

Many of Balchen's letters to the Admiralty between 1717 and 1720 concerned his efforts at mustering sufficient men onto his ships and complaining about their capabilities. Berthed at Chatham on *Shrewsbury* in March 1718, he responds to his orders for manning his ship 'to her middle complement of men, which I shall endeavour to do as soon as I can, by employing my Officers here about it', but he then goes on to ask their Lordships if he can 'send my Lieutenants up to Town [London] or not to get men' (a note from the Lords at the bottom states 'Leave it to him to do as he shall think may best contribute to the Service', implying he should press any men he can from wherever he can).[114] While on *Monmouth* in Portsmouth he referred to many of his men going ashore and 'of those absent, I fear a great many will not come, and those that are hereabouts we cannot get on board, they are too lazy, don't care to work'.[115] In a similar vein, when back on *Shrewsbury* at Spithead a few months later, he wrote: 'I bare more men than my Complement at present, but a great many of those absent, I fear will not return, and indeed some of them are good for nothing if they should; likewise many of them I have on board I would gladly part with, if I could get better.'[116] Part of the solution for the navy was to wait off the Downs roadstead for incoming merchant ships and then seize active seamen from them, regardless of nationality. Naturally, the owners and commanders of such merchantmen did their best to avoid naval ships and retain their crew members. In this context, Balchen complained to the Admiralty about his Orders 'for impressing what men I can out of ships homeward bound, which I shall endeavour to do, for I very much want men; I have my number, but very bad. The merchantmen often put their men ashore at Folkestone [to the south of the Downs] as I am informed, and sometimes go on the back of the Goodwin [Sands] to prevent their men being impressed.'[117]

Despite such travails, Balchen continued as captain of *Monmouth* and joined Admiral Sir John Norris cruising the Baltic in the summers between 1719 and 1721. Admiral Norris had previously been stationed with a fleet in the Baltic between 1715 and 1716, where Britain was supporting a coalition of Russia, Denmark and Hanover against Sweden, as one phase in what became known as the Great Northern War (1700–21) against the expansionist Swedish Empire in Northern, Central and Eastern Europe. However, with the death of King Charles XII of Sweden in 1718, Britain switched sides to protect British merchant ships and trades from Russian raiders. There are few records of Balchen's activities while serving in the Baltic on this occasion, but his cruising there came to an end when the Treaty of Nystad ended that war in 1721. Before he left *Monmouth* in order to take up a brief command of the 70-gun *Ipswich* on guardship duties at Spithead in 1721–2, Balchen had to complete his paperwork for those of his

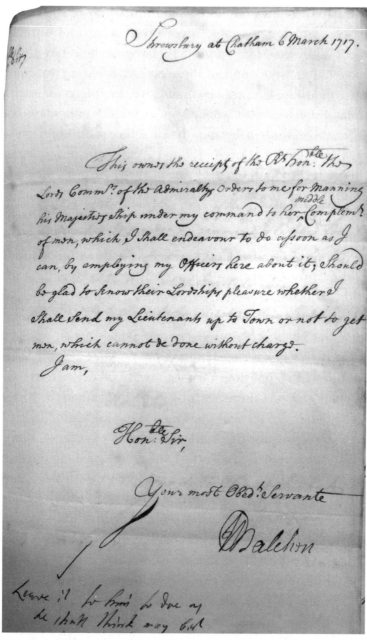

Letter written by Captain Balchen seeking Admiralty permission to send his Lieutenants to London to press more men for his ship and their scribbled comment at the bottom 'Leave it to him to do as he shall think may best contribute to the Service', 6 March 1718. (ADM 1/1472. The National Archives, Kew, London)

officers dispersing to other ships and duties. Typical of this duty and his support of those officers serving under him was his signing off for his First Lieutenant: 'These are to certify to their Hon'rs the Principal Officers and Commissioners of his Majesties Navy, that Mr Titus Smith served as First Lieutenant of his Majesties ship the *Monmouth* under my command, from the 13 March 1718, to the 19 October 1720; during which times he compl'd with the General printed Instructions annext to his Commission. Given under my hand, this 19 Day of December 1721. J Balchen.'[118]

He returned to *Monmouth* in February 1725/6, seemingly taking all his officers and crew with him from *Ipswich*. This event was captured graphically by his new Second Lieutenant, Kinzey, who was given his commission to join *Ipswich* in Portsmouth on 24 January 1725/6. In his logbook entry for that day, Kinzey wrote: 'I was under orders of Captain John Balchen. Order'd to stay in London, set up a Rendezvous & enter and Impress men for the ship.' His log entry for 23 February registered the change of plans for him and his captain: 'The Captain, Lieutenants, Officers and men were tunn'd over [from *Ipswich*] on board the *Monmouth*' though he continued to stay in London until April 'to enter and impress men for his Majesty's ship *Monmouth*'. Finally, Kinzey reports that 'by Order of Captain John Balchen I broke up my rendezvous and repair'd to meet the ship where I arrived on 18th April and went on board her'. Five days later he and *Monmouth* arrived in Copenhagen, Denmark.[119]

Balchen and the crew of *Monmouth* had joined Admiral Sir Charles Wager's large fleet back to the Baltic again. This time it was there to protect Sweden and Denmark from the threat of a recently mobilised Russian Fleet as well as protecting vital British trade interests, particularly in timber, hemp, rope and other naval-related materials from Scandinavia. The twenty-ship squadron went first to Copenhagen then across the Baltic to the port and naval base of Reval (today's Tallinn in Estonia). Wager had orders to destroy the Russian fleet if it came out into the Baltic and, though the Russians quickly demobilised, the Royal Navy remained all summer for each of the next two years to reassure Sweden. The *Monmouth*'s First Lieutenant Mr B Mansel's logbook[120] entries between 23 February 1725/6 and

October 1727 record the ship's movements around the Baltic during the summers and back home for the winters:

24 February – off Copenhagen;

30 May – off Reval;

13 June – went into Reval;

20 September – left Reval;

9 October – Copenhagen;

3 November – Spithead;

27 November – Portsmouth Harbour;

29 November – 'people went away for their six weeks leave';

23 December – 'This day I went to London with leave from Captain Balchen';

25 January – 'Returned to my Duty', Spithead;

April – The Nore;

13 May – Copenhagen;

24 July – Kronenburg;

7 August – The Nore, then Spithead;

October – St Hellens.

During the winter of 1727/28 there was no Christmas leave back home for Balchen and the crew of *Monmouth* as no sooner were they back in Portsmouth than they were off again in November to Gibraltar, via Cape St Vincent, Spain and Lagos Bay, Portugal. On 18 December they were anchored in Tangier Roads, Morocco, returning to Gibraltar in January. They eventually came back to Portsmouth Harbour in April 1728.[121]

Before Balchen left *Monmouth* for the second time, there was further evidence, already shown all through his career, of a genuine concern for the welfare of both officers and seamen. When the Admiralty received an anonymous letter from Portsmouth in February 1728/9 complaining that the crews' bread was only half baked and was less than the proscribed weight, Balchen responded: 'I had all the men on board each ship called up on the quarterdeck ... I desired them not to be afraid of speaking their minds freely', as he would not 'suffer them to be abused in any manner'. Though they said they had no reason to complain about their rations, Balchen was still concerned that there might be an issue with the bread rations. So he went to the bakery concerned and tested for himself the batch of loaves being prepared and checked that the weight and baking was to the correct standard. 'I caused 20 of them to be put into the scale and they weighed fairly forty pounds at 16 ounces to the pound, and I am well assured.' Thus satisfied with the quality of the loaves provided, he concluded, reassuringly, that 'the baker could know nothing of my design of weighing his bread, for the bread was hot. This, Sir, is fact ...'[122] So the baker and his bakery were fully exonerated by Balchen.

By then, George II had become king, succeeding George I in 1727. After his brief expedition to the Mediterranean, Balchen was back in England and, due to both his seniority and his accumulated experience both in war and peace, gained promotion to Rear-Admiral in 1729. Another phase was now to begin in the life of John Balchen, this time as an Admiral of the Royal Navy.

6

Service as Admiral John Balchen

'My point is that the admirable men of those times, the Cochranes, Byrons, Falconers, Seymours, Boscawens and the many less famous sailors from whom I have in some degree compounded my characters, are best celebrated in their own splendid actions rather than in imaginary contests; that authenticity is a jewel; and that the echo of their words has an abiding value.'

Patrick O'Brian, Author's Note, in *Master & Commander*, 1970.

As an admiral, Balchen's career became a little more mundane compared to his very active life as a captain. Administrative work had to accompany seagoing activities, though undoubtedly he preferred the latter. In between various shore-based commissions in charge of the ships and their operations at either Portsmouth or Plymouth, Balchen still took command of substantial squadrons, both in the Channel Fleet and in the Mediterranean Fleet, and, on the resumption of war in 1739, had a more substantial contribution, both at sea and in managing naval ships in the dockyards. But it was in this phase of his life that we also begin to see more of the man behind the title and obtain a greater understanding of his family life ashore.

As the new Rear-Admiral of the White Squadron, Balchen's initial responsibilities were confined to Portsmouth Harbour where he had remained on board *Monmouth*. In the same year as his promotion, he wrote to the Admiralty Secretary raising the issue of men being able to stay with their captains when there was a change of ship. He argued that 'the captains tell me that some of them are people that have been with them in other ships and are uneasy they can't go with them again'. Conversely, he also argued the case for the men as well, adding 'I am likewise informed that several men that entered in town [London] decline coming down to the ship they entered for upon hearing the captain was removed from that ship and believing they should not have liberty to go with the captains they entered for'.[1] The Admiralty Board quickly consented to Rear-Admiral Balchen's request and agreed 'to the removing such men from one ship to another who shall desire to go with the captains under whom they have formerly served'.[2] It was befitting then that, given his ongoing concern for both officers and crew, he was appointed to the Board of the 'Corporation for the Relief of Poor Sea-Officers' Widows' in 1732.[3]

Balchen's first significant sea commission as an admiral came in May 1731. His Journal for that year[4] began on 21 May with the words: 'This day I received a commission as Commander-in-Chief of his Majesty's ships at Spithead and Portsmouth Harbour with orders for holding Court Martial & and for fitting out at this port for the Sea.' He left London shortly after and arrived in Portsmouth in the evening of 26 May and 'hoisted my flag on boarding the *Dreadnought*'. This 60-gun ship had originally been built in 1706 and enlarged in 1722. However, Balchen's stay on this ship did not last long because on 6 July 1731 he noted that he had received further orders 'to put myself under the command of [Admiral] Sir Charles Wager and to get the *Princess Amelia* ready to accompany Sir Charles to the Mediterranean'. Under his command, his new flagship, the 80-gun *Princess Amelia* (she had been renamed after George II's daughter from her original name, HMS *Humber*, in 1727), was to cause Balchen much grief over the next several years. Nevertheless, on 10 July 1731 he reported that 'in the night struck my flag on board the *Dreadnought* and hoisted it on board the *Princess Amelia*'. Four days later, at 5.00am Sir Charles Wager made the signal for the mighty squadron to unmoor, with Balchen's Journal noting the thirteen men-of-war that set sail that morning: *Namur, Princess Amelia, Cornwall, Buckingham, Grafton, Hampton Court, Edinburgh, Kent, Canterbury, Exeter, Dreadnought, York* and *Kinsale*. The squadron proceeded south, spending time in Cadiz Bay and then Gibraltar Bay before proceeding to Malaga, southern Spain, in August. It appears from the Journal that the fleet was basically on a diplomatic mission, with particular emphasis on bolstering good relations with Spain. Compliments were exchanged with mutual gun salutes out of respect entering ports and various diplomatic shore exchanges and banquets for senior officials. After a visit to Cape Dragonera in Majorca, for much of September the ships were at anchor in Barcelona Port, continuing such activities there.

To the ordinary sailor, these hot days at anchor in the Mediterranean cannot have been comfortable, particularly when cooped up below decks in sultry conditions, rather than the more active at-sea duties on the upper decks and aloft. An indication of such boredom and restlessness comes from Balchen's entries in his Journal on 7 September 1731:

Court Martial for trying James Thornton belonging to the *Namur* for fighting with Rachin his mess mate who died soon after, he was acquitted of the murther [murder] but was found guilty of the 23rd Article of War & fighting on board the ship for which he was sentenced him to be whipped from ship to ship 12 lashes on his bare back.[5]

By implication, this meant he was to receive twelve lashes alongside each ship in the squadron in turn. The administering of twelve lashes was common place for being drunk or for insolence to a superior, but this escalated through various misdemeanours to twenty-four or thirty-six lashes. Such harsh punishment meted out to ordinary sailors was a common practice in the eighteenth-century Royal Navy and given some of the more serious sentencing such as this could lead to the recipient's death. The sentences were usually carried out on the quarterdeck in front of the whole crew, including officers, and usually administered by the boatswain's mates. This acted as a powerful lesson to the men to ensure the discipline of the crew at all times in the ship.

October 1731 saw Balchen and the squadron in Leghorn on the west coast of Italy, then back at Gibraltar in November and home again on 11 December. There followed sporadic shore and sea duties for him over the next few years when the long period of peace saw little in the way of action and more in terms of simply maintaining the dockyards and the many warships 'in ordinary'. This was a time when many officers were either on half-pay or even dismissed from the service while ships were laid up in port. However, Balchen maintained his active position and, unlike many of his senior colleagues as we shall see later, avoided leaving the service to pursue politics instead. Indeed, there were certainly incidents which have been recorded about him and his activities at this phase in his career.

By 1734 Balchen had been promoted again, to Vice-Admiral of the White, and was Flag Officer once more on board *Princess Amelia*. It was while he was on this ship in January 1734/5 that he fell out with Sir Jacob Acworth, Surveyor of the Navy. He wrote to the Admiralty Secretary that, while trying to get *Princess Amelia* into dry dock at Plymouth, 'she fell over against the jetty head; that scared the men in such a manner that I expect to lose half of them'. Claiming that she could have 'tumbled quite over' and that without providing additional girdling (added planking along the waterline for increased width and stability) and ballast, 'she is not fit to go to sea'. He added, what proved to be right, that 'I expect the Surveyor of the Navy will object'[6] to his complaints. A week later the Navy Board responded to the Admiralty Secretary with a narrative which, while acknowledging that the event had 'so intimidated the seamen that Vice-Admiral Balchen expects to lose half of them', intimated that Balchen was wrong in his allegations and, while counter-claiming that the ship was quite stable, only agreed that it might be advisable to girdle her and increase her ballast 'as the ship is now to labour under an unhappy character'.[7] The letter also claimed that no previous complaints had been made about the ship which 'rode light and single' even in Mediterranean storms. Balchen was clearly incensed, firmly attributing this letter to Acworth's hand. Countering the claims by Acworth that there were no complaints about *Princess Amelia* since she had been built and that there were no stability problems, Balchen gave several examples of recent events clearly demonstrating her being unstable unless almost over-ballasted. 'I beg leave to observe to their Lordships that when Sir George Walton had his flag on board her some time since, and the ship was going into Portsmouth Harbour from Spithead with reefed topsails, she then lay along in such a manner that frightened the people, they thinking she would overset', going on to say that 'I was in the ship in the Mediterranean in company with Sir Charles

Wager and had great reason to complain of her in every respect'. He also gave a robust and factual account of why his ship was so tender, and condemned Acworth for ordering work to be done to his ship 'without taking any notice to me or any other officer' and that 'he should have the good manners to ... let me know what he would have them do'. He proceeded at length to advise that even greater girdling and more ballast was required than had been recommended should be applied[8] and generally complained of the ship's design and stability.

But that was not an end to *Princess Amelia*'s troubles. In February, the Plymouth Dockyard Officers reported 'on the damage to the *Princess Amelia* by being driven ashore when the mooring chains broke after she had been undocked and the *Hampton Court* taken in. The mooring chains of the *Hampton Court*, the *Litchfield* and other ships have broken.'[9] Balchen's reaction to the instability issues with *Princess Amelia* undoubtedly paved the way for later calls to review the design and building of naval ships, particularly such 80-gun vessels, as discussed earlier and in Chapter 8, demonstrating where his legacy led to many changes in both ship designs and naval administration. *Princess Amelia* remained Balchen's flagship intermittently over the following several years, even after he was promoted again to Vice-Admiral of the Red in 1736.

By this time, tensions were rising in Europe between the colonial seafaring nations, with Britain, France, Spain and to an extent the Dutch Republic increasingly clashing over trade, particularly between Europe and the Caribbean, North American and South American colonies. The Whigs and Tories were increasingly emerging as peace and war factions and Parliamentary debates, often led by senior Admiralty officers elected as Members of Parliament (MPs), seemed to increase the sabre-rattling. By May 1738 Rear-Admiral Haddock had been sent with a squadron of eleven men-of-war to provoke the Spanish around Cadiz, Gibraltar and the Mediterranean. But things came to a head the next year and war officially broke out again, firstly with the War of Jenkins' Ear against Spain and then escalating into the War of the Austrian Succession against Spain and France.

By this time Balchen was Flag Officer in charge of ships in Plymouth, a role he held intermittently from 1739 and into the early 1740s. However, it was not long after the commencement of hostilities that he was called into action again. Writing to the Admiralty from his flagship, the 80-gun *Russell*, on 2 May 1740, Balchen reported that he had left Plymouth on 9 April with a squadron including the *Russell*, *Grafton*, *Norfolk* and *Dunkirk* (later joined by the *Deptford*), bound for cruising duties off the Atlantic coasts of Spain and Portugal where he arrived on 14 April. But the letter then continues by saying that although he acknowledges 'my orders of the 18th last month direct my leaving this station and coming to Spithead', he writes that, in the light of information he has received while stationed off Ferrol, northern Spain, regarding the number of enemy ships in that port, he therefore thinks 'it not proper to leave this station till further orders'. He adds that 'If the Cadiz squadron and those at Ferrol should attempt to joyne, I shall want more ships'.[10] But later that afternoon he received further intelligence delivered by the sloop *Swift*, from Oporto in Portugal, in a letter from the British Consul in Oporto. Indeed, amongst Balchen's letters in these same archives is a letter addressed to him, dated 1 May 1740, from John Burnaby Parker, Consul at Oporto. This letter, it states, is:

> To inform you that a squadron of nine sail of Spanish Men of War, and three Frigates, which left Cadiz some time ago, arrived the 27th past month at Ferrol, and that five ships that had sailed upon a cruise from this last Port, have return'd back again to it, so that there is now in the Harbour of Ferrol eighteen men of war, and three frigates, besides several small vessels for transports, and it is reported they are to be joined by ten more sail of men of war more, but from whence they are to come is not mentioned. Two ships have arrived lately from Buenos Aires at Santander richly laden.[11]

Having been alerted by this news, Balchen then wrote a second, more urgent letter to the Admiralty. Referring to the Consul's letter, he reported that:

> If that Intelligence is to be depended on, I am not in a condition to look them in the face, and instead of Rendezvousing off the cape and

twenty leagues north from it, I shall wait their Lordships' Orders about midway between Ushant and Cape Finisterre in Latitude 46 degrees or thereabouts for I don't think it will be advisable to expose myself with so small a force: the wind is now at S by E about 16 or 17 Leagues, as the wind being now fair for coming out of Ferrol, and they seeing Wednesday last when I stood off there, that I had but six ships it is likely they may come out in quest of me, however I shall keep a good look out, and not be surprised. I hope their Lordships will send me strength fit to cope with them, or call me in.[12]

Clearly his small squadron of six ships could not confront a Spanish fleet of up to nineteen men-of-war and several frigates, so a cautious retreat to await orders to return home or to be sent substantial reinforcements was a wise choice. In fact, Balchen remained in that holding station in the Bay of Biscay until 22 May without receiving any response or further orders from the Admiralty. So, he reported, 'then meeting no orders and the people [crew] very sickly and our beer all gone, I thought proper to make the best of my way home'. By 1 June, Balchen was near the Scilly Isles and reported from the *Russell* that his was returning to England with four other ships in his squadron, the *Norfolk*, *Grafton*, *Dunkirk* and *Severn*. He also reported that his sixth ship, the *Deptford*, had been ordered to give chase having seen 'three sail all together, one ship'. The ship was captured by the *Deptford* and it turned out to be a French privateer of 12 guns from St Sebastian, with 120 crew on board. The other two vessels were her prizes, one being a brigantine with wine from Oporto, the other a small sloop form Poole in Dorset but on her way from Cork in Ireland with provisions for Newfoundland when she was caught by the privateer. Balchen then lost sight of the *Deptford* and her prizes 'and have not seen them since'.[13]

After that excitement, though still occasionally going to sea either for convoy duties or to command the Channel Fleet or the Mediterranean Fleet during this early period of the war, Balchen often held the important post of Port Admiral in Plymouth or in Portsmouth, where mundane administration was the core part of his role. It can therefore be imagined how he must have had mixed feelings when he was called upon in August that year to assist the young Commodore George Anson in preparing for his secret but clearly exciting expedition to the South Seas in 1740. Early that year large naval forces were fitting out for war in home waters and the Caribbean, with naval dockyards and victualling departments fully stretched, leaving preparations for Anson's squadron of ships (led by the 60-gun *Centurion* and two 50-gun ships, *Gloucester* and *Severn*, accompanied by *Pearl*, *Wager* and *Tryall*) a low priority. Coinciding with this frenetic activity, England was suffering the worst typhus epidemic of the century and this had spread through the fleet, killing many seamen in the process. Instead of sending 300 able seamen that Anson had requested to make up his complement of crews, the Admiralty responded 'with men discharged from hospital, drafts brought in from the press gang and marines quartered in the neighbourhood ... [and] pensioners from Chelsea Hospital'.[14] Anson's response was a letter to Andrew Stone, secretary to the Duke of Newcastle, the Secretary of State, stating: 'I am sorry for the occasion of complaining that fourscore of the best of the invalids have been suffered to desert the night before they were embarked, and that as many more are unfit for service by infirmities and extreme old age. Vice-Admiral Balchen has made up the deficiencies with marines.'[15] And so, with Balchen's help and support, Anson's squadron eventually sailed from Spithead 'in company with Admiral Balchen, who wore the red flag at the foretopmast head on board the *Russell*, an 80-gun ship. He had a squadron of eleven sail of men-of-war under his command, besides a great number of transports, and many merchant ships that had waited for convoy.'[16] Considering how Anson's eventually triumphant voyage around the world, completed in 1744, led not only to wealth, promotion and fame for the later Lord George Anson (1st Baron Anson) and Admiral of the Fleet, Balchen would undoubtedly be pleased but probably envious of his achievements. As discussed later, Balchen and Anson's careers overlapped on several occasions, when both were engaged, on different ships, in many of the same battles and campaigns. Indeed, it was largely through Anson that Balchen's legacy was carried into the next generation of the Royal Navy.

As mentioned, for much of 1739 and the early 1740s he 'generally served as Flag Officer in charge of the ships at Plymouth'.[17] It was in this capacity that he became clearly bored by inaction and administrative duties. Commodore Philip Vanbrugh, the Naval Commissioner at Plymouth, wrote to his friend John Russell that 'Vice-Admiral Balchen is here, but no flag is hoisted, nor much to do, which gives him much trouble; whereas ease and quiet is most agreeable to me'.[18] Around the same time, when Balchen seldom went to sea except for convoy duties, he complained to his friend Admiral Haddock that he was missing out on any chance to find either fame or fortune while Admiral Vernon (who had just captured Porto Bello in Panama) 'has all the Glory, and success pursues him', adding that 'the West Indie people will be so rich there won't be Roome for them to purchase Lands; whilst I am forced to drudge from place to place for Nothing'.[19] This reflects his continued ambition and lack of new opportunities despite being such a long-serving officer.

His so-called 'drudge from place to place' can be exemplified in late September of 1740 when he sailed on board the yacht *William & Mary* from the Nore with two ships, *Guernsey* and *Port Mahon*, to Helvoit Sluice in the Dutch Republic (today's small city of Hellevoetsluis by the sea in the western Netherlands close to the Europoort shipping terminal). Although we do not know the purpose of such a trip to allied Holland, it is clear that a number of ships were involved in the expedition. Balchen reported to the Admiralty on 25 September that he had 'arrived with the *Royall Caroline* and four yachts. The three ships I took from the Nore lost company the first night … but yesterday they all came in. I hope as the wind is now at SW it will not be long before the *Argyle* and *Cruiser* Sloop arrives, it threatens durty weather and I shall be glad to see.'[20]

Boredom with shore duties or short seagoing errands such as that did not mean that he failed to continue making his mark on the administration of the navy during this renewed period of war. In 1740 it became apparent that some officers who objected to being sent to a station or ship they did not like, simply resigned temporarily due to ill health. The Admiralty therefore ordered that any application to resign by officers should be forwarded by their commanding admiral. Balchen responded: 'I believe I shall have but few Applications for that purpose, for they know I am no favourer of Quitting, they must be bad if I write for them, but it is now become a fashion, if they don't like the Ship, or Voyage they Quitt for their health, Altho' they Ayle Nothing.'[21] Conversely, it was not long after this when the Admiralty complained that 'it is frequent practice' with captains to send men ashore to the hospitals 'whose ailments are but triffling, and might be easily cured on board, in order to get rid of such men as they did not like'.[22]

Balchen was also a man who, despite issues with his seamen on *Gloucester* mentioned earlier, generally respected his crew. In 1741 the Admiralty tended to mistrust and confine everyone, volunteers and pressed men alike, when their ships came into port, but when they questioned Balchen's wisdom in allowing his men ashore in Portsmouth, he defended their trustworthiness in his retort: 'Some of them had been sent up to London in the Room of Others Imprest, and returned again. Should we confine such men, they would certainly Run the first opportunity they got ashore. In my opinion it is necessary to make some distinction between Volunteers and others.'[23]

There are two handwritten letters by Balchen kept in Godalming Museum which relate to his mundane administrative duties in Plymouth. Dated 24 October 1739[24] and 25 May 1742,[25] and addressed to Commodore Philip Vanbrugh, the Naval Commissioner at Plymouth, they are both routine administrative orders for preparing or repairing ships. In the first, addressed from the Hamoaze anchorage outside Plymouth on the estuary of the River Tamar, his instructions concern 'His Majesty's Ship the *Assistance*, having been ashore upon the rocks upon the Island and I think it necessary her bottom should be look'd on before she proceeds to sea; I have given orders to Captain Wynnall to get her ready with all dispatch possible; I desire you will please give the proper directions for her being received into the Dock accordingly.' His second letter, addressed from Plymouth Yard, concerns a sloop being prepared for sea: 'Captain Cooper of the *Hound* Sloop, acquaints me by his [letter] of this days date that upon overhauling his rigging, he finds his main & fore shrouds bad & likewise some of the sails. As he is under orders for Virginia, I desire you'll give directions to the proper Officer that the said Sloop may be fitted for her voyage accordingly.'

Such letter-writing must have been Balchen's everyday activity and was to be of even more importance and scale as a new round of frenetic naval activity was exploding around him amidst the escalating demands of war. But supervision of the Royal Dockyards and their good functioning would be an essential part of the naval war effort. At this time, he was kept in readiness in the Channel Fleet as the French appeared to be mobilising in Brest. It is evident from letters written by Plymouth Dockyard Commissioner Philip Vanbrugh that Balchen was back flying his vice-admiral's flag on the *Princess Amelia* in January 1743[26] and from a letter by his Flag Captain on the *Princess Amelia*, Captain W Hemmington, that in May that year, just before retiring, he was again at the Hamoaze anchorage off Plymouth.[27]

Nevertheless, in August 1743, Balchen advanced to the rank of full Admiral of the White Squadron. After 58 years of loyal and brave service, he deservedly retired in April 1744 on a comfortable pension of £600 per annum,[28] was knighted by King George II in May and was made Governor of Greenwich Naval Hospital. The commission appointing John Balchen as Master of Greenwich Hospital lies folded today in a leather-covered wooden box in The National Archives, Kew, still attached by red and white cords to the Great Seal, in brown wax, of the King's Privy Council. The beautifully-illustrated royal document states that it does 'constitute and appoint our Trusty and beloved John Balchen Esq to be Master of our Royal Hospital Greenwich'. It also states that a 'fee or salary of one thousand pounds by the year in the manner aforesaid under him the said John Balchen owning our pleasure'.[29] This represented a remarkable accolade by the king in recognising the loyalty and long service Balchen had given to so many monarchs during his career. This was at the age of 75, a remarkable age given the period in which he lived and the arduous career he had pursued. Unfortunately that was not the peaceful end to Balchen's career that it should have been. Somehow, it seems hardly surprising then that it was to him, albeit at his great age, that the Admiralty turned to in 1744 when they dragged him out of retirement to take command of the formidable squadron that was to unfold into such a fateful final voyage.

However, after Balchen made his way down to Portsmouth to board *Victory* and take command of the mighty combined squadron of British and Dutch warships towards the end of July, there were a few days of delay caused by the weather and by the gathering of merchant ships to be escorted south with the squadron. This gave Balchen the opportunity to undertake his final land-based piece of work for the Admiralty. And what a bizarre affair it was amongst the substantial list of orders he had undertaken in his long and glorious career in the Royal Navy: he was asked by their Lordships if, while he was moored at Spithead, he could investigate complaints of sick sailors at the Fortune Naval Hospital in Gosport (on the west side of the entrance to Portsmouth Harbour) being supplied with copious amounts of alcohol and causing anti-social behaviour in the area. Balchen's final report made on English soil was therefore of a very formal, yet down to earth nature, typical of his matter-of-fact approach to so many issues in his dealings with sailors and everyday life:

> Pursuant to your Directions to me on the Information given to their Lords Commissioners of the Admiralty, of the excessive drinking of strong liquor at Fortune Hospital, I have been there, and find that the houses about the hospital and adjoining to it, are a nest of Gin shops, who retail Spiritous Liquor to the sick, open both day and night; there being nothing to confine them within the hospital but a few pales which they would pull down if the Gates were not open to them at all hours; instead of the Agent and Proper Officers to lye within the Hospital and inspect frequently into the Wards to prevent any Disorders, there is no apartment or lodging for any, except the Contractor who is afraid to speak to them. The Nurses and Men deny that there is any Spirits brought into the Wards; but it appears by other credible witnesses that they often drink there, which liquors must be brought in by the Nurses, or such men as are capable of going abroad, or both, they being under no restraint and are often times Drinking and dancing the whole night long on the Green without the Hospital.[30]

Balchen's recommendation to the Admiralty over this issue was to suggest that the licences to sell alcoholic liquor be revoked from all the local retailers near the hospital and that proper officers be appointed to supervise affairs at the establishment.

Four days after this, Balchen set sail on his last voyage. As discussed in some detail in Chapter 2, his final commission saw him sail out of the

St Hellens anchorage off the Isle of Wight with a mighty fleet of twenty-three men of war, comprising seventeen British and six Dutch ships, on 28 July 1744. His orders were to attack any French ships he could find, to escort a vast convoy of transport ships bound for the West Indies and Virginia and eventually, and most importantly, to destroy a French squadron blockading a substantial convoy of vital transport ships in the River Tagus, Lisbon. This long-overdue convoy was bound for Gibraltar and Port Mahon, Minorca, for the desperately under-provisioned Mediterranean Fleet commanded Admiral Thomas Mathews but had been intercepted by the French and blockaded in the river anchorage. It was on this ill-fated mission that the last letters were written by Balchen before he finally went down with *Victory*. Even these letters continue to show his courage and determination to attack the enemy wherever he could find them. Having failed to lure any French warships out of Brest on his way south, despite trying his best to find the enemy, he did manage to see some action on 12 August, capturing six large French transport ships sailing from the West Indies back to French ports. He described this action in a letter to the Admiralty thus:

On the 12th instant, at 7 the *Hampton Court* made the signal for seeing ten sail, made the *Prince Frederick*, *Captain*, *Monmouth* and *Falkland* signals to chase and stood after with the rest of the squadron, at 9 saw several Guns Fired which we took to be signals, at half past 11 Tack'd to the northward, wind at NW ... by 5 came up with the chase, they proved to be six French merchant ships from Cape Francois, St Domingo, three of them bound for Nantes and the others for Bordeaux. Two [English] privateers, the *Prince Charles* of Bristol and the *Dispatch* of Plymouth were chasing them, two struck to the Dutch, two to the *Hampton Court*, one to the *Captain* and the other to the *Augusta*, viz:

Le Intrepide – Captain
La Flora – Augusta
La Laurance – Hampton Court
Le Bon Enfant – Hampton Court
Le Monarch – Edam
La Serin – Dordreight

They had been on their passage fifty days, are laden with sugar, some Indigo and a little coffee.[31]

Despite his desire for more active opportunities in his later years, Balchen was not, until after his retirement in 1744, given many such commissions or postings that could bring him either fame or fortune. As Baugh comments, Balchen 'was one of the few admirals in this period who never got rich, and he probably would have, had he not gone down in the *Victory* in 1744'.[32] Had he survived, he would have been more prosperous with the valuable prize monies for these ships. This became clear when a letter from the owners of the Plymouth-based privateer, the *Dispatch*, arrived at the Admiralty Board in October 1744. It explained that the *Dispatch*, along with the Bristol-based privateer, the *Charles*, 'drove six French merchant ships into Sir John Balchen's fleet, and were aiding and assisting in taking them', therefore 'praying that their agent ... may make out the claim of the said privatiers'.[33]

What was probably the very last letter Balchen wrote before he was drowned in the dreadful storm of 3/4 October was typical of his determination to do his duty to the crown and the Admiralty and his continuing wish to engage with the enemy and protect British ships and trade. Written on 27 August 1744, in *Victory*, at sea off Cape Finisterre, Balchen reports that he had sent back *Hampton Court* with the four prizes to Spithead and that:

Being informed of 2 French Men of War near [Cape] Finisterre and six more between that and Cape St Vincent – so escorted a trade convoy bound for Portugal & the Mediterranean ... I shall proceed off Cape St Vincent or Spartel, and having seen the Trade [convoy] so far, shall return and cruise in my former station so long as my water will allow it ... the Dutch complain of their being short of water.[34]

Sadly, it was the Dutch shortage of water that forced Balchen's decision to abandon his hope of engaging with the enemy off that station and to return home. A voyage he never completed.

Given Balchen's career and life up to October 1744, there is much to be admired in his service, his actions and his contribution to the navy that he should be remembered for much more than simply his shipwreck. He served the crown with loyalty, with conviction, with professionalism and, in the battles that he was engaged in, with courage and tenacity, and perhaps he should now be considered as one of the great seamen of his age. Even embarking from Gibraltar on his final, fatal voyage, Balchen once again showed his absolute professionalism and passionate sense of duty to serve his country over and above his own personal ambitions. *The Gentleman's Magazine* published a letter from Antigua, dated 23 July 1746, relating to a conversation had with Balchen before setting off on his final homebound voyage:

> Poor Admiral Balchen had the glory of the nation so much at heart that, when he was last out, he declared to Capt. Gregory, he would rather take half a dozen large French men of war, than two or three galleons – [if] I with every commander was of his opinion, and then we might possibly take more of the French navy than we do.[35]

This is surely a fitting eulogy to the life and career of the admiral who so deserves better recognition in the history of British sailors: Sir John Balchen.

7

Sir John Balchen: Family Man, Gentleman

'We are taught from the passages of his life which were fill'd with great and gallant actions but ever accompanied with adverse gales of fortune, that the brave, the worthy, and the good man, meets not always his reward in this world'.

> Words inscribed on the memorial monument to
> Admiral Sir John Balchen, Westminster Abbey
> in 1746 by his widow Susannah.

Behind Balchen's career and his rise through the ranks, his battles and his commands, there was a very real human side to the man and the officer. His character and his personality can be more clearly ascertained when looking into his relationships with those around him, his crew members and those he had to interact with in doing his day-to-day duties, either on board his ships or ashore. Through examining many of his letters, those of others, various Admiralty letters, State Papers and other archive material, Balchen is revealed as a sympathetic man who respected those around him, of every rank, and yet he could be very hard and forceful. In some ways he could be sensitive and react strongly if he thought he was being affronted. And yet rarely is there any significant sign of him being overly ambitious or eager to elbow his way through the system to higher office. It seems that duty and loyalty were his abiding priorities, delivered largely with honesty, sensitivity and a balance between being hard and soft. But beyond assessing these traits in his career, any estimation of his personality can only be truly undertaken when also considering his personal life outside of the navy and how he treated his own extended family and relatives.

Away from the sea, Balchen was a family man. Although he was, as we have seen, born in Godalming in Surrey, it appears from the early records of his children's baptisms that the family base was soon located somewhere in Covent Garden, London. In 1698, during his brief period ashore between his commands of *Virgin* and the fireship *Firebrand*, he married Susannah Apreece, daughter of Colonel Apreece of Huntingdonshire.[1] They had six children but only two outlived the admiral. The first child, Annesloe, was baptised at the Parish Church of St Paul, Covent Garden, on 3 March 1699 but died in her father's lifetime. Robert, baptised on 20 February 1700, died immediately. The third child, Daniel, was baptised in August 1707 but again did not survive. In between his two surviving children, Frances (baptised at the Parish Church of St Clement-le-Dane in the Strand on 5 June 1710) and George (born 1717), was Edmund, who was stillborn, being buried on 12 June 1714.[2] Balchen's surviving son, George, who rose to become a captain in the Royal Navy, survived him only a short time having been sent to the West Indies in command of *Pembroke* in 1745 and dying in the same year in Barbados.[3] Balchen's surviving daughter, Frances, married Captain Temple West in 1736.

It will be recalled that between 1710 and 1715, Balchen commanded the 54-gun *Colchester*, mainly in the Mediterranean, but also in the Channel, at a time when the War of the Spanish Succession was at full force leading up to the 1713 Treaty of Utrecht. It was also a period in which Balchen captured several ships and was due significant amounts of prize money, which often took time to be realised through the Admiralty prize courts. It comes as no surprise then that Balchen's increasing income and increasing seniority in the navy should lead him into a property better reflecting the worth of a successful eighteenth-century naval captain. So, in 1718/19, on his return from the Mediterranean, fresh from the British victory at the Battle of Cape Passaro off Sicily, Balchen became the first tenant of the newly-built four-storey Carlton House, No 15 Cheyne Walk, in affluent Chelsea, London. He made this his family home until 1742, though it seems he sublet the house in 1724 to a Captain Reginald, and again between

1725 and 1728, while he spent several commissions with the Baltic Fleet, to Captain Leonard Wynn. Balchen's tenancy of Carlton House was followed in 1742 by his son-in-law, then Commodore Temple West, and his daughter Frances. Temple West and his family left Cheyne Walk in 1755, two years before he died.[4]

Temple West was the son of Reverend Dr Richard West and Maria, daughter of Sir Richard Temple. Among her cousins were Earl Temple and William Pitt the Elder, the Prime Minister, so Frances clearly married into an aristocratic family, perhaps reflecting the status to which her father had risen by that time.[5] Significantly, given Balchen's efforts to help George Anson's fleet embarking on his famous circumnavigation of the world in 1740, Temple West was captain of the 60-gun *Devonshire* at the First Battle of Cape Finisterre in May 1747 under the command of Admiral Anson. As Flag Captain to Admiral Sir Peter Warren, his ship was one of Anson's fleet that engaged with the 74-gun French ship *Invincible* before she was captured, the ship that later became the template for all the Royal Navy's 74-gun warships.[6] This is discussed in more detail in the next chapter. By amazing, if unfortunate, coincidence, as Rear-Admiral Temple West, he was second-in-command to Admiral John Byng in May 1756 in the action which saw the French capture the British naval base at Mahon in Minorca; a loss eventually resulting in Byng's court martial and subsequent execution on his own quarterdeck on 14 March 1757. Temple West gave evidence at Byng's trial but after the verdict he resigned from the Board of Admiralty in disgust. It was John Byng's father, Rear-Admiral George Byng, who had acquitted Balchen at his court martial in 1708.

Temple West, later an admiral and a Lord of the Admiralty, died in 1757, aged 43. Today he has a marble memorial, bearing both the shields of West and Balchen, in the North Choir Aisle in Westminster Abbey[7] not far from the memorial to his father-in-law, Sir John Balchen. The long inscription includes a tribute to Balchen himself: 'To preserve to posterity his fame and his example this monument was erected by the daughter of the brave unfortunate Balchen, the wife of Temple West A. D. 1761.' They had three children, John West, Martin West and, significantly, Balchen West.

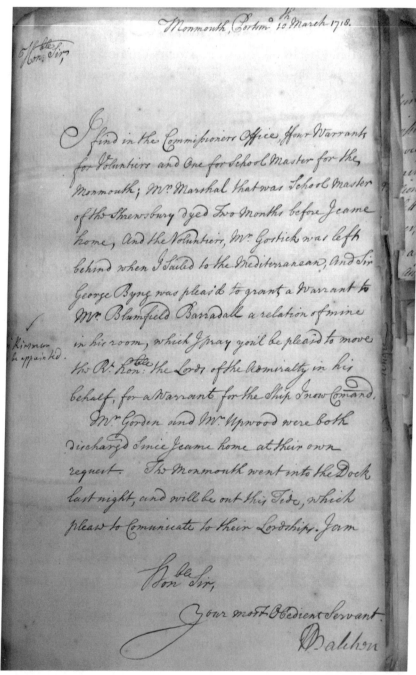

Letter written by Captain Balchen to the Lords of the Admiralty seeking their appointment of his 'relative' as schoolmaster aboard his ship HMS *Shrewsbury*, 10 March 1719. (ADM 1/1472. The National Archives, Kew, London)

Balchen's brother-in-law was also an officer in the navy, serving as a lieutenant on the ships *Hawk*, *Royal Oak* and *Dorsetshire*. When Lieutenant Apreece died in 1707 as a lieutenant of *Leopard*, Balchen wrote to the Lord High Commissioners of the Navy in January 1708 to obtain his naval pay for his own wife, Lieutenant Apreece's sister, and seeking the Lord High Admiral to 'grant me his order for the said Lieutenant's money'. In February the Commissioners confirmed that 'the wages which was due for Mr Apreece's service as Lieutenant of Her Majesty's Ships named therein, has been paid to his sister Susanna Balchen, she appearing by vertue ... to be heires at Law'.[8]

Another example of his 'concern' for members of his family (nepotism was part of naval officers' lives during this period, exemplified by Nelson's early rise through his uncle, Captain Suckling, and the employment of his brother as chaplain on board whilst he was captain of the frigate *Boreas* in the Caribbean, amongst others) was shown in a letter to the Admiralty in 1719 when he was given command of *Monmouth*, transferring from *Shrewsbury*. Receiving four warrants for volunteers and one for a schoolmaster for *Monmouth*, Balchen wrote: 'Mr Marshal that was School Master of the *Shrewsbury* dyed two months before I came home, and the Voluntiers, Mr Gostick was left behind when I sailed to the Mediterranean, and [Admiral] Sir George Byng was pleas'd to grant a warrant to Mr Blumfield Barradall a relation of mine in his room, which I pray ... for a warrant for the ship I now command'.[9] Clearly, his 'relative' was given employment on Balchen's ships to help his career.

Undoubtedly Balchen's son, George, must have benefitted from having an admiral as his father. He followed his father's footsteps into the navy and, like him, not only came to command a fireship by the time he was 23 years old, but also managed to take a prize. As Captain Balchen of the *Mercury* fireship he served under his father's good friend Admiral Haddock in the Mediterranean in 1740. At the same time that Admiral Balchen was on board his flagship *Russell*, leading his squadron of five ships cruising off the Atlantic coast of Spain, watching and avoiding the two Spanish squadrons from Ferrol in the north and Cadiz in the south, his son was off the Mediterranean coast. Writing from his flagship, *Somerset*, moored in Port Mahon in

Minorca, Admiral Haddock reported to the Admiralty that an armed privateer had been brought into the port by *Garland*, Captain Watson, 'which was taken in company of the *Mercury* Fireship, Captain Balchen, by whom she was chased so near the shore, near Leges on the coast of Catalonia, as gave the opportunity to all the sailors, except one which was killed, to get on shore'. This was clearly a significant prize, especially given the land war going on at the time, as the captured ship carried a large contingent of army personnel and war materiel. Admiral Haddock listed the privateer's cargo thus:

> There was seized in her one Colonel, four Captains, whereof one had his leg shot off and is since dead, three Subalterns, three sergeants and two companies of soldiers ... making together one hundred and six persons ... the vessel mounted six carriage guns and had 120 small arms (all loaded) on board. She had likewise in her hold a considerable number of grenade shells, sand bags, pick axes and sundry instruments of war designed for Palma on the Island of Majorca.[10]

So the young Captain George Balchen could well have gone on to be as successful in his career as his father had he not died at the age of 28, probably of yellow fever, the year after the admiral, in 1745 while in command of his ship, *Pembroke*, in Barbados.

As a family man so often away at sea, Balchen senior also had commitments at home he had to fulfil, not least providing a home, an income and family welfare. Their families' health was always a concern to seamen while they were away at sea, so any return to home waters was an occasion to support them. When Balchen returned to Spithead in *Monmouth* in 1721 he appealed to the Secretary of the Admiralty to leave his ship and go home, pleading 'I beg you be pleas'd likewise to move their Lordships for their leave for my coming to Town to see my family which is very ill'.[11] By this time, his family lived in London.

The early biographies espouse Balchen's courage and bravery, but more than that, they describe his loyalty and his devotion to duty. The earliest description we have of his character is the inscription on his memorial in Westminster Abbey erected by his widow in 1746 which, understandably, refers to 'the brave, the worthy, and the good man' and 'so zealous, so valiant, and so able a commander'.[12] It also refers to king and country 'whose interest he ever preferr'd to his own, and his unwearied zeal for their service'. Balchen, according to Baugh, 'lacked influential connections'[13] unlike so many naval officers had to sponsor their rise through the ranks. There are certainly no known references to any such benefactors, nor do the family history newsletters mention any influential connections. But, having served as lieutenant for some five years in the West Indies, Balchen himself mentioned that 'he had the honour of being commissioned by Admiral [John] Neville',[14] so it can be assumed that he did indeed rise through endeavour as much as influential sponsors, being recommended by his commanding admiral. The chronicles of Greenwich Hospital, written in 1886, also records that Balchen 'was a man of very humble parentage, and rose by his own honourable exertions'.[15] The 2004 biography describes him as 'a hardworking, thoroughgoing professional, recognized for his readiness to accept duty whenever and wherever required'.[16] This often meant he missed out on opportunities for fame and fortune, frequently being assigned to overseas stations away from action, to convoy duties or land-based flag officer administration. The early biographies espouse Balchen's courage and bravery, but more than that, they describe his humble loyalty and his honour of duty. It could be presumed that, in the aftermath of the tragic end to his life, some of these early biographies may have put emotion before reality, but that would not reflect what we now know of the man.

Unlike many other prominent admirals of the time, Balchen does not appear to have become at all seriously involved in politics. It was during Balchen's youth that British political parties, as we have come to know them, originated. The Whig party was formed by a group of MPs in 1679 who opposed the Court of Charles II's corruption and foreign policies while also opposing the Church of England's persecution of Protestant Nonconformists. They wanted to exclude the Roman Catholic Duke of York (later James II) from succeeding to the throne and managed to win three parliamentary elections between then and 1681. However, in reaction to this another group in Parliament, which passionately supported both the monarchy and the established Church, had created what became a 'Tory' ideology.

The consequent Tory ascendency then helped a relatively peaceful succession to the throne for James II when Charles II died in 1685. So Tories and Whigs formed an embryonic version of party politics in Britain. While Whigs represented mostly landed aristocratic families and the financial interests of the growing middle class, Tories became identified as being largely country gentry and squires who were against foreign wars and religious toleration and were supporters of Anglicanism. Following the Glorious Revolution of 1688 and the beginning of William and Mary's reign and through Queen Anne's reign to the Treaty of Utrecht in 1713, Tories and Whigs battled for control of government. It was into this fray that leading naval officers became embroiled. They entered politics often as prominent MPs to air their views on the state of the nation, its trade, its economy, its colonies, its foreign policies and, in particular, its naval affairs which were increasingly in the public's mind. Their political careers, however, could also be hazardous to their naval careers.

Many senior officers under whom Balchen served during his long career were deeply, often outspokenly, involved in politics. But there is no evidence of him being involved in any way. Both Admirals Sir John Norris and Sir Charles Wager were fervent Whig supporters, the former as MP for Rye in Kent and the latter as MP for Portsmouth. Although they would both be elevated to the Board of the Admiralty eventually, 1710 was not a good year for either as the election saw the Whigs lose to a Tory landslide. Despite having recently returned from commanding the Jamaica Squadron, becoming rich through the capture of a Spanish galleon filled with Peruvian silver, promoted to rear-admiral and knighted in 1709, Wager could no longer expect any important command under the new Tory administration. The same administration saw Norris relieved of the Mediterranean command in 1711. In the see-saw of politics Norris returned to active service in 1715 when a new Whig administration took over. Rising to Senior Naval Lord of the Admiralty Board in 1727, Norris lost his post again when a Tory government took control in 1730. Admiral Edward Vernon was another prominent politician who was always outspoken in naval matters, as we have seen elsewhere in this book. Issuing a series of pamphlets criticising the Admiralty, especially First Lord Winchilsea and Surveyor of the Navy Acworth, Vernon lost his post more than once. In 1738 his attacks as an MP on Prime Minister Walpole saw him stood down from his vice-admiralship. The outbreak of war in 1739, however, soon saw him reinstated and off he went to capture Portobello in Panama to the acclaim of the nation.

Politics, particularly under the long Walpole administrations between 1721 and 1742, was bound up in corruption and scandal. So Balchen's freedom from the shackles of political factionalism allowed him to pursue his career in a purely professional and loyal manner. As remarked in one of the Balchin Family Newsletters, 'unlike other senior naval figures of the time there is no hint anywhere in the records of any impropriety or scandal in Sir John's private life; the evidence all points to a happy family life'.[17]

At the end, Balchen was not a well man. His 1795 biography, referring to Balchen's final voyage, commented that: 'Such, however, were the necessities of his country, and such the spirit of this gallant man, that even at the very advanced age he had now reached, an age felt more severely in consequence of infirmities naturally induced by so long and active a service, that, in the year 1744, he accepted the command of the fleet.'[18] There is still much to learn about Balchen and his life, both in active service and in his home and personal activities. But, having examined the victualling failures that led to the need for that last voyage and then identified a series of known flaws in both ship design and shipbuilding, and particularly in the case of *Victory*, it seems natural that Balchen's widow should make a pointed reference on his Westminster Abbey memorial, to the 'many aggravating circumstances' attending his and *Victory*'s loss.[19] 'The topos of shipwreck', observed Landow in a paper written in 1975, 'has impressed itself upon the art and literature of the past two centuries as an image of major spiritual or political crisis.'[20] This neatly reflects what has now been demonstrated through the lives, loss and legacy of Balchen and his ship. His memorial in Westminster Abbey, with its sculptured depiction of the mighty *Victory* sinking below the waves, can now be seen in a new light, given our much wider knowledge of his life and achievements. Those visiting the *Victory*'s guns in future years at the National Museum of the Royal Navy in Portsmouth should also pay due homage to the admiral whose loss they now tangibly represent and the legacy he created.

Perhaps it is most fitting that John Balchen be remembered in summary by the full text inscribed on his memorial monument in Westminster Abbey, placed there by his widow. According to the Abbey's Assistant Keeper of Muniments, permission was given by the Dean and Chapter of Westminster to Lady Balchen to erect the memorial on 14 November 1745 and she paid the fee to the Abbey for the space. The white and grey marble monument has a distinct relief of a ship sinking beneath the waves during a storm. It was created by sculptor Peter Scheemakers and completed in 1746. The design for it by Scheemakers is in the Victoria & Albert Museum, London. Susannah herself died on 2 June 1752 at the age of 77. Her inscription on Balchen's memorial reads thus:

To the memory of Sir JOHN BALCHEN, Kt. Admiral of the White Squadron of his MAJESTY'S Fleet who in the year 1744 being sent out Commander in Chief of the combined fleets of England & Holland, to cruise on the enemy was on his return home in his MAJESTY'S ship the VICTORY lost in the Channel by a violent storm, from which sad circumstance of his death we may learn that neither the greatest skill, judgement, or experience, join'd to the most firm unshaken resolution can resist the fury of the winds and waves, and we are taught from the passages of his life which were fill'd with great and gallant actions but ever accompanied with adverse gales of fortune, that the brave, the worthy, and the good man, meets not always his reward in this world. Fifty eight years of faithful and painful services he had pass'd when being just retired to the Government of Greenwich Hospital to wear out the remainder of his days, he was once more and for the last time call'd out by his KING & Country whose interest he ever preferr'd to his own, and his unwearied zeal for their service ended only on his death, which weighty misfortune to his afflicted family became heighten'd by many aggravating circumstances attending it, yet, amidst their grief had they the mournful consolation to find his gracious and royal master, mixing his concern with the general lamentations of the publick, for the calamitous fate of so zealous, so valiant, and so able a commander, and as a lasting memorial of the sincere love and esteem born by his widow to a most affectionate and worthy husband, this honourary monument was erected by her. He was born Febry. Ye 2nd 1669, Married SUSANNAH the daughter of Coll: APRICE of WASHINGLY in the county of HUNTINGDON. Died October ye 7th 1744 leaving one son and one daughter the former of whom GEORGE BALCHEN survived him but a short time, for being sent to the WT.INDIES in 1745 Commander of his MAJESTY'S ship the PEMBROKE he died at BARBADOES in Decber. the same year aged 28 having walked in the steps and imitated the virtues and bravery of his good but unfortunate father.[21]

8

Their Legacy – What Happened Next?

'A thousand events interesting to contemporaries are lost to the eyes of posterity and disappear, leaving only to view great happenings that have fixed the destiny of empires. Every event that occurs is not worth recording. In this history we shall confine ourselves to that which deserves the attention of all time ...'

Jean François-Marie Arouet de Voltaire. Extract from his book
The Age of Louis XIV, published in 1751.

The end of 1744 and the following year saw the beginnings of radical change and reform for the Royal Navy. These reforms involved the whole range of naval administration, shipbuilding and ship design which transformed the British navy in the second half of the eighteenth century and the early nineteenth century. If the tragic loss of Admiral Balchen and his *Victory* in October 1744 cannot be labelled as the catalyst for these changes, then at least the event can, and should, be counted as a very significant factor influencing the subsequent catalogue of reforms. The national psyche was shocked by the loss of the largest, most prestigious ship in the fleet together with her well-known admiral and full complement of crew. This has been plain to see from the plethora of newspaper and magazine articles, art, poetry and literature that followed on the heels of the disaster. This in turn stimulated widespread reflection on the possible and probable causes of their loss and a serious examination of policies, processes and current practices across the naval infrastructure and industry that could have led to those causes.

It is quite easy to connect the Balchen tragedy in October with the almost immediate dismissal of the First Sea Lord, the Earl of Winchilsea, and his Admiralty Board in December 1744 and their replacement with a new Board on 28 December by a new government. This Board, under the Duke of Bedford as the new First Lord, included the Earl of Sandwich and Captain George Anson, all three names that would become synonymous with naval reform between 1744 and 1762. Undoubtedly the enormity of the disaster that October became a significant influencing factor, amongst others, that stimulated those appointments. The government's naval misfortunes had already been under great scrutiny following the news of the disastrous Battle of Toulon the previous February and the subsequent trial of Admiral Mathews. However, it is more difficult to prove a direct relationship between *Victory's* loss and the more distant events and reformation of the Royal Navy that occurred over the next few decades, particularly in ship design and construction. Nevertheless, there are definite threads that can be identified in the timeframe from the loss of *Victory* in October 1744 and the laying of the keel of the next *Victory* on 23 July 1759, watched by the then Prime Minister William Pitt. Indeed, it was Anson who was First Lord of the Admiralty when the decision to build the next HMS *Victory* was taken and it was Anson who represents one of those connecting threads of legacy.

Despite their difference in age, the careers of both Anson and Balchen, like those of most great sea officers of the time, criss-crossed over the years as both rose through the ranks. While Balchen commanded *Shrewsbury* at the Battle of Cape Passaro in 1718, the young Anson, promoted to lieutenant two years earlier, was on board the flagship of Admiral Sir George Byng during the battle. When, in 1740, the then Admiral Balchen helped Captain Anson in preparations for the latter's voyage around the world, he would hardly have dreamt that Anson would end up being the architect of some kind of legacy for Balchen himself and for *Victory*. Four years after Balchen and his 80-gun flagship, *Russell*, sailed from Plymouth accompanying Anson's South Seas fleet into safe waters at the start of his voyage, Anson returned a hero in June 1744, just as Balchen was preparing to depart on his own last fateful voyage. At the same time, Anson must have been aware of Admiral Vernon's bitter and very public criticisms of British warship design and his premonition that unless something was done about the crank and unstable three-decker ships there would likely be a 'fatal sacrifice'.[1] By December that year, Anson had joined the Duke of Bedford's new Admiralty Board (and the following April was promoted to Rear-Admiral of the White). He was now in a position where he could begin to work on changing the face of the Royal Navy, firstly under First Lord Bedford, then First Lord Sandwich before himself becoming First Lord of the Admiralty in 1751. Between them, these three men in charge of the navy 'were responsible for a range of reforms and developments in tactics, discipline, ship design and administration which substantially reshaped it'.[2]

In response to recent events, including the loss of *Victory* and Vernon's criticism of ship design, one of the early actions of the Board was to set up an ad-hoc Committee of Senior Officers under the chairmanship of Admiral Sir John Norris, supported by long-term Surveyor of the Navy Sir Jacob Acworth, in June 1745. The committee was 'to propose and lay before your Lordships such a solid and well digested system and establishment for building a ship of each class or rate down to a sloop inclusive, as well with respect to their principle dimensions as to their masts and yards, and whatever else might in their opinion contribute to make them complete ships of war'.[3] The Board specifically requested this committee to replace the 80-gun three-decker ship, which was deemed by their Lordships 'ill approved',[4] with a new 74-gun two-and-a-half-decked ship. Undoubtedly there is a connection between this request and Admiral Balchen's bitter confrontation with Sir Jacob Acworth in 1735 over the instability of his 80-gun *Princess Amelia*. This class of ship was generally deemed as crank, high-sided and so overloaded with guns that even in the slightest sea they were frequently incapable of opening their lower-deck gunports, being ballasted so close to the waterline (see Chapter 4). Unfortunately for the reform-minded and innovative Board, this conservative-minded committee (including the much-maligned Acworth) differed with this request and continued with the 80-gun three-deck design Establishment, rejecting a new 74-gun alternative. But, despite being strongly inclined to be experimental and innovative, the Board had to endure the deterrent to progress, Acworth, who had held office as Surveyor of the Navy since 1715, until 1747. The year 1747 became the great catalyst for dramatic innovation in British ship design.

It may be recalled from Chapter 4 that in the weeks leading up to the loss of *Victory* Admiral Vernon had been at the forefront of criticism of the design of warships in the navy, particularly their size and being overloaded with guns proportionate to their size. This criticism escalated publicly and in Parliament immediately following the loss of Balchen and *Victory*. It may also be recalled that it was Commodore Charles Knowles who wrote to the First Lord of the Admiralty on 6 January 1745, shortly after hearing the news of their loss and Vernon's criticism, complaining bitterly about dockyard management of timbers and about current British warship design. As contemporaries of Balchen, both must inevitably have seen his loss as proof of their misgivings about the state of naval dockyards and shipbuilding, and both will have been aware of Balchen's own vehement criticism of his own 'crank' ships such as the *Princess Amelia* fracas with Acworth. Their careers were often intertwined with each other's and with Balchen's. Indeed, Knowles was present with Balchen and Anson at the Battle of Cape Passaro in 1718 when he was temporarily on board Admiral Sir George Byng's flagship *Barfleur*, while Balchen commanded *Shrewsbury*, flagship of Vice-Admiral Sir Charles Cornwall. Much later, in 1740, Knowles commanded the 60-gun *Weymouth* as part of Sir Chaloner Ogle's fleet sent to reinforce Vernon in the West Indies. It can be no coincidence that both Knowles and Vernon were certainly amongst the most vociferous in calling for changes to ship design and dockyard practices both immediately prior to their colleague Balchen's loss and certainly following it. In his letter to the Admiralty, written from Antigua upon hearing of the disaster to *Victory*, Knowles begins with the words: 'I have presumed to give my opinion of the questions I see the late Admiralty asked of

Mr Vernon.' In this letter he wrote almost prophetically of his ideas on how to improve ship design which, over the next few years, would indeed emerge under Anson's leadership:

It is therefore most humbly offered to your Lordship's consideration the establishing one general and unalterable dimensions of ship of each rank, which should be as near as possible the size of those of our enemies [the French and Spaniards], and that the scantlings of their timbers and beams, number of ports alow and aloft, nature of guns, and number of men should also be the same, and then a captain whom commanded one of them could have no excuse if he did not take a ship of the enemy's of the same class; it having been of late pleaded as an excuse, on meeting with some of the enemy's ships, that they have been bigger ships than ours, carried the ports higher out of the water, had more men and heavier metal.[5]

Later in the same letter, Knowles (later Admiral Sir Charles Knowles, 1st Baronet) suggested that each shipbuilder in the naval dockyards 'should try his art till an unexceptionable ship of each class was built, and then that ship to remain as a model'.[6] Little would he know that at that very moment, just such a model upon which the navy's most successful future line of battle ships was to be developed had just been launched – ironically, in Rochefort, France.

It was indeed prophetic coincidence that at the beginning of October 1744 a brand-new 74-gun ship was ready to be launched at the French naval shipyard of Rochefort; the same week in which *Victory* was lost in the Channel. The hull of *L'Invincible*, larger than any ship of this type ever launched before, 'was cleaned and caulked and all was prepared for the next full moon which would bring with it a high spring tide, absolutely necessary in the narrow shallow waters of the [River] Charente. This came on 21 October.'[7] This ship was the second of her type (*Terrible* had been launched in 1739). *L'Invincible*, along with Anson who would go on to capture her and then copy her lines, became the foundation for the complete overhaul of the battle fleets of the Royal Navy over the next couple of decades. Close on the heels of *L'Invincible* was the launch of her slightly larger 74-gun sister ship, *Magnanime*, and then a further nine were launched in quick succession up to 1748. They were a new pedigree of fast, powerful warship designed by the French to defend her growing overseas empire.

The impasse between the innovation-minded Board and stoically conservative Acworth and his Master Shipwrights was blown apart by two major sea battles that saw the Royal Navy capturing *L'Invincible* and then several more of the new 74-gun French ships. Again, it was Anson himself that led this action and, adding another thread to the Balchen legacy, it was Captain Temple West, Balchen's son-in-law, who sailed alongside Anson in this action. At the First Battle of Cape Finisterre, on 3 May 1747, a British fleet of fourteen ships of the line under the command of Vice-Admiral Anson aboard his 90-gun flagship, *Prince George*, made contact with two French squadrons off northern Spain, with fleets of merchantmen bound to reinforce India and Canada and sailing together towards Madeira. The battle, on 4 May, was fairly one-sided with Anson taking six warships and three large Indiamen (and the next day a further eighteen of thirty-three French merchant ships were taken).[8] The last and the most significant ship to be captured during the battle was *L'Invincible*. At 5.30 in the afternoon the 60-gun *Devonshire* was engaging closely with *L'Invincible* and 'her captain, Temple West, believed she had struck to him and that the *Bristol*'s broadside was fired after that. In fact, *L'Invincible*'s pendant had merely been shot away and she had not surrendered.' Indeed, it was not until 7.00pm, when Anson's 90-gun flagship aimed her broadside at the stern of *L'Invincible*, that her admiral, St George, hauled down his flag and surrendered.[9] The log book from *Prince George* for that day describes the final action thus:

> At $\frac{1}{2}$ past 4 the rest of our Fleet began to Engage, at 5 saw a French East Indiaman struck his colours, at $\frac{1}{2}$ past made the signal for all our Ships to come to a closer Engagement, at $\frac{1}{2}$ past 6 the French Admiral struck his Flag & Colours, at 7 we got close up with the *Invincible* with in a cable's length & was that moment going to fire when He struck his colours, as did two French Men of War.[10]

It was immediately obvious to Anson that this French ship was extraordinary and also special. When he wrote to the Duke of Bedford, still First Lord of the Admiralty at the time, from his ship after the battle, he made specific reference to *L'Invincible*: 'The *Invincible* is a prodigious fine ship, and vastly larger; I think she is longer than any ship in our fleet, and quite new, having made only one voyage.'[11] The captured ship was immediately taken to Portsmouth and on 20 May the Board ordered her to be fully surveyed in a dry dock. By 14 August the Dock Officers reported to the Navy Board that 'We have taken the *Invincible* French Ship of War into the Dock, and having carefully survey'd & measured her, find her condition as follows, viz', followed by seven pages of detailed description of the ship. The report clearly reflected the damage inflicted upon her in the action, with numerous references to 'One beam and hanging knee cut away by shot', ' ... being destroyed by shot', ' ... cut out in the wake of the shot holes', 'foresheet blocks shot away' and 'being damaged by shot'.[12] Such was the determination of Anson and the Board to take the ship into the Royal Navy that only six days later, on 20 August, orders had already been received for *Invincible* and *Serieux*, both captured by Anson, having been 'surveyed in Portsmouth Harbour with all dispatch and purchased for His Majesty ... having received from the Officers at Portsmouth their survey and valuation of the *Invincible* French Ship of War, we at the same time treated with them for the purchase of that ship also and agreed with them for her at the Rate of Thirteen Pounds a Tun for her Hull'.[13] So the new 74-gun ship then became HMS *Invincible*, and a template for the mainstay of new ships of the line for the Royal Navy for years to come. She was significantly longer than British 74-gun ships at the time and sailed higher out of the water. This meant there was more space between the guns for the gun crews to work and that her lower gun ports were able to remain open even in rough weather. Her rudder was narrower and squared, meaning she did not have to slow down when exercising a quick turn, in contrast to the wider, rounded British rudders. These factors, as well as the shape of her hull, contributed to her much greater speed than the Royal Navy 74-gun ships. In fact, *Invincible*'s first commander, Captain Bentley, was sent down to Gibraltar and asked to assess how fast she could sail in a fair wind. The trial, which was somewhat compromised by her sails tearing during the exercise, saw the ship achieve over 13 knots compared to the maximum 11 knots of her British counterparts. Such was her speed and the length of rope needed to run overboard to measure her knots that Bentley ordered a 14-second sand timer to be made in place of the standard 28-second timer. This reduced the length of rope required at 13 knots from 187m to 93.4m, much to the relief of the seamen undertaking the measurements at sea.

Within a year of the capture of *Invincible*, Britain had captured nearly the whole of France's new fleet of intercontinental 74-gun ships, including *Terrible*, *Monarque*, *Neptune*, *Magnanime* and *Glorioso*. Such was the importance of these ships to the Board that on 15 June 1748 they wrote to the Lords Justices seeking to ensure that they would be purchased into the Royal Navy rather than by any other power:

May it please your Excellencies,
The ships of war named in the annexed list [as mentioned above] having been taken from his Majesty's enemies a few months ago and the captors having not yet disposed of any of them by sale, and they being ships of considerable force, it may be apprehended now hostilities are ceased and a peace expected that commissions may come from abroad to purchase them, and that they may possibly fall into unacceptable hands. We do therefore humbly propose that your Excellencies may be pleased to authorise us to have the said ships carefully and thoroughly surveyed, and that we may be at liberty to purchase for his Majesty on the cheapest terms we can get such of them as shall appear to be strong and well built and in condition to do good service, which will be no small addition of strength to the Royal Navy and disappoint any hopes of others.

We are the more induced to offer this to your Excellencies' consideration from the experience we have had of such of the enemies' large ships as we have bought in the course of the war, and employed at sea, which have fully answered all the good qualities expected in ships of war and have been greatly commended by his Majesty's flag officers and captains who have sailed in them.[14]

The Board also proceeded to commission the building of brand-new 74-gun ships in their own Royal Dockyards based specifically upon the dimensions and specifications of *Invincible*. These included *Valiant*, built at Chatham Dockyard and launched in August 1759, and *Triumph*, built at Woolwich Dockyard and launched in March 1764, both being 'copies of *Invincible*'.[15]

One could understandably ask why, if these superb French 74-gun ships were so brilliant, then how come they kept on being apparently so easily captured, one after the other, by the Royal Navy? It seems that British seamanship, gunnery and tactics, as much as overwhelming superiority in ship numbers, were the keys to this remarkable achievement. To have systematically captured so many of these clearly better ships in such a short time does indeed speak volumes about the in-depth strength of the Royal Navy in this period.

Unfortunately, *Invincible* was lost in February 1758 when she went aground on the Dean Sands, just off Portsmouth, while she was about to join Admiral Edward Boscawen's fleet bound for the ultimate capture of the French fort of Louisbourg in Nova Scotia (directly leading to Britain's capture of Quebec and the whole of Canada in 1759). However, she had given several years of service to the Royal Navy and at one stage, in December 1756, (and to continue the thread back to his father-in-law, Admiral Balchen) was under the orders of Admiral Temple West, now a Lord of the Admiralty. But as Brian Lavery concludes, 'The main historical role of the *Invincible* was to show the British how ships should be designed. The praise of those who sailed in her or saw her – Anson, Boscawen, Keppel and Bentley – served to reinforce Anson in his belief that ship design needed to be drastically improved. The *Invincible*, more than any other ship, pulled the navy out of its rut of the first half of the eighteen century.'[16]

Significantly, in the context of this story, Lavery actually uses Balchen's *Victory* of 1737 as a direct comparison to *Invincible* in describing the attributes of the new 74-gun warship, describing some

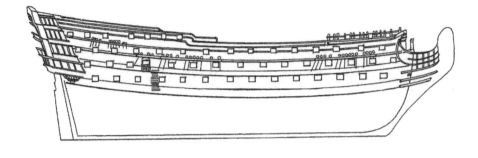

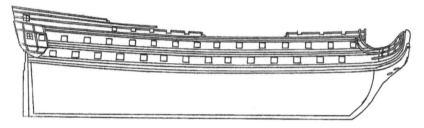

Top: The *Victory* of 1737. She was lost at almost the same time as the *Invincible* was launched, and represented the extreme of the 'floating fortress' concept of shipbuilding. She was very little longer than the *Invincible*, but carried 100 guns on three decks, and had four galleries at the stern, compared to *Invincible's* two. As a result, she was 15ft higher out of the water at the stern and sailed poorly.
Bottom: The *Invincible* to the same scale. (Reproduced from Brian Lavery, *The Royal Navy's First Invincible*, (Portsmouth: Invincible Conservations (1744-1758) Ltd, 1988)

of the lessons learnt from *Victory's* loss on the new type of ship. As well as being a fast, manoeuvrable and heavily-armed ship, well suited to increasingly global operations, *Invincible* also demonstrated some other innovative features that the navy quickly adopted. One in particular was her steering indicator which showed the helmsman exactly what angle the rudder was positioned at. Writing on 27 January 1747 while *Invincible* was still being fitted out for Royal Navy service, Portsmouth Dockyard Commissioner Richard Hughes referred to a warrant 'directing all His Majesty's ships to be fitted as the *Invincible* is, in order to show the Officer upon deck, how the ship is steered, and enable him immediately to correct any mistakes the helmsmen may commit'.[17]

Another slim thread from Balchen and his *Victory* to *Invincible* comes from the proposed attempts to recover the ships after their loss at sea. As noted earlier, the internationally-renowned diver John Lethbridge, who had successfully dived and retrieved both guns and treasure from several British and Dutch wrecks across many oceans, had sought permission to find the wreck of *Victory* in January 1745. Lethbridge believed he could 'find the place where the *Victory* was and also recover her guns, money and other valuable things that are sank in the sea'.[18] Remarkably, in 1758, some 13 years after the proposed search for *Victory*, the same name appeared amidst letters from various people to Portsmouth Dockyard Commissioner Hughes offering their services to raise the half-submerged wreck of *Invincible.* In one of his reports to the Navy Board in June 1758, Hughes mentioned that 'John Lethbridge, Diver, shall be supply'd with a Longboat, men and Lead Lines, to enable him to form a judgement, of the practicality of weighing [raising] the *Invincible*'.[19] At the same time a certain Joseph Mason was 'proposing to weigh the *Invincible*' and the next day it was reported that 'Mich'l Wooden, a shipwright, shall be supplied with a Longboat, men and Lead Lines, for forming a judgement, of the practicality of weighing the *Invincible*'.[20] However, as things turned out, *Invincible* was never recovered, though all of her guns and most of her valuables were removed from her as she lay and eventually broke up on the Dean Sands (dives in the 1980s and in 2018–19 have continued to retrieve artefacts from the wreck of *Invincible* which have been displayed at the National Museum of the Royal Navy in Portsmouth Historic Dockyard). By late July, Hughes reported that 'Michael Wooden, the shipwright has been here to take a view of the *Invincible*, but Mr Lethbridge, the diver, has not yet appeared here'.[21] Given that John Lethbridge would have been 82 years of age at this time it may be assumed that it was his son, also John Lethbridge, who had proposed to investigate the wreck. Nevertheless, there was certainly a connection between the plight of both *Victory* and *Invincible* and their eventual loss. Commenting on this connection, Michael Fardell, author of a book on John Lethbridge for the Historical Diving Society, stated 'I had thought that given his age and his son's precarious financial position the Lethbridge diving saga was over, but it seems there was at least one more throw of the dice'.[22]

A further connection forming the Balchen and *Victory* legacy in later years was Anson and the creation of the next *Victory* whose keel was laid in 1759 and launched in 1765. The two great British victories of Cape Finisterre over the French in 1747 and the actions in 1748 resulting in the capture of what now became highly-praised British 74-gun ships had confirmed the Admiralty's earlier desire for the replacement of the old three-deck 80-gun ships with the more agile and fast 74-gun two-deckers. In 1750 the Board finally obtained Privy Council approval to amend the 1745 Establishment of ship designs (where such innovation had been blocked by Surveyor Acworth) as they wished. This opened the floodgates for the Sandwich and Anson Boards to transform the navy and in 1755 Anson could at last appoint a new Surveyor of the Navy who shared his ideas, Sir Thomas Slade, who would become Britain's greatest naval architect of the eighteenth century. From this date, asserts N A M Rodger, 'the Navy was in process of rapid transformation into a superficially French-style line of battle based on seventy-four-gun two-deckers'.[23] By the time of the Battle of Trafalgar in 1805, some two-thirds of the Royal Navy's fleet was made up of 74-gun ships of the line. Of the twenty-seven ships Nelson had at the Battle of Trafalgar, sixteen were 74-gun ships based broadly on the *Invincible*'s design: *Leviathan, Conqueror, Ajax, Orion, Minotaur, Spartiate, Belleisle, Mars, Bellerophon, Colossus, Achille, Revenge, Swiftsure, Defiance, Thunderer* and *Defence*.

It was Slade who then went on to design the next *Victory* while Anson was First Lord of the Admiralty. Like the previous *Victory*, the new ship would be the largest, most expensive warship ever built for the Royal Navy. Such was its importance that the Prime Minister, William Pitt, attended the laying of the keel at Chatham Dockyard on 23 July 1759. This 104-gun ship was slightly larger than her predecessor with a length of 227.49ft (against 174ft) and a beam of 51.83ft (50ft). At the time of her being ordered and even after her keel was laid and work was well underway on this new ship, she had no name and was only a number in the dock. Before this time, there had only been five other ships in the navy named as the *Victory*. Since Balchen's *Victory* had been lost so tragically with all hands in 1744, there had been a certain stigma attached to the name and some felt it was a bad omen. However, on 20 November in the same year as the keel was laid, Admiral Edward Hawke defeated a French fleet in the Battle of Quiberon Bay, one of the greatest victories ever won by the Royal Navy. This success followed several other major victories in the Caribbean, the Indian Ocean and in European waters that year, including Admiral Edward Boscawen's victory over another French fleet off Portugal in the Battle of Lagos in August 1759. This so-called *Annus Mirabilis*, or Year of Miracles, persuaded the Admiralty to give their newest and largest ship under construction the name HMS *Victory*. She was formally named on 13 October 1760. However, those same victories also led to the order to slow down the building of a new fleet of ships in Royal Dockyards, including the new *Victory*. Instead of taking three years to build her, the yard at Chatham ceased work on her, only to resume again in 1763. She was launched in May 1765 when the Seven Years War was over. So she spent the next 12 years moored in the Medway, only being fully fitted out in 1778 when war with France broke out again. The rest, it can be said, is history.

While there can be no absolutely proven connections between the loss of Balchen and his crew on the ill-fated *Victory* and the amazing reformation of the Royal Navy that followed it, it is clear that the event of their passing had very widespread ripples that flowed through the country, the government and the Admiralty. Balchen's *Victory* certainly represented many of the problems relating to the unreformed navy and can be contrasted with the next generation of warships. Threads of their legacy can be traced through any number of those developments between October 1744 and the launch of the next *Victory* in May 1765. Vernon, Knowles, Anson, Temple West, Lethbridge, *Princess Amelia*, Surveyor Acworth, *Invincible*, Surveyor Slade, and many others can be associated with Balchen and should certainly be considered as foundations for his enduring legacy.

Fame, as has been noted, comes in many guises. Balchen and his story, especially in its ending as the story of a disastrous shipwreck, deserves a significant portion of fame due in part to his contribution to a reformed navy that soon became commander of the oceans for years to come.

9

The Wreck: Rest in Peace?

Psalm 107, verses 23 to 30:

23 They that go down to the sea in ships: and occupy their business
    in great waters;
24 These men see the works of the Lord: and his wonders in the
    deep.
25 For at his word the stormy wind ariseth: which lifteth up the
    waves thereof.
26 They are carried up to the heaven, and down again to the deep:
    their soul melteth away because of the trouble.
27 They reel to and fro, and stagger like a drunken man: and are at
    their wits' end.
28 So when they cry unto the Lord in their trouble: he delivereth
    them out of their distress.
29 For he maketh the storm to cease: so that the waves thereof are
    still.
30 Then are they glad, because they are at rest: and so he bringeth
    them unto the haven where they would be.

Psalms of David, New English Bible

The wreck of HMS *Victory* was discovered by Florida-based deep
sea exploration company Odyssey Marine Exploration in 2008.
She lies deep in the English Channel, some 100km west of the Channel
Islands, around 80km south-east of Plymouth, and approximately
75m below the surface of the sea, outside British and French territorial
waters. With the exception of a few of her guns, the remains of *Victory*

and some of her crew still lie there today, albeit probably somewhat disturbed by currents and, possibly, by deep-sea trawling gear. Ten years after her discovery, however, there were still ongoing arguments over whether some of her remains should be salvaged for historical research and artefacts recovered for preservation, museum display and education, or whether she should remain as a war grave and be left to rest in peace. Today, one of the *Victory's* 42-pounder bronze guns lies on display in the National Museum of the Royal Navy in Portsmouth, another 12-pounder is in storage there and a third gun allegedly lies in a Netherlands museum store, apparently having been illegally looted by Dutch salvors. This chapter explores the rollercoaster of claims and counter-claims over the future of the wreck, the troubled waters of political and legal wrangles arising, as well as the more emotive questions raised by the descendants of Admiral Sir John Balchen whose final resting place remains somewhere with the wreckage of his ship.

For more than 250 years the exact location of the wreck remained a mystery. It will be recalled that at the time of the loss of *Victory* all the evidence, including supposed sightings, the sounds of guns fired in distress during the night of the storm and the wreckage thrown onto the shores of Alderney, Guernsey and France over the coming days and weeks, pointed towards her being wrecked on the infamous Les Casquets reef, 13km west of Alderney. Ever since that disastrous night, divers have sought the remains of the ship all around the vicinity of these treacherous rocks. From John Lethbridge's original request to the Admiralty in January 1745 to dive near the Casquets in pursuit of the wreck of *Victory*, there have been innumerable professional and amateur nautical archaeology divers and teams searching the area – all in vain. One such professional diver, Richard Keen, from Guernsey, who began searching for the *Victory's* wreck in the waters around the Casquets from 1973, was quoted by the BBC as suggesting that *Victory* 'was the wreck that every wreck-finder wanted to find'.[1] Once the wreck was finally discovered, in the middle of the English Channel, some 80km south-east of Plymouth, it could now be assumed that it must have been the ferocity of the storm itself as well as the fierce currents that carried lots of the masts, rigging, sails, gun carriages and other wreckage onto the beaches of the Channel Islands and France immediately after her loss.

Although found in 2008, it was not until 2009 that the wreck was positively identified as that of *Victory*. Having discovered the wreck, Odyssey Marine Exploration obtained permission from the British Ministry of Defence (MOD) to recover two of the guns to aid in its positive identification. Subsequently, the 42-pounder and the 12-pounder were presented to the United Kingdom Receiver of Wrecks, at the direction of the MOD. They were confirmed as belonging to *Victory* and handed over to the National Museum of the Royal Navy to undergo conservation and restoration. According to the museum, the manufacture of the cannons was overseen by Andrew Schalch, whose name appears on their exterior. Amazingly, while undergoing conservation, excavation of their interior revealed that they were still fully loaded with hemp rope wadding, gunpowder and a roundshot, ready to fire.[2] But the confirmation of the discovery of *Victory* also led to the firing of other proverbial guns in the battle over the future of the wreck itself; a battle that would last over ten years.

Initially, the MOD and the UK Department for Digital, Culture, Media and Sport (DCMS) held a joint public consultation on options for the management of the wreck site. A range of organisations and commentators provided views and opinions on different approaches to managing the site. Some sided with the idea to salvage as much as possible in order to preserve artefacts from further deterioration or damage, natural or man-made, while others argued for preservation in situ as the best solution. As an example, Dr Sean Kingsley of Wreck Watch International wrote a paper edited by Odyssey Marine Exploration on deep sea fishing impacts on the shipwrecks of the English Channel and Western Approaches. The Joint Nautical Archaeology Policy Committee (JNAPC) published a response paper in 2009 by Professor Dave Parham, commenting that the Odyssey paper 'expresses a number of unsubstantiated opinions that may reflect a lack of familiarity with the material which it is discussing and fails to consider alternative causations to those which it is presenting'.[3] It was hardly surprising therefore that in their response to the MOD/DCMS consultation on options for the management of the wreck in June 2010, the JNAPC 'recommends management in situ as the clearly preferred option taking into account of best archaeological practice'.[4]

But, after completing the public consultation exercise, on 24 January 2012, the MOD, then under the UK's Conservative and Liberal Democrat coalition government, made the controversial announcement that 'the wreck of the historically important HMS *Victory* from 1744 has been gifted to the Maritime Heritage Foundation'.[5] The Maritime Heritage Foundation was a very new organisation which had only been formed as a registered charity in April 2011 by its chairman, Lord Lingfield (previously Sir Robert Balchin, as discussed later in more detail). Unsurprisingly, perhaps, the announcement by the government referred twice to 'Admiral Sir John Balchin' as opposed to the more accurate spelling of Balchen. Nevertheless, it was acknowledged that the wreck was 'of unique importance to British naval heritage as the remains of British "First Rate" warships from the period of history are rare', adding: 'In its day, the ship represented the pinnacle of naval technology, and was fitted with a complete arsenal of bronze cannons.' Therefore, it claimed, an agreement had been reached with the Maritime Heritage Foundation for it to 'undertake the future management of the wreck site'. It quoted Andrew Robathan, Minister for Defence Personnel, Welfare and Veterans, as saying the 'gift' of the *Victory* to the Maritime Heritage Foundation 'should give better protection to the wreck which is very important to British naval heritage'. The announcement concluded thus:

> It [the Maritime Heritage Foundation] has been established especially to recover, preserve and display in public museums artefacts from HMS *Victory* (1744) and to promote knowledge and understanding of our maritime heritage, particularly through educational projects.
>
> The foundation will be supported by an advisory group, with representatives from English Heritage and the National Museum of the Royal Navy.

The group will advise on the extent to which actions proposed by the Foundation are consistent with the archaeological principles set out in Annex A to the UNESCO (United Nations Educational, Scientific and Cultural Organisation) Convention on the Protection of the Underwater Cultural Heritage.[6]

This announcement sparked off a row that would see numerous media articles, 'Letters to the Editor' and even questions being raised in the House of Commons and House of Lords. Of particular note, perhaps, was a Letter to the Editor of *The Times* published on 23 June 2012, written by Richard Temple West:

I have been following with increasing dismay the fate of the wreck of HMS *Victory*, which was Admiral Sir John Balchen's flagship, lost in 1744 with all hands. Admiral Balchen is my direct ancestor and I am deeply concerned about the fate of his war grave.

The Culture Secretary, Jeremy Hunt, recently oversaw a process by which the Ministry of Defence under the Secretary of State Philip Hammond, 'gifted' the wreck to the newly formed Maritime Heritage Foundation which in turn has made an arrangement with a salvage company, Odyssey Marine Exploration.

What concerns me most is that it appears deals over the fate of HMS *Victory* are being done behind closed doors. Meanwhile scant regard is being taken for the concerns of the descendants of the crew. This is after all a grave.

We recognise the historical importance of HMS *Victory*, but out of respect for that and the memory of all her crew who died serving their country, any investigation of the site must be painstaking, guided by independent experts with no financial interest and carried out for the benefit of the people of our nation.

Most important of all, my ancestor's name must not be used by advertising men to pretend that the profit-seeking activities of a treasure-hunting company are archaeology done in the public interest. RICHARD WEST.[7]

The next day, 24 June 2012, the same Richard Temple West released a public statement 'regarding the suggestion published in a press release by Odyssey Marine Exploration on 2 February 2009, and repeated in other media including the BBC, that Sir Robert Balchin, now Lord Lingfield, is a "descendant" of Admiral Sir John Balchen'. Referring to professionally-researched genealogies, including the Society of Genealogists, he asserted that this research 'makes it clear that Lord Lingfield cannot be a direct descendant of Admiral Sir John Balchen'. On behalf of the West/Temple West family, the statement concluded: 'We deplore even more the attempt to use that claim of kinship as the authority for the disturbance of Admiral Balchen's grave for its commercial profit by Odyssey Marine Exploration Inc.'

It will be recalled, in the context of Richard West's letter and statement, that Admiral Balchen was survived by only two of his six children. His surviving son, George, a captain in the Royal Navy, died soon after his father in Barbados while commanding *Pembroke* in 1745. His daughter, Frances, married Captain (later Admiral) Temple West in 1736. Temple West was the son of the Reverend Dr Richard West and Maria, daughter of Sir Richard Temple. Nor, it seems, is Richard West the only 'direct descendant' of Balchen. In another Letter to the Editor, this time in *The Daily Telegraph* on 5 January 2013, the script was signed off from Richard West, 'Direct descendant of Admiral Sir John Balchen' and Riccardo Tomacelli, 9th Prince of Boiano, also 'Direct descendant of Admiral Sir John Balchen', as well as Robert Yorke, Chairman, Joint Nautical Archaeology Policy Committee. This letter, under the title 'Respect for *Victory*', claimed that 'the effect of the *Victory* deal, if it stands, will be to see the British Government allow the deliberate disturbance of another military grave for the private profit of the banks and hedge funds which invest in Odyssey. The wreck site is the last known resting place of over 1,000 Royal Navy sailors who died on active duty. However, under the deed of gift, the Government has the right to veto work on HMS *Victory*' and therefore called on the Government to veto any further work by the Maritime Heritage Foundation and Odyssey.[8]

The debate flared up again when, in February 2013, the Discovery Channel in the United States showed a three-part miniseries claiming to show the activities of Odyssey during the summer of 2012. In the third part, 'Odyssey's Victory', filming appeared to show a human skull, apparently recently disturbed by excavation. Temple West immediately wrote an 'open letter', on 23 March 2013, to Mark Francois MP, Minister of State for Defence Personnel, Welfare and Veterans, claiming that neither 'Odyssey, nor its employer, the Maritime Heritage Foundation chaired by Lord Lingfield, held a licence from the Marine Management Organisation, which is required to conduct such excavation work' and that they had 'allowed the television cameras to show remains of dead Royal Navy personnel, possibly even the remains of my direct ancestor Admiral Sir John Balchen, which is deeply distasteful'.

On the other hand, pressure continued to be applied for work to proceed on the wreck. A website developed by the Maritime Heritage Foundation with assistance from Odyssey Marine Exploration and Wreck Watch International, www.victory1744.org, claimed that Odyssey's visual surveys, starting in 2008 and continuing through 2013 'has confirmed a pattern of ongoing natural and man-made impacts that are continuously eroding the shipwreck's structural integrity and leading to artefacts' losses. The site cannot be considered stable or to have reached a state of equilibrium where further impacts would be benign. The impacts have resulted in a significant loss of archaeological data and knowledge about the wreck.' It lists general fishing impacts, damage to cannon surfaces, artefact displacement and looting. In the latter case, it claimed that in July 2011 a Dutch salvage vessel had used a hydraulic grab to illegally remove a 24-pounder gun from the wreck and had it taken to the Netherlands where it was 'confirmed through royal arms and stamps (including the founder's name SCHALCH and the year 1723) that the cannon originated from HMS *Victory* (1744)'.[9]

With this argument, and contrary to the pleas from Balchen's descendants, Odyssey Marine Exploration was then pleased to announce on 24 October 2014 that it 'welcomes today's statement by the United Kingdom's Secretary of State for Defence giving consent to proceed with the archaeological investigation and recovery of at-risk artefacts from the HMS *Victory* (1744) wreck site in accordance with the project design that has been approved by the UK Ministry of Defence (MOD) and Department for Digital, Culture, Media & Sport (DCMS)'.[10]

But that was not the end of the matter. On 23 December 2014 a Judicial Review Pre-Action Protocol Letter was sent to the Ministry of Defence by lawyers on behalf of Robert Yorke, chairman of the JNAPC, Vice-President of the Nautical Archaeology Society and former Commissioner on the Royal Commission on the Historical Monuments of England. The intention, it stated, 'is to commence a claim for judicial review of the decision of the Secretary of State for Defence on or around 24 October 2014 to permit the Maritime Heritage Foundation ("MHF") to recover at-risk surface items from the site of the wreck of HMS Victory 1744 ("the Contested Decision")'. He believed that the Contested Decision was unlawful.

Politics also ensured that arguments would continue. One of the most ardent opponents of the whole scheme and in particular of Odyssey and the Maritime Heritage Foundation was Kevan Jones, Labour MP for North Durham. On 29 January 2015 he made a statement in the House, first reminding listeners that in 2010 under the previous government, Margaret Hodge, 'in her capacity as a Minister at the Department for Culture, Media and Sport and I in my capacity as a Defence Minister, launched a consultation on the management of the HMS *Victory* wreck site, laying out various options and seeking expert opinions on the best way forward', adding: 'when the consultation reported back in July 2011', following the 2010 general election:

It recommended that the Government set up an independent charitable trust to manage the site. It recommended the Sir John Balchin Maritime Heritage Foundation, a charity that had only recently been established by Lord Lingfield, formerly Sir Robert Balchin, who had just been ennobled as a Conservative peer by the Prime Minister. Sir Robert was introduced as a direct descendant of Admiral Balchen of the *Victory*, and he described the admiral in a TV interview as his forebear. It has since been demonstrated that Sir Robert Balchin, spelled B-A-L-C-H-I-N, is not a direct descendant of Admiral Balchen, spelled B-A-L-C-H-E-N. Odyssey deliberately changed the spelling of Admiral Balchen's name to match that of Sir Robert Balchin for reasons we can only speculate about. When it was pointed out that Odyssey and Sir Robert had changed the spelling of Balchen to Balchin, Sir John's name was quickly dropped from the name of the charity. At about the same time as HMS *Victory* was found and Odyssey became involved with Sir Robert Balchin, the spelling of the admiral's name on the Balchin Family Society website was changed to match that of Sir Robert. Balchen's true descendants, the Temple West family, contacted Odyssey's chief executive officer, Gregg Stemm, to protest and raise their understandable concerns about the fraudulent nature of Lingfield's claims.[11]

Jones went on to criticise Odyssey, its motives and its track record. Bringing the debate back to the day in January 2015, Jones concluded that there were 'serious questions about the procedures that led to the Ministry of Defence gifting the wreck to MHF in January 2012' and that 'the Government should immediately cancel the arrangement with Odyssey and the Maritime Heritage Foundation'. Responding in the House was Edward Vaizey, the Minister for Culture and the Digital Economy, who reminded Jones that the MOD's decision 'is currently subject to a judicial review action', but ended the debate by saying 'I certainly pledge now in the House that I will take the Hon. Gentleman's points very seriously indeed, go back and consult my officials'.[12] This debate indeed saw some serious reconsideration. In the same year, Robert Yorke, chairman of the JNAPC, filed for a judicial review to reverse the decision.

Such was the controversy over the 'gift' and the 'deal' made of the *Victory*'s wreck site to the Maritime Heritage Foundation and Odyssey Marine Exploration that work on the wreck remained on hold, still subject to judicial review. But the arguments from both sides still continued in the press, with mounting frustration over delays in the decision-making process and pressure seemingly mounting on government to let salvage attempts begin. On 29 April 2018 *The Sunday Times* carried an article entitled 'Saving of navy wreck sinks in sea of experts'. Claiming that *Victory* had become 'mired in politics', it quoted Sean Kingsley, 'the *Victory* project's lead archaeologist', as saying: 'It is time to make the public aware of the shocking treatment imposed on arguably the most important British shipwreck since the *Mary Rose*' and claiming that 'repeated attempts to start had been halted by an army of government advisers and heritage experts moving goalposts after countless meetings'. The same article also quoted Lord Lingfield as chairman of the MHF, saying 'leaving the *Victory* marooned ... is a lose-lose situation for everyone. The site will only continue to be endangered as its chances to survive and educate erode.'[13] A month later, on 20 May 2018, the *Sunday Express* waded into the argument with the headline: 'Victory to rise again'. 'The Maritime Heritage Foundation', it stated, 'is hoping Defence Secretary Gavin Williamson will give his consent to push ahead with the salvage before the wreck – which lies 50 miles south of Plymouth – is further damaged by tides, deep-sea trawlers and looters.' The article stated that conservation work had been stalled by 'the differing views among the six bodies making up the Government's advisory group'. Again, Sean Kingsley was quoted as saying: 'The Foundation has presented a multi-million pound scientific project to government to cover the excavation, study and conservation of *Victory*. The MOD holds a bond for £390,000 as assurance any artefacts recovered will be properly conserved.' And Lord Lingfield was again quoted with the 'lose-lose situation' statement repeated.[14] Pressure was clearly mounting to get the salvage project back on its feet so excavation could begin.

Then, in October 2018, there was a spectacular about-turn by the Government when the MOD and the DCMS made a decision not to grant permission to the Maritime Heritage Foundation, and its contractor Odyssey Marine Exploration, to excavate the wreck of HMS *Victory* and made the following statement:

MOD and DCMS have reached an agreed position over the future management of the HMS *Victory* 1744 wreck site and consider that:

1. The V1744 site is environmentally stable.
2. While there is some evidence of damage or disturbance by either trawlers or illegal salvage activity; the risk of further damage or

disturbance can now be mitigated and maritime traffic can be monitored.

3. Other authorities can mobilise at short notice to investigate any vessels suspected of illegal activity over the site to protect the site from further damage.

4. To allow permission to remove items from the wreck would be in clear contravention of the rules of the Annex of the UNESCO Convention for the Protection of Underwater Cultural Heritage.

MOD therefore considers that the HMS *Victory* 1744 site and her associated artefacts should be left in situ. This decision is final but, in the future, if evidence suggests that the risk to the site changes, MOD will review if appropriate.[15]

Given their official response to the Government's public consultation in 2010, it is no surprise that the JNAPC was very pleased with this decision. Having noted the conclusion that the site 'is environmentally stable and that the site is best managed by preservation in situ', the Committee added: 'JNAPC particularly welcomes the application of technology to safeguard the site enabling 24/7 monitoring, which brings with it substantial reduction in any threat to the site from unauthorised interference.'[16]

Despite the Government's assertion that their decision was 'final', the arguments continued, both in the media and the courts. Indeed, on 14 February 2019 the BBC reported that 'this decade-long saga now faces a further twist though, as the Foundation [MHF] has now been granted permission to launch a judicial review of the Government's decision not to allow preliminary archaeological work on the wreck', adding 'the launch of legal proceedings at the Royal Courts of Justice on 6 February [2019] has been acknowledged by the MOD'.[17] Reporting on this judicial review in April 2019, Rebecca Reynolds of the Institute of Art & Law, referred to the Maritime Heritage Foundation and its ties with Odyssey who apparently seek to monetise salvage operations which 'goes against the principles of the UNESCO Convention on the Protection of the Underwater Cultural Heritage (in particular Article 2 (7))'.[18]

Parallel to these legal proceedings, the press became a forum for the arguments to continue in public from both sides. A particular example of this was delivered by *The Times* newspaper on 20 February 2019 under the heading 'Salvagers fight to raise the other HMS *Victory*'. Describing the wreck as being 'regarded by many as the most important shipwreck after the *Mary Rose*', the article commented that 'the salvagers argue that the wreck is at risk of being damaged by trawlers, erosion and illegal salvage, and that bringing it up will save it for future generations. Opponents accuse them of being treasure hunters motivated by profit.' The article quoted Robert Yorke, chairman of the JNAPC, as saying 'it is a very important wreck. Any work on it needs to be undertaken in a professional and properly funded manner. If any artefacts are brought up, they need to go in a museum, they need to be conserved. This costs an enormous amount of money.' He added that there was no evidence that the Maritime Heritage Foundation could fund such an operation. 'This is a war grave', he concluded, 'they have already found two skulls on board. You don't go digging up churchyards, in the hope of finding gold under bodies.'[19]

On cue, two days later, on 22 February, Dr Sean Kingsley, marine archaeologist for the *Victory* Shipwreck Project, had a Letter to the Editor published in *The Times*, beginning with the phrase 'shipwrecks elicit strong emotions and waterlogged thinking' and claiming that Robert Yorke's belief that the shipwreck was a 'war grave' was simply wrong. 'British wrecks have to be designated such under the Protection of Military Remains Act 1986, which *Victory* has never been,' said Kingsley. He therefore argued that 'the very few precious human remains on *Victory* should be carefully recorded, recovered, studied and interred with full naval honours'.[20] This was, predictably perhaps, followed by a further Letter to the Editor published in *The Times* on 28 February 2019, from Robert Yorke. He wrote that Kingsley 'does a disservice to his cause and his clients by claiming that HMS *Victory* is not a "war grave" because it has not been designated under the Protection of Military Remains Act 1986'. He continued: 'were he to check his facts before maligning me, Dr Kingsley would find that the

1986 Act can only be used to designate wrecks that sank after August 4, 1914, or sank less than 200 years ago, depending on the type of site. *Victory* was lost in 1744 – it has never been designated under the 1986 Act because it never could.' Yorke concluded '*Victory*'s sailors rest in peace; why not let them remain so?'[21]

The High Court clearly agreed with this conclusion. In September 2019 the court ruled that the artefacts on the wreck should remain with the ship, meaning defence ministers won their case having been challenged by the Maritime Heritage Foundation chaired by Lord Lingfield. After analysing evidence at a High Court Hearing in London, a judge dismissed the Foundation's challenge. On 27 September 2019 the BBC News reported that 'Mrs Justice Lieven said in a written ruling, the decision by the ministry [MOD] was lawful and not irrational'. Adding that the wreck contained at least forty-one bronze cannons, ship-borne artefacts, iron ballast, wooden fixtures and fittings, parts of two anchors and a rudder, the judge also said there was 'no direct evidence' to support the claims that the ship was carrying gold bullion. The BBC reported that Mrs Justice Lieven said the MOD had concluded the wreck was at 'minimal risk' and could be 'appropriately monitored'.[22]

Even now echoes of the debate still resonate. In an article in *The Times* on 18 June 2020, entitled 'Spanish retrieve lost treasure from depths', it was reported that Spain had recovered hundreds of artefacts from the wreck of an early nineteenth-century ship, the *Nueva Senora de las Mercedes*, 'that was sunk by the British and looted by treasure hunters'. It reported that 'a US salvage company took 594,000 gold and silver coins worth £308 million from the site in 2007' and that this had been 'by Odyssey Marine Exploration company, which had it flown to Tampa, Florida. A court in 2012, however, forced the treasure hunters to return the haul to Spain.'[23] This fact had been raised back in 2013 in Richard Temple West's open letter to the MOD as evidence of the 'conduct on the part of Odyssey'.

So, at the time of writing this chapter, the wreck of HMS *Victory* remained where it has lain for more than 250 years, at the bottom of the English Channel. It seems now that she will remain there, undisturbed, while the retrieved gun now on display at the National Museum of the Royal Navy in Portsmouth will give everyone a profound reminder of the fate of the ship and the lives of her thousand sailors, her captain, Samuel Faulknor and her Admiral, Sir John Balchen, who were lost with her. May they indeed all rest in peace.

10

Conclusion

'Entirely unexpected, within seconds of entering [Westminster] Abbey, every visitor is confronted with an image of the Royal Navy. You expect to be awed by British reverence for God but within seconds you are awed by British reverence for seapower.'

Sam Willis, in *The Glorious First of June:*
Fleet Battle in the Reign of Terror

There are still many unanswered questions about the loss of *Victory* and Admiral Balchen which will probably always remain so. Until now, both Balchen and *Victory* (1737) have, as demonstrated through the literature and art that has followed them through the ages since their disappearance, been seen and subsequently submerged in the story of a tragic shipwreck. Having thoroughly reconsidered their individual lives, the circumstances leading up to their loss, and the event itself, perhaps their individual and collective stories can be better understood for their service at the time and in their subsequent legacy. Between them, the contemporary prominence of their lives and the enormity of their loss brought to the attention of the British public the serious flaws in naval shipbuilding and design as well as the poor administration of the naval dockyards. The newspapers and journals of the day ensured through their reporting of the wreck and the circumstances surrounding it, that questions would be asked in Parliament and that the Admiralty Board would be called to account. Without doubt this was a contributory catalyst to the fall of Winchilsea's Board a mere two months after the catastrophe. It is equally inevitable that the shipwreck itself, rather than the admiral or the ship, should be the centre of their individual stories in the vast array of subsequent art and literature.

Now that one of the two retrieved and restored guns from *Victory* has gone on public display at the Historic Dockyard in Portsmouth, it is timely that the admiral and his ship should be recognised and properly understood in their wider historical context. Their sinking in the storm of October 1744 has been attributed to several proven defects in shipbuilding and design at the time. Balchen was at the forefront of criticising the Surveyor of the Navy, Acworth, for producing unstable ships in 1735 and his remarks must have been influential in the decision by the Admiralty Board to review the design of ships in 1740 with input from Sir John Norris, and the move by the new Admiralty Board in 1745 to set up a committee of sea officers to recommend a new Establishment for ship designs. Rightly, therefore, the later ships that emerged from Britain's dockyards, including Nelson's *Victory*, whose keel was laid in Chatham in July 1759, can be seen as a major legacy of the loss of Balchen, *Victory* and her guns.

Balchen had few opportunities to gain significant historical stature due in part to the period in which he served and in part to the roles and stations to which he was ordered. In the same way, he never got rich, unlike several admirals of his time. War, and the potential opportunity to make his name in a major engagement, came at an early period of his career and then, 26 years later, towards the end of his service. But even then, when the earlier battles came his way, the overwhelming advantage of the enemy fleets ensured that he had the ignominy of surrendering two of his ships in successive engagements. However, the courts martial in 1708 and 1709 demonstrate clearly that he fought bravely to the end, even when his ship was completely shattered by far superior forces. He can be seen still, through the court reports, standing on his quarterdeck amidst the carnage as the victorious boarding parties seized him. In contrast, his several subsequent years commanding *Colchester* saw him capturing several enemy merchantmen and warships, thus proving that, given the opportunity, he could indeed demonstrate his worth to the navy. The following years of peace stripped him of further opportunities for pursuing glory in battle, but nevertheless saw his career advance and his successful rise through the ranks. When his final opportunity came to engage the enemy in a full fleet action in 1744, his own vast Anglo-Dutch squadron was so threatening that the enemy chose to stay in the protection of Cadiz and Brest rather than confront such a superior force. But the success of his final mission probably saved the entire Mediterranean Fleet and Port Mahon, thereby contributing greatly to eventual victory in the war. In between the wars, he was an active officer and demonstrably contributed to the welfare of his officers and crew as well as influencing ship design.

As discussed in earlier chapters, fame comes in different colours. In an article examining 'Admirals as Heroes', it was asserted that: 'Naval biographers have assumed that the popularity of admirals flowed naturally and spontaneously from their spectacular victories and exemplary feats of valour. This may be taken as a truism. But it does not entirely explain their appeal.'[1] Indeed, Admiral Byng is famous for being shot on his quarterdeck for alleged cowardice in the face of the enemy, not for the glorious engagements he did win. On the other hand, victorious sea battles won have invariably led to fame for the commanders on the winning side. From the Elizabethan heroes, Raleigh, Drake and Blake, to the Rodneys and Hoods of the eighteenth century, the examples of English and British admirals have found their names emblazoned in song, plays, art and print and many in the marbled memorials of Westminster Abbey or St Paul's Cathedral. On entering Westminster Abbey in particular, as mentioned by Sam Willis at the beginning of the chapter, it could be anticipated that one was entering a religious house of prayer and worship, but within minutes of walking down the ranks of naval memorials to great sea commanders and the vaulted tombs beneath the central aisle where Admiral Cochrane lies, one would be forgiven if one thought it was a place of celebration to the greatness of the Royal Navy over those hundreds of years. That Balchen's memorial adorns a place in the abbey is alone a testament to his life and achievements.

But Balchen will never be seen as a famous admiral in British naval history. There can be little comparison between his albeit long and loyal service and the great exploits of other far more prominent naval characters; those before him, in his time or after him. In many respects, the legacy of Nelson has come to overshadow many of his predecessors and contemporaries alike. True, Admiral Sir Edward Hawke retains his fame for the Battle of Quiberon Bay and Admiral Richard Howe is famed for 'The Glorious First of June' victory over the French. However, even these great names and their tremendous achievements, some have argued, have been somewhat diminished in the wake of Nelson's fame. In his book on 'The Glorious First of June', Sam Willis aims to raise Howe to 'his rightful position' by demonstrating that 'Howe does not exist in the shadows of Nelson, but Nelson exists in the shadow of Howe'. He asserts that for too many years Nelson's influence 'has wrongly been allowed to go backward as well as forward in time', concluding 'that must now change'.[2] This story also argues that, though his legacy might not be so glorious as Howe's nor his achievements even approach the heights of those other above-mentioned admirals, Admiral Balchen's contribution should at least be better recognised as having an intrinsic value, and that he and his ship should assume a more visible position in naval history. He was clearly well-known and admired in his day for his long, loyal service and briefly attained wider recognition through the tragedy of his shipwreck. His being acknowledged for this event only 'briefly' was due to being overtaken and overshadowed by those names delivering many greater achievements in more important naval events that followed. Such is the nature of history, especially naval history. But sometimes either an event or some other catalyst can re-ignite some degree of historical recognition that has faded or even disappeared over the centuries.

The finding of the wreck of *Victory* and the putting of one of the two mighty bronze guns retrieved from her wreck on public display must be the trigger that will bring both Balchen and his ship back into historical significance. Their story, placed in the wider context of a mid-eighteenth century navy in desperate need for change and reform, which they, in their loss, were able to bring about by triggering Anson's sweeping reforms in the second half of the century, can now be better acknowledged. The discovery of the wreck gives us a great opportunity to look beyond the tragic event of the shipwreck itself and to reveal the person and the ship whose names can now emerge once again onto the platform of eighteenth century naval history: John Balchen and *Victory*, who perished together and who can now deservedly be more widely recognised and perhaps, in time, who may even be acclaimed.

Appendix 1

Survey Question Sent by Email on 29 December 2017

'On the night of 3/4 October 1744, Admiral Sir John Balchen and 1,100 souls perished in the storm that wrecked HMS *Victory*, the greatest warship in the world at the time. Having served in the Royal Navy for 58 years, been captured by the French twice and twice exonerated by courts martial, retired and then brought back for this final, fatal commission, Admiral Balchen has, apart from his memorial in Westminster Abbey and his portrait in the National Maritime Museum, all but disappeared from history. In the sixteen or so recently published books on naval history and naval shipwrecks, neither the admiral nor the ship are even mentioned in passing. Why, in your own opinion, do you think the man and the ship are no longer of any importance or relevance to naval, or even national, history today?'

Response from Andrew Lambert on 1 January 2018

'Good question ... history remembers heroes and the villains, not the solid sort who do most of the work, and carry the heavy loads. Balchen did not win a great battle, or get shot for not doing his best, and there are others who attract more attention. Historical memory is neither sophisticated nor inquisitive, it tends to follow trends, and Balchen is a casualty. He teaches us no obvious lessons, and his career lacks both glory and humour. He is long overdue for a serious reconsideration. I suspect he was very capable officer, with good political skills, hence his last mission. The top-heavy *Victory* was overwhelmed by a storm, Balchen did not do anything so un-seamanlike as to run into the well-know and widely avoided Casquets. His death was caused by sending out the ship in winter, when she was only fit for summer service.

A host of other capable sea officers who have shared his fall into historical oblivion, because the nation has lost sight of the sea, the Navy and the past. It is our job to reverse that trend.'

Response from Nicholas Rodger on 2 January 2018

'Thank you for your message. I don't at all agree that Balchen and the *Victory* are no longer of any importance to history. The recent discovery of the wreck of the *Victory* caused quite a flurry of interest, as no doubt you noticed from the internet, but even if ship and admiral had been quite forgotten, it would tell us nothing about their intrinsic importance. You will agree that the absence of a current event from the national newspapers does not tell us that it did not happen, or did not matter, and the same is true with history.'

Response from Frank Scott (via *The Society for Nautical Research Forum*), 5 February 2018

Frank Scott
Participant
If a ship is 'lost with all hands' the circumstances of that loss can only be a matter of conjecture. When it was believed that Balchen's *Victory* had run up on the Casquets, it was not unreasonable to ascribe that to her relatively poor windward performance. Although her later namesake, Nelson's *Victory*, sailed very well, three-deckers were optimised for firepower, and tended to be much less handy than the two-deckers that formed the bulk of any battlefleet of the period. Now that we know that she was not driven onto that notorious reef, the assumption must be that she was overwhelmed in some way by the storm. Exactly how that took place is anyone's guess.

There is a very good contemporary model of Balchen's *Victory*. However, I have not seen any formal analysis of her design and potential performance (particularly stability) done by a naval architect. Comments such as 'she was top heavy' have no weight unless backed up with figures. By the way, although the concept of the metacentre was established in the 18th century, it was not until the second half of the 19th century that the inclining test was developed, and the actual range of stability (as opposed to potentially misleading initial stiffness) could be established.

The loss of Balchen's *Victory* is covered by David J Hepper, *British Warship Losses in the Age of Sail 1650-1859* (Rotherfield, 1994), albeit with the erroneous location that was accepted until the wreck was found.

For a short discussion of the problems of sailing ship stability see Frank Scott, *A Square Rig Handbook* (2nd edn) (London: Nautical Institute, 2001), pp 97–110.

March 1, 2018 at 10:53 am #160

Response from Sam Willis, 2 March 2018

'I think it's much more complicated than you think.

"Apart from his memorial in Westminster Abbey and his portrait in the National Maritime Museum". I would argue that that means that they are fundamentally NOT forgotten. They are cared for and curated and on public display.

The motivation of every author who has published recently cannot be considered as a group. It is too individual. They may very well have known all about the wreck but chosen not to write about it for editorial reasons.

The problem is how do you measure if something is forgotten?'

Appendix 2

The Loss of the *Victory* Man of War

Good People all, pray give attention,
    To this fatal Tragedy,
    Which I am bound to mention,
Of the gallant Victory:
Fourteen hundred Souls did perish,
And are to the Bottom gone,
Oh! The dismal Grief and Horror,
    Of their Widows left alone.

When we first from *Spithead* sailed,
    Convoy unto Lisbon bound,
They with good Flip and Punch regaled,
    A brave new Ship both right and Sound:
A hundred and ten Guns she mounted,
    All of Brass so smart and clean,
The best Ship of the Navy counted,
    But alas! No more is seen.

But the Voyage proved fatal,
    As by the Sequel we shall find;
For as she was Home returning,
    She was, off *Scilly*, left behind:
In a dreadful Storm of Lightning,
    And of Hail and Thunder too;
And has never since been heard of,
    The Fatherless have cause to rue.

From *Alderney* we've Information
>That they heard that Stormy Night,
At least Ninety Guns to fire,
>Which did them something affright:
But as the more the Storm increased,
>It gave them more room to guess,
That some Ship upon the Ocean,
>Was in sad and deep Distress.

We saw floating, some Days after,
>Some spare yards were drove on Shore,
On which was the Name Victory,
>This gave us suspicion more:
That the noble Ship was stranded
>On the Gaskets, was our fear,
Long we waited with Impatience,
>But no News of them could hear.

The brave gallant Admiral *Balchen*
>With fourteen hundred Men beside,
If she's lost, went to the Bottom,
>And all at once together died:
Oh! The dismal grief and Horror,
>If one had been there to see,
How they all were struck with Horror,
>When sunk down the Victory.

O: the sad and dismal Story,
>I griev'd when I the same relate,
So many blasted to their Glory,
>And at once share the same fate:
Some thinking of their Wives and Children,
>And some of their Parents dear,
Sunk to the Bottom in a Moment,
>And no time to say a prayer.

O Victory! thou wast unlucky,
    But once before was out at Sea,
In the Night run foul of the Lion,
    And her Carved-work took away:
Now thou art gone to the Bottom,
    With a jovial Company,
An Admiral, Marines and Sailors,
    Most Unhappy Victory!

Oh! the Grief of the mournful Widows,
    And their Children fatherless,
And the Grief of tender Parents,
    Is more than what I can express:
Some lamenting for their Sweethearts,
    Overwhelm'd with Grief we see,
Each one laments his dear relation,
    Oh! the fatal Victory!

Children crying for their Fathers,
    Widows weeping in Distress,
God will surely be their Comfort,
    And protect the Fatherless.
He'll be husband to the Widow,
    That loves honest Industry,
And does give them his protection,
    Farewell, fatal Victory!

Source: John Aston (ed), *Real Sailor Songs*
(London: The Leadenhall Press, 1891).

Appendix 3

To the Memory of the Rev. Mr Charles Prince, late Chaplain on board His Majesty's Ship the *Victory*

If piety, if innocence, could save
From sad disaster, or the early grave;
If comliest form, and more, a beauteous mind,
With all that's good, and excellent, conjoin'd,
If outward graces, and an honest heart,
Could stop the tyrant, or avert his dart,
Prince then had liv'd; had liv'd from perils free,
Fulfill'd our hopes, and bless'd his friends and me.
But happier man! Thy shortliv'd toil is done,
And thou art crown'd ere half thy race was run;
Heav'n saw thy anguish, heard thy ardent pray'r,
And snatch'd thee hence, his more peculiar care,
To realms above; so his best servants fare.
Nor think that Balchen, or his heroes, die;
Led by their heav'nly guide, they triumph in the sky.

C.P.

Source: *The Gentleman's Magazine*,
Vol 14, November, 1744, p 614.

Appendix 4

Extract from William Hyland's play *'The Ship-Wreck: A Dramatick Piece'*. London: 1746

See Night comes on with growing Rage,
The whistling Winds are rising high;
Too Sure the Swelling Seas presage
An impetuous Tempest night.

No Glympse of Light, nor starry Spark,
Around the battling Whirlwinds fly;
And threat'ning Billows dash the Bark,
And dreadful Thunder rends the Sky.

Wind, Lightning, Thunder, Rain and Hail,
With furious Rage assault the Ship
Now splits the Mast, now rends the Sail,
And all are Swallowed in the Deep.

Thus Balchen and his hapless Fate,
And suffer'd an untimely Death:
A thousand Souls, the unhappy Freight,
All perish'd in a single Breath.

(Courtesy of Cathryn Pearce, 18 August 2017)

Appendix 5
John Balchen and Godalming

(This note explores John Balchen's family background in Godalming, Surrey, and the region's connections with the sea and the Royal Navy, enticing him to join the navy. Comparisons are made with the other local maritime hero, Jack Phillips, the telegrapher of RMS *Titanic* fame, also born in the same borough as Balchen.)

W̲e know from the Surrey Parish Register that John Balchen was born in Godalming in 1669 [1670], one of five children belonging to John Baltchin and Ann Edsur. Another entry refers to his father as John Balchin. It was quite usual at the time for the clerk or presiding priest to use phonetics to scribe names, so any similar-sounding names could be written with different spellings. Although it is true that there was (and still is to some extent) a Balchin 'dynasty' of yeoman farmers in the Godalming-Bramley areas of Surrey, Balchen himself always signed his name with an 'e', not the 'i' of the Balchin wing. Virtually every letter ever written between Balchen and the Admiralty and in any other letters in the multitude available in archival records refers to Balchen and almost never to Balchin. Records in the Surrey History Centre in Woking demonstrate, through estate deeds, civil parish records and other documents, that the extended BALCHEN family did indeed have extensive land and property interests across Surrey at the time. There are references to: a Thomas Balchen and his wife Sarah in the St Mary, Ewell Parish Records of the 1750s;[1] an 'Exemplification of Common Recovery' concerning extensive acres of farmland, meadows, pastures woodland and heath in Dunsfold, Catteshall, Godalming and Shalford, where Uriah Balchen, tenant, and his wife Elizabeth's names are given as 1st Vouchee, on 28 November 1752;[2] a Memorandum of Agreement between a Philip Carteret Webb and John Balchen, regarding the lease of Comb Farm in Dunsfold, filed between 1756 and 1761;[3] an insurance policy on a 'house, Malthouse, brick field, etc, in the tenure of James Balchen, Maltster, in Shalford,' dated 7 April 1786;[4] and names of fields 'in Mr Balchen's Farm in Shere, with acreage of fields, including 88 acres within Park Pales' circa 1800.[5] So evidence suggests that John Balchen was not necessarily from such a humble family background, but from a wider, clearly landed yeoman 'dynasty' in Surrey.

Nevertheless, even in Godalming, John Balchen's own birthplace in 1670, he is little known by the community. Godalming Museum has a single one-sided sheet of information on Balchen, a colour copy of his portrait and two of his hand-written letters. Moreover, in Godalming's County Library the script of a lecture given on 14 February 1968, by Stanley Charles Dedman, then curator of Godalming Museum, summarised Balchen's career and 'considered him the greatest single Godalming individual to have made his mark in history'.[6] However, Balchen is, like many other great men in history, overshadowed by another, more recent maritime hero from the area. In that same lecture, Dedman referred to 'the other Godalming sailor who is honoured by his town':[7] John George 'Jack' Phillips, the Chief Marconi Wireless Operator on RMS *Titanic*, which sank on 15 April 1912 on her maiden voyage. Jack Phillips was born in the nearby village of Farncombe, a chorister in St John the Evangelist Parish Church, and worked in Godalming Post Office where he learned telegraphy. He is well-known in the area as the hero of the *Titanic*, repeatedly sending out the world's first use of the distress signal 'SOS' as the ship sank. His fame here is perpetuated by the extensive *Phillips Memorial Grounds* alongside the river, the *Phillips Memorial Cloister* adjacent to St Peter's and St Paul's Parish Church in Godalming, the memorials to him in St John's Church, Farncombe, and in the nearby Nightingale Road Cemetery, not to mention the Jack Phillips Wetherspoons bar-restaurant in Godalming High Street.

It is a somewhat unfortunate contrast that Admiral Balchen is so little known to the public today, either locally in the communities connected to Godalming or amongst the wider general public, compared to Jack Phillips. The 26-year-old Jack Phillips perished along with more than

1,500 souls when the *Titanic*, the largest ship afloat at the time, sank. The 75-year-old Admiral Balchen, having served in the Royal Navy for 58 years under six monarchs, fought in many naval engagements, was captured by the French twice, then perished along with more than 1,100 souls when the *Victory*, the largest warship in the world at the time, was wrecked in a storm. They are two very different careers and achievements, albeit with such similar tragic endings, but such a contrast in their fame in Godalming and beyond is another good reason to unearth Balchen's story.

Having already established that Balchen was not from such 'very obscure parentage' but of a yeomanry farming family in Surrey, how then did he end up joining the Royal Navy at the age of 15, having no known naval connections? Most sailors went to sea to do what their fathers did: fishermen or sailors were brought up in maritime communities. Analysis of the birthplaces of sailors between 1650 and 1775 shows that well over 90 per cent of provincial sailors were born in maritime counties and 'the great majority of these within sight of the sea and ships, in port towns, coastal villages or on navigable rivers'.[8] However, sailors were not badly paid with promotion a good possibility and 'such a chance to move up in the world was not easily available in other occupations'.[9]

His early lure to the sea can be explained by the fact that Godalming lies mid-way between London and Portsmouth Harbour, providing a major transportation hub for naval officers, ships' victuals and the raw materials required for building and maintaining Britain's growing fleet of warships. The Portsmouth Road (today's A3) seems to have been used during the Tudor period and, by 1703, according to local historian John Nichols, Godalming had become 'a town of some importance on this road with commodious inns ranged along the High Street' and 'the mid-weekly market seems now to have been mainly concerned with the sale of corn which was supplied for the [Royal Navy's] Victualling Department at Portsmouth and for the growing population of London'.[10] It is not by chance then that on the south side of Godalming, on today's Ockford Road but then the Portsmouth Road, sits the 'Anchor Inn' public house. Although demolished and rebuilt in 1911, deeds from 1699 to 1702 refer to the original Anchor

Inn (Public House) and a messuage ⸢dwelling house and outbuilding⸥ in Godalming,[11] illustrating the maritime or naval connections with Godalming's small community at the time Balchen was in his early career in the navy.

Another significant maritime trade connection and influence within the area was the arrival of the canal system. As early as 1651 an Act was passed by Parliament authorising the River Wey to be made navigable and canalised from the Thames at Weybridge to Guildford,[12] a few miles north of Godalming. Regarded as part of the Commonwealth efforts to build a powerful fleet to counter the Dutch, England's most powerful maritime rivals, 'the canal served to convey gunpowder from ⸢nearby⸥ Chilworth, oaks for ship timbers, and heavy iron cannon from the Wealden iron works – all essential material for armaments at the time'.[13] It wasn't until 1760 that the River Wey Navigation Act extended the waterway four and a half miles from Guildford to Godalming, but by then 'considerable amounts of government stores were brought down from London to Godalming by water and carried from there by road to Portsmouth'.[14]

To the young John Balchen growing up in Godalming, all these surrounding transport links and ship-related activities must have drawn his interest towards the navy. He must also have been aware of the local industries that were increasingly driven by warship demands. South-west Surrey was on the edge of the Wealden iron industry which, from the Middle Ages onwards, used local ironstone and charcoal for fuel to produce 'cast iron ingots ... with a high carbon content' which 'were recast into guns, cannon balls and other iron objects'.[15] In nearby Chiddingfold was Ibham's Furnace which operated in the seventeenth century and 'was recorded in 1664 as equipped to cast guns'. And recently a pond has been identified there 'as a boring mill pond, to provide power for boring cannon'.[16]

Hardly any town, village or hamlet in England at that time would be in any way far removed from naval or maritime influence, such was the scale of the industrial and agricultural voracity of shipbuilding and sailors engaged in seaborne activity – in peacetime as well as during the years of naval warfare. It should also be recalled that Balchen was born at a time when thousands of English were emigrating to the New

World – Virginia, New England and Newfoundland especially – driven overseas by poverty, famine and the religious upheavals and Civil War in the first half of the seventeenth century. English ports from London to Bristol were actively engaged in shipping emigrants to the New World and bringing back raw materials, particularly tobacco and later, sugar. In large families, with many mouths to feed, it became an escape route for the younger children to seek opportunities either overseas or on the seas. But Godalming seemed particularly engaged with the sea and its supporting industries. So it was probably quite natural for the young Balchen to leave his near and extended family of tenant farmers, widespread across the rolling hills and valleys of Surrey, and make his way to the sea and to the Royal Navy.

Notes

1: Introduction

1. *The Sunday Times*, London, 29 April 2018, News, p 14.

2. A full list is in the bibliography but indicative titles include, by date published: Richard Hough, *The Great Admirals* (London: Weidenfeld & Nicolson, 1977); Jack Sweetman (ed), *The Great Admirals: Command at Sea, 1587-1945* (Annapolis: US Naval Institute, 1997); Alastair Wilson and Joseph F Callo, *Who's Who in Naval History: from 1550 to the present* (Abingdon, Routledge, 2004); N A M Rodger, *The Command of the Ocean: A Naval History of Britain, 1649-1815* (London: Penguin Books, 2004); Andrew Lambert, *Admirals: The Naval Commanders who made Britain Great* (London: Faber & Faber, 2008); Quintin Colville and James Davey (eds), *Nelson, Navy & Nation: The Royal Navy & the British People, 1688-1815* (London: Conway for NMM, 2013).

3. David Ritchie, *Shipwrecks – an encyclopaedia of the World's Worst Disasters at Sea* (New York: Facts on File, 1996), Sam Willis, *Shipwreck – a History of Disasters at Sea* (London: Quercus Editions Ltd, 2008), Serena Cant, *England's Shipwreck Heritage – from log-boats to U-boats* (London: English Heritage, 2013) and Peter Charles Smith, *Sailors on the Rocks: Famous Royal Navy Shipwrecks* (Barnsley: Pen & Sword Maritime, 2015).

4. See Appendix 1 for full survey responses.

5. James Davey, Andrew Lambert, Brian Lavery, N A M Rodger, Frank Scott, Chris Ware and Sam Willis.

6. Sam Willis, email response on 2 March 2018.

7. N A M Rodger, email response on 2 January 2018.

8. Andrew Lambert, email response on 1 January 2018.

9. Ibid.

10. Sean A Kingsley, 'The Sinking of the First Rate *Victory* (1744): A Disaster Waiting to Happen?', *Odyssey Papers 45* (Odyssey Marine Exploration, 2015), 1. Accessed on 22 March 2017 via www.victory1744org/publications.html.

11. Andrew Lambert, email response to this author's survey, 1 January 2018.

12. Alan M Smith, *Admiral Sir John Balchen (1670-1744): Should Godalming's 'obscure' naval hero be better known?*, Research Project, MA Naval History, University of Portsmouth, 16 March 2018.

13. Daniel A Baugh, 'Balchen, Sir John (1670-1744)', *Oxford Dictionary of National Biography* (hereafter *ODNB*) (Oxford: Oxford University Press, 2004); online edn, January 2008, accessed on 12 October 2017 via http://www.oxforddnb.com/view/article/1152.

14. Michael Palin, *EREBUS The story of a ship* (London: Arrow Books, 2018), p 274.
15. Hilary L Rubinstein, *Catastrophe at Spithead – The Sinking of the Royal George* (Barnsley: Seaforth Publishing, 2020), pp 235, 236.

2: The Shipwreck of 1744

1. M S Anderson, *Europe in the Eighteenth Century, 1713-1789* (London: Longman, 1961; Pearson Education Ltd, 4th Edition, 2000), p 189.
2. Brian Lavery, *The Ship of the Line, Vol I: The Development of the Battlefleet 1650-1850* (Greenwich: Conway Maritime Press, 1983), p 84.
3. Daniel A Baugh (ed), *Naval Administration 1715-1750*, Navy Records Society, Vol. 120 (London: 1977), p 6.
4. Edward Pearce, *The Great Man – Sir Robert Walpole: Scoundrel, Genius and Britain's First Prime Minister* (London: Pimlico, 2008), p 395.
5. Ibid, p 7.
6. ADM 1/381, Admiral Thomas Mathews to Admiralty Secretaries, 17 September, 1742, cited in Baugh (ed), *Naval Administration 1715-1750*, p 366.
7. SP 42/27/42, State Paper report, 21 March 1744, TNA (hereafter TNA).
8. ADM 110/13, Victualling Board to Admiralty Secretary, 7 March 1744, cited in Baugh (ed), *Naval Administration 1715-1750*, p 445.
9. ADM 3/47, 12th December 1743; ADM 110/13, 2 February 1744, cited in Daniel A. Baugh, *British Naval Administration in the Age of Walpole* (Princeton, NJ, Princeton University Press, 1965), p 446.
10. ADM 3/48, Admiralty Board Papers, 5 March 1744, chaired by Rt. Hon. Earl of Winchilsea, TNA.
11. ADM 110/13, Victualling Board to Admiralty Secretary, 7 March 1744, cited in Baugh (ed), *Naval Administration 1715-1750*, p 445.
12. A Society of Gentlemen, *The Biographical Magazine or, complete historical library* (London: F. Newbery, 1776), p 133.
13. ADM 3/48, Admiralty Board Papers, 1 June 1744, TNA.
14. Baugh (ed), *British Naval Administration 1715-1750*, p 447.
15. Society of Gentlemen, *The Biographical Magazine*, p 133, and *The Lives of British Admirals* (E. Newberry, London, 1787), p 31, and *Lives of the Most Celebrated British Admirals; containing a concise account of the characters, and an accurate detail of the Gallant Achievements of the most distinguished Naval Heroes* (Lane, Newman & Co, 1808), p 106. The latter in the Caird Library reference 92:355:33 (42): 094, PBD4884, TN: 67322.
16. ADM 3/48, Admiralty Board Papers, 13 July 1744, TNA.
17. SP 42/27 State Papers, *Commissioners of Lord High Admiralty to Sir John Balchen*, 14 July 1744, TNA.
18. ADM 3/48, Admiralty Board Papers, 13 July 1744, TNA.
19. ADM 1/87, Channel Fleet – Admirals Hardy, Martin, Balchen, Anson 1743–1747, letter from Admiral Balchen to Thomas Corbett, 18 July 1744, TNA.
20. SP 42/27 State Papers, *Commissioners to Sir John Balchen, 23 July 1744*, TNA.
21. ADM 3/48, Admiralty Board Papers, 23 July 1744, TNA.
22. ADM 1/87, Channel Fleet - Admirals, letter from Admiral Balchen to Thomas Corbett, 24 July 1744, TNA.
23. ADM 3/48, Admiralty Board Papers, 13 August 1744, TNA.
24. Ibid, 24 August 1744.

25. John Charnock, *Biographia Navalis, or Impartial memoirs of the lives & characters of Officers of the Navy of Great Britain from the year 1660 to the present time* (London: R. Faulder, 1795), p 160.
26. ADM 1/87/496, Channel Fleet – Admirals, Line of Battle, July 1744, TNA.
27. ADM 1/87, Channel Fleet – Admirals, letter from Admiral Balchen to the Admiralty on *Victory* at sea, 17 August 1744, TNA.
28. Society of Gentlemen, *The Biographical Magazine*, p 133, and *The Lives of The British Admirals*, p 31.
29. SP 42/27/128, Lords of the Admiralty to Admiral Balchen, 13 September 1744, TNA.
30. SP 42/27/130, Lords of the Admiralty to Admiral Balchen, 14 September 1744, TNA.
31. SP 42/27/145, Lords of the Admiralty to Admiral Balchen, 25 September 1744, TNA.
32. Baugh, 'Balchen, Sir John', *ODNB*, p 2.
33. Charnock, *Biographia Navalis*, p 161.
34. *Daily Post*, Wednesday, 10 October 1744, Issue 7833, 17th & 18th Century Burney Collection Newspapers and also repeated in *The Gentleman's Magazine*, 14 October 1744, p 562.
35. Charnock, *Biographia Navalis*, p 159.
36. Society of Gentlemen, *The Biographical Magazine*, p 133.
37. ADM/B/128, *Navy Board Letters to 30 April 1745*, Caird Library Archives, National Maritime Museum (hereafter NMM).
38. Ibid.
39. Zelide Cowan, 'John Lethbridge, Diver', *History Today* (journal), Vol 28, Issue 12 (December 1978), p 825.
40. ADM 106/1012/167, Letters to the Commissioners of His Majesty's Navy, John Lethbridge, Diver, to the Commissioners, 15 January 1745, TNA.
41. ADM/B/127, Board of Admiralty in-letters, 1745, Navy Office letter, 11 February 1745, Caird Library Archives, NMM.
42. *The Leeds Intelligencer*, Tuesday, 2 September 1766; Issue 651, p 3. British Library Newspapers, Part III: 1741–1950, quoting the *London Sunday Post*, 30 August 1766.
43. ADM 3/49, Admiralty Board Minutes, 10 October 1744, TNA.
44. Ibid, 11 October 1744.
45. Ibid, 31 October 1744.
46. Ibid, 17 December 1744.
47. ADM 36/4410, Ship's Musters, HMS *Victory*, 6 February 1743, to 31 July 1744, TNA.
48. PROB 11/736/243, PROB 11/738/337, PROB 11/736/43 and PROB11/745/158 respectively.
49. *Hampshire Telegraph and Naval Chronicle*, Portsmouth, Saturday, 21 July 1900; Issue 6200. British Library Newspapers, Part I: 1800–1900.
50. PROB 11/736/171, TNA.

3. The Lamentations, the Literature and the Artistic Legacy

1. Society of Gentlemen, *The Biographical Magazine*, *The Lives of British Admirals*, and Charnock, *Biographia Navalis*.
2. *Lives of the Most Celebrated British Admirals* (London: Lane, Newman & Co, 1808) in The Caird Library, NMM, Code 92:355:33 (42):094, PBD4884, TN: 67322.
3. Baugh, 'Balchen, Sir John', *ODNB*.
4. Ibid, p 1.
5. Timothy Jenks, *Naval Engagements – Patriotism, Cultural Politics, and the Royal Navy 1793-1815* (Oxford: Oxford

University Press, 2006), pp 2 and 3.

6. *The Gentleman's Magazine*, Vol 10, August 1740, p 403.

7. *The Birmingham Gazette*, Thursday, 16 November 1741, 1, Issue 1. British Library Newspapers, Part III; 1741–1950.

8. *Daily Post*, Wednesday, 10 October 1744, Issue 7833. 17th & 18th Century Burney Collection Newspapers, repeated in *The Gentleman's Magazine*, Vol 14, October, 1744, p 562.

9. *Daily Advertiser*, Friday, 12 October 1744, Issue 4359. 17th & 18th Century Burney Collection Newspapers.

10. *Daily Advertiser*, Monday, 15 October 1744, Issue 4361. 17th & 18th Century Burney Collection Newspapers.

11. *General Advertiser*, Monday, 15 October 1744, Issue 3095. 17th & 18th Century Burney Collection Newspapers.

12. *Caledonian Mercury*, Tuesday, 16 October 1744 (Courtesy of Cathryn Pearce).

13. *London Evening Post*, Tuesday, 16 October 1744, Issue 2644. 17th & 18th Century Burney Collection Newspapers.

14. *The Gentleman's Magazine*, October, 1744, Vol 14, p 563.

15. Cited in *The Gentleman's Magazine*, November 1744, Vol 14, p 594.

16. *The Gentleman's Magazine*, October 1744, Vol 14, p 557.

17. Dr Julia Bishop is a Research Fellow at the Elphinstone Institute, University of Aberdeen, and responded on 17 November 2017 to an email enquiry about the origins of the ballard.

18. Steven Roud is creator of the *Roud Folk Song Index*, and a researcher at the University of Aberdeen, and responded on 28 November 2017, to an email enquiry about the origins of the ballard.

19. Cited in John Aston (ed), *Real Sailor-Songs* (London: The Leadenhall Press, 1891).

20. https://www.traditionalmusic. co.uk/naval-songs-ballads/naval-songs-ballads-0393.htm, accessed 12 October, 2020.

21. Michael Brydon, 'Forms of Prayer to be used at Sea', article in *The Prayer Book Society Review*, Number 79, Trinity, 2016, p 24.

22. *The Gentleman's Magazine*, November 1744, Vol 14, p 616.

23. William Hyland, *The Ship-Wreck: A Dramatick Piece or The Farmer on the coast* (London: J. Millan, 1746).

24. George P Landow, 'Swim or Drown: Carlyle's World of Shipwrecks, Castaways, and Stranded Voyagers', *Studies in English Literature, 1500-1900*, Vol 15, No 4, Nineteenth Century (1975), pp 641–55, accessed via DOI:10.2307/450017 on 31 October 2017.

25. Bernard Richards, Review article on George P Landow, *Images of Crisis: Literary Iconology, 1750 to the Present* (London: Routledge & Kegan Paul, 1982), in *Modern Language Studies Journal*, Vol 13, No 2 (Spring 1983), pp 105–07, accessed via DOI: 10.2307/3194493 on 31 October 2017.

26. *The Hampshire Advertiser and Salisbury Guardian*, 2 October 1852, 7, Issue 1519. British Library Newspapers, Part II: 1800–1900.

27. *The Dundee Courier & Argus and Northern Warder*, Friday, 31 August 1877; Issue 7522. British Library Newspapers, Part II: 1800–1900.

28. Commander Chas N Robinson, RN, 'England's Drowned Admirals', *The Graphic*, Saturday, 15 July 1893; Issue 1233. The British Library Newspapers, Part I: 1800–1900.

29. *Hampshire Telegraph and Naval Chronicle*, Portsmouth, Saturday, 21 July 1900; Issue 6200. The British Library Newspapers, Part I: 1800–1900.

30. Rev. A G L'Estrange, *The Palace and the Hospital; or Chronicles of Greenwich* (London: Hurst & Blacketh, 1886), p 158.

31. Ibid, p 161.

32. Frank Howard, *Sailing Ships of War 1400-1860* (Greenwich: Conway Maritime Press, 1979), Lavery, *The Ship of the Line Vol I* and David J Hepper, *British Warship Losses in the Age of Sail: 1650-1859* (Rotherfield: Jean Boudriot Publications, 1994).

33. Rif Winfield, *First Rate: the Greatest Warships of the Age of Sail* (Barnsley: Seaforth Publishing, 2010).

4: HMS *Victory*'s Story

1. ADM/A/1773/5, Admiralty to Chatham Officers, 3 March 1690, The Caird Archives, NMM.

2. Ibid, Admiralty Office, 5 March 1690.

3. Lavery, *The Ship of the Line Vol I*, p 161.

4. Rodger, *The Command of the Ocean*, pp 149–50.

5. Ibid, p 150.

6. ADM/A/1795/96, In-Letters or orders received by the Navy Board, 9 May 1693, The Caird Archives, NMM.

7. ADM/A/1795/240, In-Letters or orders received by the Navy Board, 29 May 1693, The Caird Archives, NMM.

8. Rodger, *The Command of the Ocean*, p 220.

9. ADM/A/1822/41, In-Letters or orders received by the Navy Board, 5 August 1695, The Caird Archives, NMM.

10. ADM/A/1824/97, In-Letters or orders received by the Navy Board, 8 October 1695, The Caird Archives, NMM.

11. ADM 106/483/259, Court Martial held on 2 September 1696 on board *Victory*, Vice-Admiral Matthew Aylmer, President, TNA.

12. ADM 106/483/256, Court Martial held on 3 September 1696 on board *Victory*, Vice-Admiral Matthew Aylmer, President, TNA.

13. Baugh (ed), *Naval Administration 1715-1750*, p 197.

14. ADM/A/1838/104, Extract of a letter from Vice-Admiral Aylmer to the Lords of the Admiralty, 12 January 1697, The Caird Archives, NMM.

15. ADM/A/1838/104, Admiralty Office, 13 January 1697, The Caird Archives, NMM.

16. ADM/A/1838/103, Admiralty Office, 13 January 1697, The Caird Archives, NMM.

17. ADM 106/584/193, Letter from Commissioner Captain Sir William Gifford, Portsmouth, 14 June 1704, TNA.

18. Lavery, *The Ship of the Line Vol I*, p 165.

19. Ibid.

20. Winfield, *First Rate*, p 56.

21. Baugh, *British Naval Administration in the Age of Walpole*, p 247.

22. ADM 106/792/123, Letter to the Navy Board from Portsmouth Dock, 17 March 1726, TNA.

23. Winfield, *First Rate*, p 56.

24. ADM 106/847/251, Letter to the Commissioners of the Navy from Portsmouth Dock, 14 September 1733, TNA.

25. ADM 106/890/18, Letter from Commissioner Richard Hughes, Portsmouth, 12 January 1737, TNA.

26. ADM 106/891/6, Letter to the Navy Board, 4 July 1737, TNA.

27. ADM 106/923/247, Letter to the Navy Board, 26 April 1740, TNA.

28. *The Gentleman's Magazine*, Vol 10, July 1740, article dated 17 July 1740, p 356.

Notes

29. ADM/L/V/60, Lieutenants'
Logs HMS *Victory* 1740–1744,
Lieutenant Sheldrake Laton,
17 July, 1740, The Caird Archives,
NMM.
30. ADM 106/921/42, letter from
Hughes, Portsmouth Dock to
Commissioners of the Navy, 19 July
1740, TNA.
31. Aston (ed), *Real Sailor Songs*,
'Loss of the Victory Man of War',
verse eight.
32. ADM 106/954/178, In-letters,
Navy Board, Captain Faulkner, the
Victory, Portsmouth, 21 February
1742, TNA.
33. SP 36/63/132, State Papers,
25 February 1743/4, TNA.
34. ADM 106/987/51, letter from
William Moreland to the Hon.
Commissioner Brown, Deal,
25 February 1743/4, TNA.
35. Charnock, *Biographia Navalis*,
p 159.
36. Sean A Kingsley, 'The Sinking
of the First Rate *Victory* (1744):
A Disaster Waiting to Happen?',
Odyssey Papers 45 (Odyssey
Marine Exploration, 2015), p 1.
Accessed on 22 March 2017 via
www.victory1744org/publications.
html.
37. Andrew Lambert, email response
to this author's survey, 1 January
2018.
38. Frank Scott, posting of 5 February
2018 on *The Society for Nautical
Research Forum* via: https://snr.
org.uk/snr-forum/topic/admiral-
sir-john-balchen-1670-1744-hms-
vistory-1744/
39. Ibid.
40. 'Digital Modelling in the
evaluation of the sinking of
HMS *Victory* 1737' paper
given at the Royal Institution
of Naval Architects' Historic
Ships Conference, London,
7-8 December 2016, accessed
on 2 July 2020 via Https://
academia.edu/30574034/

Ball_et_al_Digital_Modelling_in_
the_evaluation_of_the_Sinking_
of_HMS_Victory_1737_Royal_
Institution_of_Naval_Architects_
Historic_Ships_Conference_12_
December_2016
41. Sir Jacob Acworth, Surveyor of
the Navy, to Joseph Allin, Master
Shipwright at Portsmouth, 14
April 1740, cited in John B.
Hattendorf (ed), *British Naval
Documents 1204-1960*, Navy
Records Society, Vol 131 (1993),
Document 282, 484/pdf 520.
42. Ibid.
43. ADM 1/796, letter from Admiral
Balchen to Admiralty Secretary,
Princess Amelia, The Hamoaze,
17 January 1735, cited in Baugh
(ed), *Naval Administration 1715-
1750*, pp 212–13.
44. Lavery, *The Ship of the Line Vol I*,
p 79.
45. Winfield, *First Rate*, p 59.
46. Ibid, p 57.
47. Howard, *Sailing Ships of War*,
p 182.
48. Andrew Lambert, email response
to this author's survey, 1 January
2018.
49. Royal Museums Greenwich,
description of model SLR0449.
50. Winfield, *First Rate*, p 51.
51. Daniel G Harris, *F H Chapman –
The First Naval Architect and his
Work* (London: Conway Maritime
Press, 1989).
52. National Maritime Museum,
Picture reference ZAZ0145.
53. Frank Scott, *A Square Rig
Handbook – Operations, safety,
training, equipment* (2nd Edition,
London, Nautical Institute, 2001)
(1992 1st Edition), pp 103 and 105.
54. Curatorial description for
Peter Monamy painting Image
BHC0361, National Maritime
Museum, Greenwich.
55. Lavery, *Ship of the Line Vol I*, p 84.
56. ADM 1/578, Vernon to Lord
Commissioners of the Admiralty,
18 June 1744, TNA.

57. Ibid.
58. Baugh (ed), *Naval Administration 1715-1750*, pp 195–7.
59. Ibid, pp 197–8.
60. *The Gentleman's Magazine*, Vol 14, October 1744, 19 October, p 563.
61. *The Gentleman's Magazine*, Vol 14, November 1744, 3 November, p 594.
62. Commodore Charles Knowles to Lord Winchilsea, First Lord of the Admiralty, *Superbe*, Antigua, 6 January 1745, cited in Hattendorf (ed), *British Naval Documents 1204-1960*, Navy Records Society, Document 284, 486/pdf 522.
63. Ibid, 489/pdf 525.
64. Ibid, 486/pdf 522.
65. Winfield, *First Rate*, p 56.
66. *British Tars, 1740-1790:* February 2017, accessed on 12 October 2017 via www.britishtars.com/2017/02.
67. Curator's comments, British Museum collections website for *The Famous Ship Victory*, Museum Number 1992, 0620.15, Image AN164566001.
68. ADM 106/899, letter from Commissioners of the Navy to Portsmouth Dockyard, 17 March 1737, TNA.
69. ADM 1/3651, letter from Richard Haddock to Bunchett, Navy Office, 15 August 1737, TNA.
70. Ibid., letter from Admiral Haddock, HMS *Somerset*, at Port Mahon, to Commissioners of the Navy, 1 August 1738, TNA.
71. D. B. Horn and Mary Ransome (eds), *English Historical Documents, 1714-1783* (London: Eyre & Spottiswoode, 1957), p 594.
72. Memorandum from Sir John Williams, Surveyor of the Navy, to the King, 11 January 1774, cited in *British Naval Documents 1204-1960*, Navy Records Society, 484/pdf 520. Accessed on 31 October 2017 via https://www.navyrecords.org.uk/british-naval-documents-1204-1960/.
73. ADM 3/49 Board Minutes, 28 December 1744, New Board present: Duke of Bedford, Earl of Sandwich, Lord Admiral Hamilton, George Anson, TNA.
74. Lavery, *The Ship of the Line Vol I*, p 90.
75. Matthew Sheldon, *HMS Victory*, The National Museum of the Royal Navy (Pitkin, 2014), p 3.

5: Captain John Balchen's Adventures

1. Hilary L Rubenstein, *Catastrophe at Spithead: The Sinking of the Royal George* (Seaforth: Barnsley, 2020).
2. In December 2017 and January 2018 a survey was conducted of 147 members of the public at The National Museum of the Royal Navy, Portsmouth, The National Maritime Museum, Greenwich, and in Godalming, Surrey, to establish if anyone could recognise Admiral Balchen's portrait. None could.
3. Baugh, *British Naval Administration in the Age of Walpole* and Baugh (ed), *Naval Administration, 1715-1750*.
4. W G V Balchin, 'Admiral Sir John Balchin (1660-1744)', *Mariner's Mirror* 80 (1994), pp 332–5.
5. M E Matcham, *A Forgotten John Russell* (1905), H W Richmond, *The Navy in the War of 1739-48* (1920), and T Lediard, *The Naval History of England* (1935), and J H Owen, *War at Sea under Queen Anne, 1702-1708* (1938).
6. A Society of Gentlemen, *The Biographical Magazine*.
7. *The Lives of the British Admirals*.
8. Charnock, *Biographia Navalis*.
9. Alan Smith, *Admiral Sir John Balchen*, Research Project, MA Naval History, University of Portsmouth, 2018.
10. Ann Laver, *Admiral Sir John Balchen (1669/70-1744)* (data

sheet, Godalming Museum
Library, 2009), p 1.

11. John Baptiste de Medina, *Admiral
Sir John Balchen, 1670-1744*
(Object ID: BHC2525, oil on
canvas painting, circa 1705,
National Maritime Museum,
Greenwich, London, Greenwich
Hospital Collection).

12. Ibid.

13. Ibid.

14. Geoff Quilley, *Empire to Nation –
art, history and the visualization
of maritime Britain 1768 – 1829*
(New Haven & London, Yale
University Press, 2011), pp 209
and 210.

15. Edward Hawke Locker, *Catalogue
of the Portraits of Distinguished
Naval Commanders, and
Representations of their Warlike
Achievements, Exhibited in the
Naval Gallery of Greenwich
Hospital* (London: 1836), p 4,
cited in ibid, p 210.

16. *Surrey, England, Church of
England Baptisms, Marriages and
Burials, 1538-1812*, illustration
accessed and supplied on 26
November 2017 by Jennifer
Goldsmith via https://www.
ancestry.co.uk. Also verified in
the printed version in Godalming
Museum, Accession Number
B003.408, *The Parish Register of
Godalming, Surrey, 1582-1688,
Volume II, Baptisms* (Surrey Parish
Register Society, 1904), p 136.

17. Surrey Parish Register Society,
The Parish Register of Godalming,
p 89.

18. Balchin, 'Admiral Sir John Balchin
(1669-1744)', pp 332–5.

19. Baugh, 'Balchen, Sir John (1670-
1744)', *ODNB*.

20. Surrey Parish Register Society,
The Parish Register of Godalming,
respectively pp 131, 134, 136
and 139.

21. Jean François Voltaire, *The Age
of Louis XIV* (1751), translated by

Martyn P Pollack (London: J M
Dent & Sons, 1969), p 76.

22. Ibid, p 332.

23. Ibid, pp 332–3.

24. A Society of Gentlemen, *The
Biographical Magazine*, p 132.

25. No.12 Letter from Nelson to
Frances Nisbet, 19 August 1786,
Boreas, English Harbour, cited in
George P B Naish (ed), *Nelson's
Letters to his Wife and Other
Documents, 1785-1831,* Vol 100
(1958), p 34.

26. No. 3 Letter from Nelson to
Francis Nisbet, 13 December 1785,
Boreas, English Harbour, cited in
ibid, p 21.

27. ADM 106/424/78, Letter
from Captain Vickars, *Dragon*,
Portsmouth, to the Navy Board, 22
August 1692, TNA.

28. ADM 106/424/79, Letter from
Captain Vickars to the Navy
Board, 23 August 1692, TNA.

29. ADM 106/441/151, Letter
from Rear-Admiral Sir Francis
Wheeler describes his West Indies
Squadron, 4 June 1693, TNA.

30. PROB 11/416/440, Will of
Lieutenant Thomas day of the
Dragon, to the Navy Board, 28
October 1693, TNA.

31. PROB 11/417/461, Will of
Lieutenant Peter Devett of the
Dragon, in Barbados, 13 December
1693, TNA.

32. PROB 11/427/465, Will of Charles
Vickars, Mariner, the *Dragon*,
bound for the West Indies, 31
October 1695, TNA.

33. ADM 106/443/323, Report to the
Navy Board, 20 September 1694,
TNA.

34. ADM 106/449/145, Report to the
Navy Board, 22 December 1694,
TNA.

35. SP 89/16/216, State Papers, 27
December, 1694, TNA.

36. ADM 106/486/305, Report to
the Navy Board from Portsmouth,
9 March 1696, TNA.

37. ADM 106/511/71, Letter to the Navy Board from Vice-Admiral Neville, 27 April 1697, TNA.
38. ADM 106/501/383, Report to the Navy Board, December 1697, TNA.
39. Baugh, 'Balchen, Sir John (1670-1744)', *ODNB*, p 1.
40. ADM 106/506/313, Letter from Captain William Julius, *Colchester*, Port Royal, Jamaica, to the Navy Board, 12 August 1697, TNA.
41. A Society of Gentlemen, *The Biographical Magazine*, p 132.
42. Quoted in Baugh, 'Balchen, Sir John (1670-1744)', *ODNB*.
43. ADM/L/V/117, Logbook of HMS *Vulcan* 1701 – 1703, Caird Library Archives, The National Maritime Museum.
44. Ibid.
45. A Society of Gentlemen, *The Biographical Magazine*, p 132.
46. Ibid.
47. HCA 32/60/36, High Court of Admiralty, High Court of Appeals for Prizes, 1702-1703, TNA.
48. Rodger, *The Command of the Ocean*, p 166.
49. Baugh, 'Balchen, Sir John (1670-1744)', *ODNB*, p 1.
50. ADM 106/569/287, Letter from the Navy Board to the Portsmouth Commissioner, 1 May 1703, TNA.
51. ADM 106/569/354, Letter to the Navy Board, 20 June 1703, TNA.
52. Baugh, 'Balchen, Sir John (1670-1744)', *ODNB*, p 1.
53. ADM 106/581/51, Letter to the Navy Board, Captain John Balchen, the *Adventure*, Nore, 11 February 1703/4, TNA.
54. John Baptiste de Medina, *Admiral Sir John Balchen, 1670-1744* (Object ID: BHC2525), NMM.
55. ADM 106/596/290. Letter to the Navy Board from John Balchen, 9 July 1705, TNA.
56. ADM 106/596/291. Letter from John Hockaday, 9 July 1705, TNA.
57. ADM 106/597/266. Letter from James Conch, 12 August 1705, TNA.
58. ADM 106/596/324. Letter from Captain John Balchen, 2 September 1705, TNA.
59. ADM 106/596/334. Letter from Captain John Balchen, Portsmouth Harbour, 14 September 1705, TNA.
60. ADM 106/596/337. Letter from Balchen, the *Chester*, Spithead, 18 September, 1705, TNA.
61. ADM 106/606/221, In-letters, the Navy Board, 19 July 1705, TNA.
62. ADM 1/1468, Letters, Balchen, HMS *Chester*, slave ship off Guinea, 23 November 1706, TNA.
63. Voltaire, *The Age of Louis XIV*, p 207.
64. ADM 106/625/129, Report to the Navy Board, 25 April 1707, TNA.
65. Charnock, *Biographia Navalis*, p 155.
66. Ibid, p 156.
67. David J Hepper, *British Warship Losses in the Age of Sail: 1650-1859* (Rotherfield, Jean Boudriot Publications, 1994).
68. John R Hutchinson, *Press-Gang Afloat & Ashore*, 1913, electronic book, 1 March 2006, p 45.
69. ADM 1/5267, Court Martial, Spithead, Monday 27 September 1708, on HMS *Royal Anne*, by George Byng, Admiral of ye blue Squadron, TNA.
70. Frederick Hervey, *The Naval History of Great Britain; from the earliest times to the rising of the Parliament in 1779, Volume III* (J. Brew, London, 1779), p 202.
71. Ibid, p 201.
72. ADM 1/1468-9, Letters from Captains – Surname B, 1706–1707 & 1708–1709, 4 February 1709, TNA.
73. Ibid, 2 May 1709.
74. ADM 106/638/354, Letter from Balchen, the *Gloucester*, Deptford, 19 August 1709, TNA.
75. ADM 106/638/354, Letter from Balchen, the *Gloucester*, Deptford, 24 August 1709, TNA.
76. ADM 106/638/370, Letter from Captain Balchen, the *Gloucester*,

Longreach, 11 September 1709, TNA.

77. ADM 1/1468-9, Letters from Captains – surname B, 1706–1707 & 1708–1709, on the *Gloucester*, Longreach, 13 September 1709, TNA.

78. ADM 106/638/380, Letter from Captain Balchen, the *Gloucester*, Longreach, 20 September 1709, TNA.

79. ADM 1/1468-9, Letters from Captains – Surname B, on the *Gloucester*, in the Downs, 29 September 1709, TNA.

80. ADM 106/638/387, Letter from Captain Balchen, on the *Gloucester*, The Downs, 29 September 1709, TNA.

81. ADM 1/1468-9, Letters from Captains - B, London, 3 December 1709, TNA.

82. ADM 1/5267, Court Martial, River Thames, 14 December 1709, on HM Yacht *Peregrine*, by Sir John Jennings, Admiral of ye White Squadron, TNA.

83. https://enacademic.com/dic.nsf, accessed 20 March 2020.

84. *The Times*, 27 December 1919, via thetimes.co.uk/archive.

85. HCA 32/50/119 High Court of Appeals for Prizes, 27 May 1710, TNA.

86. HCA 32/54/47 High Court of Appeals for Prizes, 1710, TNA.

87. HCA 32/55/39 High Court of Appeals for Prizes, 1710, TNA.

88. ADM 1/1470, cited in Baugh, 'Balchen, Sir John (1670–1744)', *ODNB*, p 1.

89. HCA 32/54/26 High Court of Appeals for Prizes, 18 November 1710, TNA.

90. A Society of Gentlemen, *The Biographical Magazine*, p 132.

91. ADM 106/665/33, Letter to the Navy Board, 26 October, 1711, TNA.

92. ADM 106/674/64, Dockyard Proceedings, 12 March 1712, TNA.

93. SP 42/68/109, State Papers, Sir John Jennings' letter, 31 January 1713, TNA.

94. ADM 106/684/64, Letter, Sir John Jennings, Admiral, HMS *Blenheim*, Isle de Hyeres, 26 October 1713, TNA.

95. B.M. Add (Additional manuscripts in the British Museum). 35, 898, ff.89-92,15 September 1715, cited in Baugh (ed), *Naval Administration 1715-1750*, pp 43–4.

96. ADM 106/696/48, Balchen, the *Diamond*, at Woolwich, to the Navy Board, 14 February 1714/5, TNA.

97. ADM 106/696/62, Balchen, the *Diamond*, Woolwich, 20 February 1714/5, TNA.

98. ADM 106/696/86, Balchen, the *Diamond*, at Longreach, 25 March 1715, TNA.

99. ADM 106/696/132, Balchen, the *Diamond* in Port Royal Harbour, Jamaica, 20 June 1715, TNA.

100. ADM 106/699/159 Samuel Page, Deputy Commissioner, St Jago de la Vega, Jamaica, to Navy Board, 31 August 1715, TNA.

101. ADM 106/696/202 Balchen, the *Diamond*, Port Royal Harbour, Jamaica, 12 November 1715, TNA.

102. Baugh (ed), *Naval Administration 1715-1750*, p 325.

103. ADM 1/1472 Letters from Captains - Surname B 1717-1723, Balchen to the Lords of the Admiralty, 26 February 1716, TNA.

104. ADM 106/703/94, Balchen, the *Diamond*, off Dover, 4 May 1716, TNA.

105. T 1/201 Treasury Board Papers, *Captain Balchen to the Admiralty*, HMS *Orford*, The Nore, 22 November, 1716, TNA.

106. William Balchin, *The Balchin Family Newsletter, Issue 2*, July 1995, pp 4–7. Compilation of Newsletters, Godalming Museum, 920 BAL BAL.

107. T 1/201 Treasury Board Papers, *Admiralty Office to Commissioners of His Majesty's Customs, 28 November 1716*, TNA.

108. ADM 1/1472, Letters from Captains – Surname B, 1717–1723, Balchen to the Lords of the Admiralty, 26 January 1717, TNA.

109. ADM 1/1472 Letters from Captains – Surname B 1717–1723, Balchen to the Lords of the Admiralty, 10 March 1718, TNA.

110. ADM/L/S/280 Lieutenants' Logs HMS *Shrewsbury* 1716–1719, Charles Drummond, Third Lieutenant of His Majesty's Ship *Shrewsbury*, 18 March 1718 to 9 March 1719, The Caird Library Archives, NMM.

111. Newberry, *The Lives of the British Admirals*, p 27.

112. ADM/L/S/280, Lieutenants' Logs HMS *Shrewsbury* 1718 –1719, Charles Drummond, Third Lieutenant HMS *Shrewsbury*, The Caird Library Archives, The National Maritime Museum (Note, strangely this extract comes from Drummond's logs from 31 July to 2 August 1718 whereas the battle occurred on 11 August).

113. ADM 1/1472 Letters, Balchen to the Lords of the Admiralty, 8 March 1719, TNA.

114. Ibid. Balchen to the Lords of the Admiralty, 6 March 1718, TNA.

115. Ibid. Balchen to the Lords of the Admiralty, 15 March 1719, TNA.

116. Ibid. Balchen to the Lords of the Admiralty, 16 May 1719, TNA.

117. Ibid. Balchen to the Lords of the Admiralty, 20 May 1720, TNA.

118. ADM/L/M/235, Lieutenants' Logbooks, HMS *Monmouth*, 1719–1729, The Caird Library Archives, NMM.

119. ADM/L/M/235, Journal kept by 2nd Lieutenant Kinzey on HMS *Ipswich* and HMS *Monmouth*, 24 January 1725/6 to 30 June 1726, The Caird Library Archives, NMM.

120. Ibid, Logbooks of 1st Lieutenant B Mansel, 23 February 1725/6 to 31 December 1726 and 1 July 1726 to October 1727, The Caird Library Archives, NMM.

121. Ibid, Journal of HMS *Monmouth*, 9 September 1727 to 13 April 1728, The Caird Library Archives, NMM.

122. ADM 1/899, Letter from Admiral John Balchen to Admiralty Secretary, *Monmouth*, Portsmouth, 27 February 1728/9, cited in Baugh (ed), *Naval Administration 1715-1750*, p 432.

6. Service as Admiral John Balchen

1. ADM 1/899, Letter from Admiral John Balchen to Admiralty Secretary, *Monmouth*, Portsmouth, 4 March 1729, cited in Baugh (ed), *Naval Administration 1715-1750*, p 107.

2. ADM 3/37, Admiralty Minute, 6 March 1729, cited ibid.

3. Balchin, *The Balchin Family Newsletter*, Issue 2, July 1995, p 6.

4. ADM 50/28, Admiral's Journals, A Journal kept by John Balchen, Esq. Rear-Admiral of the White between 21 May 1731 and 11 December 1731, TNA.

5. Ibid.

6. ADM 1/796, letter from Admiral John Balchen to Admiralty Secretary, *Princess Amelia*, The Hamoaze, 17 January 1735, cited in Baugh (ed), *Naval Administration 1715-1750*, pp 212–13.

7. ADM 1/3649, letter from the Navy Board to Admiralty Secretary, 24 January 1735, cited in ibid, p 213.

8. ADM 1/796, letter from Admiral John Balchen to Admiralty Secretary, *Princess Amelia*, Plymouth, 2 February 1735, cited in ibid, pp 214–15.

9. ADM 106/874/16, Letter from the Plymouth Officers to the Navy Board, 14 February 1735, TNA.

10. ADM 1/380, Letters from Commanders-in-Chief, Mediterranean: including Admirals Haddock, Ogle and Balchen. Letter from Admiral Balchen at sea on the *Russell*, 2 May 1740, TNA.

11. Ibid. Letter from John Burnaby Parker, Consul at Oporto, to Admiral Balchen, 1 May 1740, TNA.

12. Ibid. Letter from Admiral John Balchen, at sea on the *Russell*, 2 May 1740, TNA.

13. ADM 1/380, Letter from Admiral John Balchen to the Admiralty, 1 June 1740, Near Scilly, TNA.

14. Glyndwr Williams (ed), *Documents relating to Anson's Voyage Round the World 1740-1744*, Navy Records Society, Vol 109 (1967), p 47.

15. ADM 1/4109/Doc.42, Anson to Andrew Stone, Spithead, 18 August 1740, cited in ibid, p 50.

16. Journal of Lawrence Millechamp, to Rt Hon Benjamin Fitzwalter, HM Privy Council, 'A narrative of Commodore Anson's Voyage into the Great South Sea and Round the World, 18 September 1740 - 15 June 1744, NMM. MS 9354/JOD 36, cited in Williams, *Documents relating to Anson's Voyage*, p 67.

17. Baugh, 'Balchen, Sir John (1670-1744)', *ODNB*.

18. Cited in Baugh, *British Naval Administration in the Age of Walpole*, p 291.

19. BL, Egerton MS 2529, fol.220, cited in Baugh, 'Balchen, Sir John (1670-1744)', *ODNB*, 1.

20. ADM 1/518, Letters from Admirals Byng (later Lord Torrington), Aylmer and Balchen: Letter from Admiral Balchen to the Admiralty, 25 September 1740, TNA.

21. ADM 1/904, Balchen to the Lords of the Admiralty, 15 August 1740, cited in ibid, and Baugh, *British*

Naval Administration in the Age of Walpole*, p 117.

22. ADM 3/49 Board Minutes, 22 November 1744, TNA.

23. ADM 1/905, Balchen to the Lords of the Admiralty, 4 February 1741, cited in Baugh, *British Naval Administration in the Age of Walpole*, p 230.

24. Letter from Vice-Admiral Balchen to Commodore Philip Vanbrugh, Naval Commissioner at Plymouth Yard, 24 October 1739, Godalming Museum, Accession Number 1776/1 TRB 293/1 5070/1.

25. Letter from Vice-Admiral Balchen to Commodore Philip Vanbrugh, Naval Commissioner at Plymouth Yard, 25 May 1742, Godalming Museum, Accession Number 1776/2 TRB 293/1 5070/2.

26. ADM 106/982/8, Letter, Commissioner Philip Vanbrugh, Plymouth, 7 January 1743, TNA.

27. ADM 106/976/50, Letter, Captain W Hemmington, the *Princess Amelia*, Hamoaze, TNA.

28. Baugh, 'Balchen, Sir John (1670-1744)', *ODNB*, p 2.

29. SP 9/72, State Papers, Commission appointing John Balchen Esq, Master of Greenwich Hospital, TNA.

30. ADM 1/87, Channel Fleet – Admirals Hardy, Martin, Balchen, Anson 1743 – 1747, letter from Admiral Balchen to the Admiralty, 24 July 1744, TNA.

31. ADM 1/87, Channel Fleet – Admirals Hardy, Martin, Balchen, Anson 1742 – 1747, letter from Admiral Balchen, at sea on the *Victory*, 17 August 1744, TNA.

32. Baugh (ed), *Naval Administration 1715-1750*, p 41.

33. ADM 3/49, Admiralty Board Minutes, 11 October 1744, TNA.

34. ADM 1/87, Channel Fleet – Admirals 1743 – 1747, letter from Admiral Balchen to the Admiralty, on the *Victory*, at sea off Cape Finisterre, 27 August 1744, TNA.

35. *The Gentleman's Magazine,* Vol 16, November, 1746, p 576.

7: Sir John Balchen: Family Man, Gentleman

1. Baugh, 'Balchen, Sir John (1670-1744)', *ODNB*, p 1.
2. Balchin, *The Balchin Family Newsletter, Issue 2,* July 1995, p 6.
3. Inscription on Memorial to Sir John Balchen, Westminster Abbey, North Transept.
4. https://www.british-history.ac.uk/survey-london/vol2/pt1/pp50-53 accessed on 12 October 2020.
5. Balchin, *The Balchin Family Newsletter, Issue 13,* January 2001, p 17.
6. Brian Lavery, *The Royal Navy's First Invincible* (Portsmouth, Invincible Conservations [1744-1758] Limited, 1988), p 22.
7. Marble stone carving, North Choir Aisle, Westminster Abbey.
8. ADM 1/1469-9, Letters from Captains – Surname B, 29 January, 1708, and February 1708, TNA.
9. ADM 1/1472, Letters from Captains – Surname B, 1717–1723, Balchen to the Lords of the Admiralty, 10 March 1719, TNA.
10. ADM 1/380, Letters from Commander-in-Chiefs, Mediterranean: including Admirals Haddock, Ogle and Balchen, letter from Admiral Haddock, on board the *Somerset,* Mahon Harbour, 10 April 1740.
11. Ibid. Balchen to the Lords of the Admiralty, 29 October 1721, TNA.
12. Memorial to Sir John Balchen, Westminster Abbey, North Transept.
13. Baugh, 'Balchen, Sir John (1670-1744)', *ODNB*, p 1.
14. Cited in ibid.
15. The Rev. A G L'Estrange, *The Palace and the Hospital; or Chronicles of Greenwich* (London: Hurst and Blackheath, 1886),

p 158, The Caird Library Archives, 914.216, LES 585, NMM.
16. Baugh, 'Balchen, Sir John (1670-1744)', *ODNB*.
17. *The Balchin Family Newsletter, Issue 2,* July 1995, Godalming Museum 920 BAL BAL, p 7.
18. Charnock, *Biographia Navalis,* p 159, National Museum of the Royal Navy, Library and Archives.
19. Memorial to Sir John Balchen, Westminster Abbey, North Transept.
20. Landow, 'Swim or Drown', p 642.
21. Memorial to Sir John Balchen, Westminster Abbey, North Transept.

8. Their Legacy – What Happened Next?

1. ADM 1/578, Vernon to the Lords Commissioners of the Admiralty, 18 June 1744, TNA.
2. Rodger, *The Command of the Ocean,* p 244.
3. ADM 95/2, Ad Hoc Committee of Senior Officers to Admiralty Board, 27 November 1745, referenced in Baugh (ed), *Naval Administration 1715-1750,* p 227.
4. Ibid, p 230.
5. Commodore Charles Knowles to Lord Winchilsea, First Lord of the Admiralty, *Superbe,* Antigua, 6 January 1745, cited in Hattendorf, ed., *British Naval Documents 1204-1960,* Navy Records Society, Document 284, 486/pdf525.
6. Ibid, 488.
7. Lavery, *The Royal Navy's First Invincible,* p 10.
8. Lambert, *Admirals,* p 134.
9. Lavery, *The Royal Navy's First Invincible,* pp 22–4.
10. ADM 1/4297 Part 7 folios 38-40, *Log Book of HMS Prince George,* TNA.
11. Anson to Bedford, 11 May 1747, Russell, *Duke of Bedford II,* pp 213–15, referenced in Lambert, *Admirals,* p 136.

12. ADM/B/136, Board of Admiralty, In-letters, 14 August 1747 and POR/D/9, Dock Officers' reports to the Navy Board, 1746 to 1749, 14 August 1747, The Caird Library Archives, NMM.
13. ADM/B/136, Board of Admiralty, In-letters, 14 August 1747, The Caird Library Archives, NMM.
14. ADM 7/340, Admiralty Memorial to the Lords Justices, 15 June 1748, TNA, referenced in Baugh (ed), *Naval Administration 1715–1750*, p 234.
15. Lavery, *The Ship of the Line Vol I*, p 174.
16. Lavery, *The Royal Navy's First Invincible*, p 104.
17. ADM 106/1059/39, Commissioner Richard Hughes letter, 27 January 1749, TNA.
18. ADM 106/1012/167, Letters to the Commissioner of His Majesty's Navy, John Lethbridge, Diver, to the Commissioners, 15 January 1745, TNA.
19. POR/F/11, Resident Commissioner Hughes's reports to Commissioners of the Navy Board (1757-1760), 28 June 1758, The Caird Library Archives, NMM.
20. Ibid, 2 and 3 July 1758.
21. Ibid, 21 July 1758.
22. Email response from Mike Fardell, 12 April 2019.
23. Rodger, *Command of the Ocean*, p 414.

9: The Wreck: Rest in Peace?

1. Rob Byrne, *HMS Victory: The English Channel's 'abandoned shipwreck'*, BBC News Online, 14 February 2019, accessed on 21 February 2019 via https://www.bbc.co.uk/news/uk-england-47044932.
2. Cited on the website of the National Museum of the Royal Navy, www.nmrn.org.uk, accessed on 27 May 2020.
3. Dave Parham, *Comments on Odyssey Paper 4 – Deep-sea Fishing impacts on the shipwrecks of the English Channel and Western Approaches*, accessed on 4 June 2020 via www.jnapc.org.uk.
4. Consultation papers, June 2010, accessed on 4 June 2020 via www.jnapc.org.uk.
5. Ministry of Defence, 24 January 2012, cited in www.gov.uk/government/news/hms-victory-1744-a-rare-gift-to-foundation, accessed on 22 March 2017.
6. Ibid.
7. *The Times* (London: England), Saturday 23 June, 2012, issue 70607, p 25. Gale Document Number IF504395238.
8. *The Daily Telegraph*, 5 January 2013, accessed on 4 June 2020 via Admiral Sir John Balchen's Descendants Society website at https://sites.google.com/site/adsirjohnbalchendescendant/
9. www.victory1744.org accessed on 4 June 2020.
10. Odyssey Marine Exploration website accessed on 27 May 2020 via ir.odysseymarine.com/press-releases.
11. Wreck of HMS Victory 1744, 29 January 2015, Volume 591, House of Commons Hansard, accessed on 22 March 2017 via www.hansard.parliament.uk/commons/2015-01-29/debates/15012952000002/wreckofhmsvictory1744.
12. Ibid.
13. 'Saving of navy wreck sinks in sea of experts', *The Sunday Times*, London, 29 April 2018, p 14.
14. 'Victory to rise again', The *Sunday Express*, London, 20 May 2018, p 85.
15. Joint Nautical Archaeology Policy Committee Report of Activities in 2018, accessed on 24 May 2020 via www.jnapc.org.uk.
16. Ibid.
17. Rob Byrne, *HMS Victory: the English Channel's 'abandoned shipwreck'*, BBC News Online,

14 February 2019, accessed on 27 May 2020 via www.bbc.co.uk/news/uk-england-47044932.

18. Rebecca Reynolds, 10 April 2019, on the Institute of Art & Law website accessed on 27 May 2020 via https://ial.uk.com/judicial-review-undertaken-for-hms-victory-salvage/

19. *The Times,* 20 February 2019, p 15.

20. *The Times,* 22 February 2019, Letters to the Editor.

21. *The Times,* 28 February 2019, Letters to the Editor.

22. BBC News, 27 September 2019, accessed on 27 May 2020 via https://www.bbc.co.uk/news/uk-england-devon-49854546.

23. *The Times,* 18 June 2020, World, p 33.

10. Conclusion

1. Gerald Jordan and Nicholas Rogers, 'Admirals as Heroes: Patriotism and Liberty in Hanoverian England', DOI: https://doi.org/10.1086/385935, published online by Cambridge University Press, 2014, *Journal of British Studies,* Volume 28, Issue 3, July 1989, 201-224 (accessed 16/01/2020 via www.cambridge.org).

2. Sam Willis, *The Glorious First of June: Fleet Battle in the Reign of Terror* (Quercus, London, 2011), p 322.

Appendix 5: John Balchen and Godalming

1. Surrey History Centre (SHC ref. 3831) Ewell, St Mary: Civil Parish Records, 1759–1895.

2. Surrey History Centre (SHC ref. 212/40/17) Properties and families in Surrey: Deeds 13th century – 1901, dated 28 November 1752.

3. Surrey History Centre (SHC ref. G5/11/48) The Webb Family of Whitley, Deeds and Papers (1354–1855), file 4 December 1756–29 September 1761.

4. Surrey History Centre (SHC ref. G111/7/5) Godwin Austen Family of Shalford Estate (1572–1864), Sun Fire Insurance Policy (No. 212582), dated 7 April 1786.

5. Surrey History Centre (SHC ref. 1322/4/53) Duke of Northumberland's Surrey Manors Records (1390–1937), Manor of Albury Rentals (1405–1905), dated c. 1800.

6. Stanley C Dedman, *Some Personalities of Godalming's History,* Lecture notes given on 14 February 1968, as No. 6 in his series of lectures on *Godalming: Growth of a Town* (Godalming Museum Library, Accession Number B003.250), compiled in 1971, with reference to John F Nichols, *Godalming: General description and historical summary* chapter in *The Borough of Godalming, Surrey, Official Handbook 1954* (Pyramid Press, 1954).

7. Ibid.

8. Peter Earle, *Sailors: English Merchant Seamen 1650-1775* (London: Methuen Publishing Ltd, 1998), p 19.

9. Ibid, p 17.

10. Nichols, *Borough of Godalming, Official Handbook,* p 14.

11. Surrey History Centre (SHC ref. 212/52/32).

12. P A L Vine, *London's Lost Route to the Sea* (Midhurst: Middleton Press, 5th Edition, 1996), p 10.

13. Ibid, p 14.

14. P A L Vine, *London to Portsmouth Waterway* (Midhurst: Middleton Press, 1994), p 55.

15. Glenys Crocker (ed), *A Guide to the Industrial History of the Borough of Waverley* (Surrey Industrial Heritage Group, 2003), p 2.

16. Ibid, p 3.

Bibliography

Primary Sources
NMM = The National Maritime Museum, Greenwich, London.
TNA = The National Archives, Kew, London

Archival Sources
ADM 106/424/78: *Captain William Vickars, HMS Dragon, Portsmouth*, August 22, 1692. TNA.
ADM 106/424/79: *Captain Vickars, HMS Dragon, Portsmouth*, August 23, 1692. TNA.
ADM 106/441/151: *Rear-Admiral Sir Francis Wheeler letter*, June 4, 1693. TNA.
ADM 106/443/323: *Letter to Navy Board*, September 20, 1694. TNA.
ADM 106/449/145: *Letter to Navy Board*, December 22, 1694. TNA.
ADM 106/486/305: *Report on 'Spanish Expedition' back in Portsmouth*, March 9, 1696. TNA.
ADM 106/483/259: *Court Martial on Victory, Admiral Matthew Aylmer*, September 2, 1696.TNA.
ADM 106/483/256: *Court Martial on Victory, Admiral Matthew Aylmer*, September 3, 1696. TNA.
ADM 106/511/71: *Vice-Admiral John Neville, HMS Cambridge, Barbados*, April 27, 1697. TNA.
ADM 106/506/313: *Captain William Julius, HMS Colchester, Port Royal, Jamaica*, August 12, 1697. TNA.
ADM 106/501/383: *Letter to Navy Board*, December, 1697. TNA.
ADM 106/569/287: *Letter, Portsmouth Commissioners ref, HMS Moderate and HMS Assurance Prizes*, May 1, 1703. TNA.
ADM 106/569/354: *Letter, Portsmouth, HMS Moderate Prize has been launched*, June 20, 1703. TNA.
ADM 106/581/51: *Captain Balchen, HMS Adventure, the Nore*, February 11, 1704. TNA.
ADM 106/584/193: *Letter from Commissioner Sir William Gifford, Portsmouth*, June 14, 1704. TNA.
ADM 106/596/290: *Balchen, HMS Chester, Portsmouth Harbour, to the Navy Board*, July 9, 1705. TNA.
ADM 106/596/291: *John Hockaday, HMS Chester, Portsmouth Harbour, to the Navy Board*, July 9, 1705. TNA.
ADM 106/597/266: *James Conch, HMS Chester, to the Navy Board*, August 12, 1705. TNA.
ADM 106/596/324: *Balchen, HMS Chester, Portsmouth Harbour, to the Navy Board*, September 2, 1705. TNA.
ADM 106/596/334: *Balchen, HMS Chester, Portsmouth Harbour, to the Navy Board*, September 14, 1705. TNA.

ADM 106/596/337: *Balchen, HMS Chester, Spithead, to the Navy Board*, September 18, 1705. TNA.

ADM 1/1468 & 9: *Letters from Captains, Surname B*, 1706–1707 & 1708–1709. TNA.

ADM 106/606/221: *Report from Spithead to the Navy Board*, July 19, 1706. TNA.

ADM 1/1468: *Balchen, HMS Chester, Slave Ship off Guinea*, November 23, 1706. TNA.

ADM 1/1468 & 7: *Courts Martial Papers*, January 1, 1705–June 30, 1708 & January 1, 1708–July 31, 1710. TNA.

ADM 1/5267: *Courts Martial, Spithead, HMS Royal Anne, by Admiral George Byng*, September 20, 1708. TNA.

ADM 106/638/354: *Balchen, HMS Gloucester, Deptford, to the Navy Board*, August 19, 1709. TNA.

ADM 106/638/358: *Balchen, HMS Gloucester, Deptford, to the Navy Board*, August 24, 1709. TNA.

ADM 106/638/370: *Balchen, HMS Gloucester, Longreach, to the Navy Board*, September 11, 1709. TNA.

ADM 106/638/380: *Balchen, HMS Gloucester, Longreach, to the Navy Board*, September 20, 1709. TNA.

ADM 106/638/387: *Balchen, HMS Gloucester, The Downs, to the Navy Board*, September 29, 1709. TNA.

ADM 1/5267: *Courts Martial, River Thames, HM Yacht Peregrine, by Admiral Sir John Downing*, December 14, 1709. TNA.

ADM 106/665/33: *Letter to Navy Board, Lisbon*, May 26, 1711. TNA.

ADM 106/674/64: *Dock Proceedings, Leghorne*, March 21, 1712. TNA.

ADM 106/684/64: *Sir John Jennings, Admiral, HMS Blenheim, Iles de Hyeres*, October 26, 1713. TNA.

ADM 106/696/48: *Balchen, HMS Diamond, at Woolwich*, February 14, 1714/15. TNA.

ADM 106/696/62: *Balchen, HMS Diamond, Woolwich*, February 20, 1714/15. TNA.

ADM 106/696/86: *Balchen, HMS Diamond, at Longreach*, March 25, 1715. TNA.

ADM 106/696/132: *Balchen, HMS Diamond, Port Royal Harbour, Jamaica*, June 20, 1715. TNA.

ADM 106/699/159: *Samuel Page, Deputy Commissioner, St Jago de la Vega, Jamaica*, August 31, 1715. TNA.

ADM 106/696/202: *Balchen, HMS Diamond, Port Royal Harbour, Jamaica*, November 12, 1715. TNA.

ADM 106/703/94: *Balchen, HMS Diamond, off Dover*, May 4, 1716. TNA.

ADM 1/1472: *Letters from Captains – Surname B*, 1717–1723. TNA.

ADM 106/792/123: *Portsmouth Dock to Hon. Navy Board*, March 17, 1726. TNA.

ADM 106/785/96: *Balchen, HMS Monmouth, Spithead*, February 21, 1727. TNA.

ADM 50/28: *Admirals' Journals, J Balchen*, May 1731–December 1731. TNA.

ADM 106/847/251: *Portsmouth Dock to Commissioners of the Navy*, September 14, 1733. TNA.

ADM 1/3649: *Navy Board to Admiralty*, January 24, 1735. TNA.

ADM 1/3649: *Navy Board to the Admiralty*, January 24, 1734. TNA.

ADM 1/796: *Admiral John Balchen to Admiralty Secretary*, January 17, 1735 and February 2, 1735. TNA.

ADM 106/874/16: *Plymouth Officers' Report*, February 14, 1735. TNA.

ADM 106/890/18: *Letter from Commissioner Richard Hughes, Portsmouth*, January 12, 1737. TNA.

ADM 106/899: *Commissioners of the Navy to Portsmouth Dockyard*, March 17, 1737. TNA.

ADM 106/891/6: *Commissioners of Portsmouth Dockyard*, July 4, 1737. TNA.

Bibliography

ADM 1/3651: *Richard Haddock to Bunchett, Navy Office*, August 15, 1737. TNA.

ADM 106/899: *Adm. Haddock to Commissioners of the Navy, HMS Somerset, Port Mahon*, August 1, 1738. TNA.

ADM 1/380: *Letters from Commanders-in-Chief, Mediterranean: including Admirals Haddock, Ogle and Balchen*, 1738–1742. TNA.

ADM 1/518: *Letters from Admirals Byng (later Lord Torrington), Aylmer and Balchen*, 1715–1740. TNA.

ADM 106/923/247: *Letter from Sir John Norris*, April 26, 1740. TNA.

ADM 106/921/42: *Hughes to Commissioners of the Navy, Portsmouth Dock*, July 19, 1740. TNA.

ADM 6/16: *Seal of the Office of Admiralty Commissions & Warrant Books*, January 4, 1741–September 18, 1745. TNA.

ADM 106/954/178: *Letter from Captain Samuel Faulkner*, February 21, 1742. TNA.

ADM 106/982/8: *Letter from Commissioner Philip Vanbrugh, Plymouth*, January 7, 1743. TNA.

ADM 106/987/51: *William Moreland to the Hon. Commissioner Brown, Deal*, February 25, 1743. TNA.

ADM 106/976/50: *Letter from Captain W Hemmington, the Princess Amelia, Hamoaze*, May 30, 1743. TNA.

ADM 1/87: *Letters from Flag Officers, Channel Fleet: including Admirals Hardy, Martin, Balchen and Anson*, 1743–1747. TNA.

ADM 106/1012/167: *John Lethbridge, Diver, to the Commissioners of His Majesty's Navy*, January 15, 1745. TNA

ADM 36/4410: *Ship's Musters, HMS Victory*, February 6, 1743 to July 31, 1744. TNA.

ADM 1/578: *Vernon to Lord Commissioners of the Admiralty*, June 18, 1744. TNA.

ADM 1/87: *Letters from Flag Officers, Channel Fleet, including Admirals Hardy, Martin, Balchen and Anson*, Balchen letters from 13 July to 27 August 1744. TNA.

ADM 3/48: *Admiralty Board Minutes*, from March 5, 1744 to October 9, 1744. TNA.

ADM 3/49: *Admiralty Board Minutes*, from October 10, 1744 to December 23, 1744. TNA.

ADM 1/4297: *Log Book of HMS Prince George*, Part 7, Folios 38-40, May 2 to May 8, 1747. TNA.

ADM/1773/5: *Letter, Board of Admiralty*, March 3, 1690. Caird Library Archives, NMM.

ADM/1824/97: *Navy Board in-letter*, October 8, 1695. Caird Library Archives, NMM.

ADM/A/1838/103 & 104: *Vice-Admiral Aylmer to the Admiralty*, January 12, 1697, Caird Library Archives, NMM.

ADM/L/V/117: *Logbook HMS Vulcan 1701-1703*, Caird Library Archives, NMM.

ADM/L/O/24: *Logbooks and Journals of Officers between 17 September 1716 and 20 November 1717, HMS Orford*, Caird Library Archives, NMM.

ADM/B/127: *Board of Admiralty in-letters, 1745*, Caird Library Archives, NMM.

ADM/B/128: *Navy Board Letters to April 30, 1745*, Caird Library Archives, NMM.

ADM/L/S/280: *Lieutenants' Logs HMS Shrewsbury 1716-1719*, Caird Library Archives, NMM.

ADM/L/M/235: *Lieutenants' Logs and Journals HMS Monmouth 1721-1728*, Caird Library Archives, NMM.

ADM/L/V/60: *Lieutenants' Logs HMS Victory 1740-1744*, Caird Library Archives, NMM.

A ship in Distress, design'd to represent the loss of the 'Victory', Etching, Peter Monamy (artist), Pierre Charles Canot (engraver), John Bowles (publisher), 1745–1746, National Maritime Museum, Object PAH, Image 1024.

Balchen, Sir John, *Letters to Commodore Philip Vanbrugh, Naval Commissioner at Plymouth Yard*, Godalming Museum Library Archives, 24 October 1739 (Accession No. TRB 293/1, 5070/1) and 25 May 1742 (Accession No. TRB 293/1, 5070/2).

Caledonian Mercury, Tuesday, October 16th, 1744 (courtesy of Cathryn Pearce).

Calm: HMS Royal James, a royal yacht and other shipping, oil painting by Van de Velde in 1675, National Maritime Museum, Object BHC3608.

Daily Advertiser, October 12, 1744, Issue 4359. 17th & 18th Century Burney Collection Newspapers.

Daily Advertiser, October 15, 1744, Issue 4361. 17th & 18th Century Burney Collection Newspapers.

Daily Post, October 10, 1744, Issue 7833. 17th & 18th Century Burney Collection Newspapers.

First rate HMS 'Victory' (1695) carrying eight hundred men and one hundred and four guns built by Mr Lee of Chatham, etching by Jan Kip after Isaac Sailmaker, 18th Century. NMM, Object PA16675.

General Advertiser, October 15, 1744, Issue 3095. 17th & 18th Century Burney Collection Newspapers.

HCA 32/60/36: *High Court of Admiralty, High Court of Appeals for Prizes*, 1702–1703. TNA.

HCA 32/50/119: *High Court of Admiralty, High Court of Appeals for Prizes*, 1710. TNA.

HCA 32/54/47: *High Court of Admiralty, High Court of Appeals for Prizes*, 1710. TNA.

HCA 32/54/26: *High Court of Admiralty, High Court of Appeals for Prizes*, November 18, 1710. TNA.

HCA 32/55/39: *High Court of Admiralty, High Court of Appeals for Prizes*, 1710. TNA.

Loss of HMS 'Victory', 4 October 1744, oil painting by Peter Monamy, 1745–1746, NMM, Object BHC0361.

London Evening Post, October 16, 1744, Issue 2644. 17th & 18th Century Burney Collection Newspapers.

London Evening Post, November 10, 1744, Issue 2655. 17th & 18th Century Burney Collection Newspapers.

Memorial: *Sir John Balchen*, Marble statue, North Transept, Westminster Abbey, designed by Scheemakers, erected 1746.

Memorial: *Vice-Admiral Temple-West (1714-1757)*, North Choir Aisle, Westminster Abbey.

Model of First rate 100-gun warship 'Victory' (1737). A contemporary full hull model of 'Victory' in Scale 1:34.3, National Maritime Museum, Object SLR0449, Image L3241-004.

Plan of the body of Victory, by Frederick Chapman, 1754, NMM, Object ZAZ 0145.

Portrait of Admiral Sir John Balchen, oil painting by John Baptiste de Medina in 1705, NMM, Object BHC2525.

Portrait of Admiral Sir John Balchen, oil painting in the style of Sir Godfrey Kneller, probably 1744, Godalming Borough Hall, Godalming, Surrey.

Portrait of Admiral Edward Vernon (1684-1757), oil painting by Charles Philips, mid-1730s–1743, NMM, Object BHC3068.

Probate records of the Prerogative Court of Canterbury, PROB 11/736/43, PROB 11/738/337 and PROB 11/745/158, PROB 11/736/171, PROB 11/417/461, PROB 11/416/440, PROB 11/427/465, et al. TNA.

SP 89/16/216: State Papers: *Report capture of French warship SPHAERE by HMS Dragon*, December 22, 1693. TNA.

SP 42/68/109: State Papers: *Sir John Jennings to Dartmouth*, January 31, 1713. TNA.

SP 42/27: State Papers: *Commissioners of Lord High Admiralty to Sir John Balchen*, July 14, 1744, and August 13, 1744. TNA.

SP 42/27/128: State Papers: *Commissioners of Lord High Admiralty to Sir John Balchen*, September 13, 1744. TNA.

SP 42/27/130: State Papers: *Commissioners of Lord High Admiralty to Sir John Balchen*, September 14, 1744. TNA.

SP 42/27/145: State Papers: *Commissioners of Lord High Admiralty to Sir John Balchen*, September 25, 1744.

SP 36/63/132: State Papers: *Victory damaged by fierce storm*, February 25, 1744. TNA.

SP 42/27/42: State Papers: *Letter expressing Admiral Mathews' fears of the interception of Sir Charles Hardy's victualling convoy*, March 21, 1744. TNA.

SP 42/27/131: State Papers: *List of the Squadrons with Sir John Balchen, Captain Osborne and Vice-Admiral Davers*, September 14, 1744. TNA.

SP 36/52/55: State Papers: *Minutes of a meeting of the Lord Justices ref. orders to Vice-Admiral Balchen at Portsmouth*, August 22, 1740, TNA.

SP 9/72: *Original Letters Patent appointing John Balchen, Esq., Master of the Royal Hospital at Greenwich, at a salary of £1,000. [The Great Seal, brown wax, on plaited red and while cords. The whole in a leather covered wooden box]*. March 19, 1744. TNA.

Surrey, England, Church of England Baptisms, Marriages and Burials, 1538-1812, illustration accessed and supplied on 26 November 2017 by Jennifer Goldsmith via https://www.ancestry.co.uk.

Surrey History Centre, Woking, records:

SHC ref. 3831: Ewell, St Mary: Civil Parish Records (1759–1895).

SHC ref. 212/40/17: Properties & Families in Surrey. Deeds 13th century–1901),document dated 28 November 1752.

SHC ref. G5/11/48: The Webb family of Whitley, Deeds & Papers (1354–1855), Memorandum of Agreement, (4 December 1756–29 September 1761).

SHC ref. G111/7/5: Godwin Austen family of Shalford Estate (1572–1864), Sun Fire Insurance Policy (No. 212582), dated 7 April 1786.

SHC ref. 1322/4/53: Duke of Northumberland's Surrey Manors Records (1390–1937), Manor of Albury Rentals (1405–1905), dated c. 1800.

SHC ref. 212/52/32. Anchor Inn (Public House) and a messuage, Deeds (1699–1702) and Deeds (1762–1890).

The Famous Ship Victory, artist unknown, 1744, woodcut to print, Accession Number AN 164566001, British Museum.

The Gust: a storm battered English Warship drifts rudderless on the high waves, oil painting by Willem van de Velde II in 1680, The Rijksmuseum, Amsterdam, The Netherlands.

The Birmingham Gazette, November 16, 1741; Issue 1, 1. British Library Newspapers, Part III: 1741–1950.

The Dundee Courier & Argus and Northern Warder, August 31, 1877, Issue 7522. British Library Newspapers, Part II: 1800–1900.

The Hampshire Advertiser and Salisbury Guardian, October 2, 1852, Issue 1519, 7. British Library Newspapers, Part II: 1800–1900.

The Hampshire Telegraph, July 21, 1900, Issue 6200. British Library Newspapers, Part I: 1800–1900.

The Leeds Intelligencer, September 2, 1766; issue 651. British Library Newspapers, Part III: 1741–1950, quoting the *London Sunday Post*, August 30, 1766.

The Norfolk Chronicle, August 9, 1777, Issue 43, 1. British Library Newspapers, Part III: 1741–1950.

The Gentleman's Magazine, Vol 10, 1740.

The Gentleman's Magazine, Vol 14, 1744.

The Gentleman's Magazine, Vol 16, 1746.

The Graphic, London, July 15, 1893, Issue 1233, British Library Newspapers, Part 1: 1800–1900.

Two bronze guns retrieved from wreck HMS *Victory* (1737) under restoration, Bay 3, Conservation Building, National Museum of the Royal Navy, HM Naval Base, Portsmouth.

T 1/201: Treasury Board Papers: *Admiralty Office to Commissioners of his Majesty's Customs*, November 28, 1716, TNA.

T 1/201: Treasury Board Papers: *Captain Balchen to Admiralty*, November 22, 1716, TNA.

Published Primary Sources

A Society of Gentlemen, *The Biographical Magazine or, Complete Historical Library*, London: F Newbery, 1776.

Aston, John (ed), *Real Sailor Songs*, London: The Leadenhall Press, 1891.

Baugh, Daniel A (ed), *Naval Administration 1715-1750*. London: Navy Records Society, Vol 120, 1977.

Charnock, John, *Biographia Navalis; or, Impartial Memoirs of the Lives and Characters of Officers of the Navy of Great Britain from the year 1660 to the Present Time. Vol. III*, London: R Faulder, 1795. National Museum of the Royal Navy Archives, Portsmouth.

Cranmer-Byng, J L (ed), *Pattee Byng's Journal 1718-1720*, Navy Records Society, 1950.

Hattendorf, John B, Knight, R J B, Pearsall, A W H, Rodger, N A M, and Till, G (eds), *British Naval Documents, 1204-1960*. London: Navy Records Society, Vol 131, 1993. Accessed 31 October 2017 via https://www.navyrecords.org.uk/british-naval-documents-1204-1960/

Hervey, Frederic, *The Naval History of Great Britain; from the earliest times to the rising of Parliament in 1779, Vol. III*, London: J Bew, 1779. 355.49 (42): 094, TN: 67325, The Caird Library, NMM.

Hodges, H W and Hughes, E A (eds), *Select Naval Documents*, Cambridge, 1936.

Horn, D B and Ransome, Mary (eds), *English Historical Documents, 1714-1783*, London: Eyre & Spottiswoode, 1957.

Hyland, William, *The Ship-wreck: A Dramatick Piece* or *The Farmers on the Coast*, London: J. Millan, 1746.

Newberry, E, *The Lives of the British Admirals. Displaying, in the most striking colours, the Conduct and Heroism of the Naval Commanders of Great Britain and Ireland, whose intrepidity has convinced the World that Britannia is the sovereign of the Ocean, Part I*, London: E Newbery, 1787.

Naish, George P B (ed), *Nelson's letters to his wife and other documents, 1785-1831*, Vol 100, 1958.

The Lives of the most Celebrated British Admirals, London: Lane, Newman & Co, 1808. 92:355:33 (42): 094, PBD 4884, TN: 67322. The Caird Library, NMM.

The Parish Registers of Godalming, Surrey, 1582-1688, Volume II, Baptisms, Surrey Parish Register Society, 1904. Godalming Museum Library Archives, Accession No. B003.408.'

Voltaire, Jean François Marie Arouet de, *The Age of Louis XIV*, Berlin, 1751. Translated by Pollack, Martyn P, London, J M Dent & Sons Ltd, 1969.

Williams, Glyndwr (ed). *Documents relating to Anson's Voyage Round the World 1740-1744*. London: Navy Records Society, Vol 109, 1967.

Bibliography

Secondary Sources

Published Material

Anderson, M S, *Europe in the Eighteenth Century 1713-1789*, London: Longmans, 1961, in 4th Edition, London: Pearson Education, 2000.

Baugh, Daniel A, 'Balchen, Sir John (1670-1744)', *Oxford Dictionary of National Biography*, Oxford: Oxford University Press, 2004.

Baugh, Daniel, *British Naval Administration in the Age of Walpole*, Princeton, NJ: Princeton University Press, 1965.

Baugh, Daniel (ed), *Naval Administration 1715 – 1750, Vol. 120*, London: Navy Records Society: London, 1977.

Cant, Serena, *England's Shipwreck Heritage – from Log-boats to U-boats*, London: English Heritage, 2013.

Colville, Quintin and Davey, James (eds), *Nelson, Navy & Nation: The Royal Navy & the British People, 1688-1815*, London: Conway, 2013.

Crocker, Glenys (ed), *A Guide to the Industrial History of the Borough of Waverley*, Surrey Industrial Heritage Group, 2003.

Dedman, Stanley C (ed), *Godalming: Growth of a Town*, Godalming County Branch Library and Borough Museum, 1971. Godalming Museum Library Archives, LOC REF: 942.21 GOD DED, Accession No. B003.250.

Dedman, Stanley C, *Some Personalities of Godalming's History*, lecture in Godalming, 14 February 1968, Godalming Library.

Earle, Peter, *Sailors: English Merchant Seamen 1650-1775*, London: Methuen Publishing Limited, 2007.

Ellen, Gill, *Naval Families, War and Duty in Britain, 1740-1820*, Woodbridge: Boydell Press, 2016.

Elliott, J H, *Imperial Spain 1469–1716*, London: Penguin Books, 1963.

Harris, Daniel G, *F H Chapman – The First Naval Architect and his Work*, London: Conway Maritime Press, 1989. Caird Library, NMM.

Hartmann, Cyril Hughes, *The Angry Admiral – the later career of Edward Vernon, Admiral of the White*, London: William Heinemann Ltd, 1953. PBD 6769, TN: 67324. Caird Library, NMM.

Heathcote, T A, *The British Admirals of the Fleet, 1734-1995: A Biographical History*, Barnsley: Leo Cooper, 2002.

Hepper, David J, *British Warship Losses in the Age of Sail: 1650-1859*, Rotherfield: Jean Boudriot Publications, 1994.

Hough, Richard, *The Great Admirals*, London: Weidenfeld & Nicolson, 1977.

Howard, Frank, *Sailing Ships of War 1400-1860*, Greenwich: Conway Maritime Press, 1979.

Hutchinson, John R, *Press Gangs Afloat & Ashore*, 1913, e-Book, 1 March 2006.

Janaway, John, *The Story of Godalming*, Newbury: Local Heritage Books, 1983, republished as *Godalming: A Short History*, Godalming: Ammonite Books, 1993.

Jenks, Timothy, *Naval Engagements – Patriotism, Cultural Politics, and the Royal Navy 1793-1815*, Oxford: Oxford University Press, 2006.

Lambert, Andrew, *Admirals: The Naval Commanders who made Britain Great*, London: Faber & Faber, 2008.

Land, Isaac, *War, Nationalism and the British Sailor, 1750-1850*, Basingstoke: Palgrave Macmillan, 2009.

Laver, Ann, *Admiral Sir John Balchen (1669-1744)*, Local History data sheet, Godalming Museum Library, 2009.

Lavery, Brian, *The Ship of the Line Vol. I: The Development of the Battlefleet 1650-1850*, Greenwich: Conway Maritime Press, 1983.

Lavery, Brian, *The Royal Navy's First Invincible*, London: Invincible Conservations (1744–1758) Limited, 1988.

Lavery, Brian, *Empire of the Seas*, London: Conway Bloomsbury, 2009.

L'Estrange, A G, *The Palace and the Hospital; or Chronicles of Greenwich*, London: Hurst and Blacketh, 1886. 914.216.LES.585, Caird Library, NMM.

Nichols, J F, *The Borough of Godalming, Surrey, Official Handbook, 1954*, London: Pyramid Press, 1954. Godalming Museum Library Archives, Accession No. 2732.

Pearce, Edward, *The Great Man. Sir Robert Walpole: Scoundrel, Genius and Britain's First Prime Minister*, London: Pimlico, 2008.

Quilley, Geoff, *Empire to Nation – art, history and the visualization of Maritime Britain, 1768-1829*, New Haven & London: Yale University Press, 2011.

Ritchie, David, *Shipwrecks – an Encyclopaedia of the World's Worst Disasters at Sea*, New York: Facts on File, 1996.

Rodger, N A M, *The Wooden World: an Anatomy of the Georgian Navy*, London: Collins, 1986.

Rodger, N A M, *The Command of the Ocean: A Naval History of Britain, 1649-1815*, London: Penguin Books, 2004.

Rubenstein, Hilary, *Catastrophe at Spithead: The sinking of the Royal George*, Barnsley: Seaforth Publications, 2020.

Sheldon, Matthew, *HMS Victory*, Portsmouth: National Museum of the Royal Navy, 2014.

Scott, Frank, *A Square Rig Handbook; operations, safety, training, equipment*, 2nd Edition, London: The Nautical Institute, 2001.

Smith, Peter Charles, *Sailors on the Rocks: Famous Royal Navy Shipwrecks*, Barnsley: Pen & Sword Maritime, 2015.

Sweetman, Jack (ed), *The Great Admirals: Command at Sea, 1587-1945*, Annapolis: US Naval Institute, 1997.

Tomlinson, Barbara, *Commemorating the Seafarer Monuments, Memorials and Memory*, National Maritime Museum: The Boydell Press, 2015.

Vine, P A L, *London to Portsmouth Waterway*, Midhurst: Middleton Press, 1994.

Vine, P A L, *London's Lost Route to the Sea*, Midhurst: Middleton Press, 5th Edition, 1996.

Ware, Chris, *Admiral Byng: his Rise and Execution*, Barnsley: Pen & Sword Maritime, 2009.

Willis, Sam, *Shipwreck: a History of Disasters at Sea*, London: Quercus Editions Ltd, 2008.

Willis, Sam, *The Glorious First of June: Fleet Battle in the Reign of Terror*, London: Quercus, 2011.

Wilson, Alastair and Callo, Joseph F, *Who's Who in Naval History: from 1550 to the present*, Abingdon: Routledge, 2004.

Winfield, Rif, *British Warships in the Age of Sail 1714-1792, Vol. II*, Barnsley: Seaforth Publishing, 2007.

Winfield, Rif, *First Rate: the Greatest Warships of the Age of Sail*, Barnsley: Seaforth Publishing, 2010.

Articles

Balchin, William, 'Admiral Sir John Balchin (1669-1744)', *The Mariner's Mirror*, Vol 80, Issue 3, August 1994, pp 332–5. Accessed via http://dx.doi.org/10.1080/00253 359.1994.10656508 on 12 October 2017.

Brydon, Michael, 'Forms of Prayer to be Used at Sea', *Faith & Worship*, Number 70, Trinity 2016, The Prayer Book Society, p 24.

Bibliography

Cowan, Zelide, 'John Lethbridge, Diver', *History Today*, Vol 28, Issue 12, p 825.

Jordan, Gerald and Rogers, Nicholas, 'Admirals as Heroes: Patriotism and Liberty in Hanoverian England, *Journal of British Studies*, Vol 28, Issue 3, July 1989, pp 201–24. Accessed 16 January 2020 via DOI: https://doi.org/10.1086/385935 online published by Cambridge University Press, 10 January 2014.

Kingsley, Sean A, 'The Sinking of the First Rate *Victory* (1744): A Disaster waiting to Happen?', *Odyssey Papers 45*, Odyssey Marine Exploration, 2015. Accessed via www.victory1744.org/publications.html on 22 March, 2017.

Landow, George P, '"Swim or Drown": Carlyle's World of Shipwrecks, Castaways, and Stranded Voyagers', *Studies in English Literature, 1500-1900*, Vol. 15, No. 4, Nineteenth Century, 1975. DOI: 10.2307/450017.

Leggett, Don, 'Navy, Nation and Identity in the Long Nineteenth Century', *Journal for Maritime Research*, Vol 13, 2011, pp 151–63. Accessed on 22 December 2017 via http://doi.org/10.1080/21533369.2011.622880.

Lincoln, Margarette, 'Shipwreck narratives of the eighteenth and early nineteenth century: indicators of culture & identity', *British Journal of Eighteenth Century Studies*, Vol 20, No 2, 1997, pp 155–72.

Richards, Bernard, Review article on Landow, George P, *Images of Crisis: Literary Iconology, 1750 to the Present*. London: Routledge & Kegan Paul, 1982, in *Modern Languages Journal*, Vol 13, No 2 (Spring), 1983, pp 105–07. DOI: 10.2307/3194493 accessed on 31 October 2017 via http://www.jstore.org/3194493.

Robinson, Commander Chas N, 'England's Drowned Admirals', *The Graphic* (London), 15 July 1893, Issue 1233. British Library Newspapers, Part I: 1800–1900.

Rodger, N A M, 'Recent books on the Royal Navy of the eighteenth century', *Journal of Military History*, Vol. 63, Issue 3, 1999, pp 683–703. Accessed on 22 December 2017, via http://dx.doi.org/10.2307/120501.

The Balchin Family Society Newsletters, Compiled in Vols 1–13, Godalming Museum Library and Archives, LOC REF: 920 BAL BAL, 1995–2001.

The *Sunday Express*, London, 20 May 2018, News, p 85.

The *Sunday Times*, London, 29 April 2018, News, p 14.

The Times, London, 23 June 2012, Letters to the Editor, p 25.

The Times, London, 20 February 2019, *Salvagers fight to raise the other HMS Victory*, p 15.

The Times, London, 22 February 2019, Letters to the Editor.

The Times, London, 28 February 2019, Letters to the Editor.

The Times, London, 18 June 2020, World, p 33.

Websites (not included in the above references):

http://www.balchin-family.org.uk: *Admiral Sir John Balchin (1669-1744)*.

http://www.navyrecords.org.uk/british-naval-documents-1204-1960/

https://www.nmrn.

https://www.threedecks.org : 'Sir John Balchen', *Warships in the Age of Sail.*

https://snr.org.uk/snr-forum/topic/admiral-sir-john-balchen-1670-1744-hms-vitory-1744/: *The Society for Nautical Research Forum.*

https://www.bbc.co.uk/news/uk-england-devon-49854546.

https://www.bbc.co.uk/news/uk-england-47044932.

https://www.victory1744.org.

https://jnapc.org.uk.

https://ir.odysseymarine.com.

https://www.ial.uk.com.

https://sites.google.com/site/adsirjohnbalchendescendants/

https://unesco.org.

https://www.hansard.parliament.uk/commons/2015-0129/debates/15012952000002/wreckofhmsvictory1744.

https://www.academia.edu/30574034/Ball_et_al_Digital_Modelling_in_the_evaluation_of_the_Sinking_of_HMS_Victory_1737_Royal_Institution_of_Naval_Architects_Historic_Ships_Conference_12_December_2016

https://www.traditionalmusic.co.uk/navel-songs-ballads/naval-songs-ballads-0393.htm

https://www.british-history.ac.uk/survey-london/vol2/pt1/pp50-53

Index

Index